READING
MATTHEW

To Edward E. Garland

CONTENTS

EDITOR'S FOREWORD

"Reading the New Testament" is a commentary series that aims to present cutting-edge research in popular form that is accessible to upper-level undergraduates, seminarians, seminary educated pastors, and educated laypeople, as well as to graduate students and professors. The volumes in this series do not follow the word-by-word, phrase-by-phrase, verse-by-verse method of traditional commentaries. Rather they are concerned to understand large thought units and their relationship to an author's thought as a whole. The focus is on a close reading of the final form of the text. The aim is to make one feel at home in the biblical text itself. The approach of these volumes involves a concern both for *how* an author communicates and *what* the religious point of the text is. Care is taken to relate both the *how* and the *what* of the text to its milieu: Christian (NT and non-canonical), Jewish (scriptural and post-biblical), and Greco-Roman. This enables both the communication strategies and the religious message of the text to be clarified over against a range of historical and cultural possibilities. Moreover, a section of commentary on a large thought unit will often contain a brief excursus on some topic raised by the material in the unit, sometimes sketching OT, post-biblical Jewish, Greco-Roman, NT, and non-canonical Christian views on the subject. Throughout, the basic concern is to treat the NT texts as religious documents whose religious message needs to be set forth with compelling clarity. All other concerns are subordinated to this. It is the hope of all participants in this project that our efforts at exposition will enable the NT to be understood better and communicated more competently.

Charles H. Talbert, General Editor

AUTHOR'S PREFACE

It is with hesitation that one adds to the growing number of commentaries on the New Testament, but I find some comfort in a remark by Gershom Scholem about the Rabbis: "It is not systematic exposition, but the commentary that is the legitimate form through which the truth can be developed" (cited by D. Winston, "Philo and the Contemplative Life," *Jewish Spirituality,* ed. A. Green [New York: Crossroad, 1986], 1:201). I am grateful to the editor, Charles Talbert, for giving me the opportunity to pursue that truth in this commentary of Matthew's Gospel that attempts to capture its religious message.

I have been indebted to many more during the preparation of the manuscript. The trustees as the Southern Baptist Theological Seminary granted me a year's sabbatical leave to complete the commentary. Vic Eldridge, principal of Morling College, the Baptist Theological College of New South Wales, and his colleagues were generous hosts to me and my family during our year in Australia. Professor Edwin Judge was also generous in giving his time and in sponsoring me as an Honorary Fellow of New Testament at Macquarie University.

My wife, Diana, deserves special appreciation. She took time from her own research and the writing of two books during the year to read many drafts and give welcomed encouragement and support. My children, John and Sarah, brought joy to life and put the writing of commentaries in its proper perspective. My mother-in-law, Dorsie Richmond, shared the time with us during the year and helped to make the time richer and more fun. Our Australian community of faith accepted us warmly and made our stay a delightful experience. Alan Tomlinson also helped by reading the final draft. Students over the years have also been helpful in teaching me what Matthew means while I was trying to teach them. Finally, I am grateful to the many who have interpreted this Gospel before me and regret that my debt to them could not always be acknowledged.

David E. Garland

ABBREVIATIONS

Journals and Series

AnBib	Analecta Biblica
ANRW	*Aufstieg und Niedergang der römischen Welt*
ANTJ	Arbeiten zum neuen Testament und Judentum
AusBR	*Australian Biblical Review*
BDF	Blass, Debrunner, Funk, *A Greek Grammar of the New Testament*
Bib	*Biblica*
BWANT	*Beiträge zur Wissenschaft vom Alten und Neuen Testament*
BZ	*Biblische Zeitschrift*
BZNW	Beihefte zur *ZNW*
CBQ	*Catholic Biblical Quarterly*
ExpT	*Expository Times*
HBT	*Horizons in Biblical Theology*
IBS	*Irish Biblical Studies*
Int	*Interpretation*
JBL	*Journal of Biblical Literature*
JETS	*Journal of the Evangelical Theological Society*
JSNT	*Journal for the Study of the New Testament*
JSNTsup	Journal for the Study of the New Testament – Supplement Series
JSOTsup	Journal for the Study of the Old Testament – Supplement Series
NovT	*Novum Testamentum*
NovTSup	Novum Testamentum, Supplements
NTS	*New Testament Studies*

OBO	Orbis biblicus et orientalis
PG	J. Migne, *Patrologia graeca*
RevExp	*Review and Expositor*
SBLSP	*Society of Biblical Literature Seminar Papers*
SBLDS	Society of Biblical Literature Dissertation Series
SBT	Studies in Biblical Theology
SJT	*Scottish Journal of Theology*
SJOT	*Scandanavian Journal of Old Testament*
SNTSMS	Society for New Testament Studies Monograph Series
ST	*Studia theologica*
TDNT	*Theological Dictionary of the New Testament*
TQ	*Theologische Quartalschrift*
WUNT	Wissenschaftliche Untersuchungen zum Neuen Testament
ZNW	*Zeitschrift für die neutestamentliche Wissenschaft*

Articles and Books

Barth, "Matthew's Understanding of the Law":
  G. Barth, *Tradition and Interpretation in Matthew,* London: SCM, 1963.
Borg, *Conflict, Holiness and Politics:*
  M. J. Borg, *Conflict, Holiness and Politics in the Teachings of Jesus,* Lewiston, N.Y./Queenston, Ont.: Edwin Mellen, 1984.
Brown, *Birth:*
  R. E. Brown, *The Birth of the Messiah,* New York: Doubleday, 1977.
Bruner, *Christbook:*
  F. D. Bruner, *The Christbook: A Historical/Theological Commentary: Matthew 1–12,* Waco: Word, 1987.
Bruner, *Churchbook:*
  F. D. Bruner, *Matthew, Volume 2: The Churchbook, Matthew 13–28,* Dallas: Word, 1990.
Caragounis, *Peter and the Rock:*
  C. C. Caragounis, *Peter and the Rock,* BZNW 58, Berlin/New York: Walter de Gruyter, 1990.
Carmody, "Matthew 18:15–17":
  T. R. Carmody, "Matthew 18:15–17 in Relation to Three Texts from Qumran Literature (CD 9:2–8, 16–22; 1QS 5:25–6:1)," *To Touch the Text,* ed. M. P. Horgan and P. J. Kobelski, New York: Crossroad, 1989, 141–58.

Davies, *Setting:*
W. D. Davies, *The Setting of the Sermon on the Mount,* Cambridge: Cambridge University Press, 1966.

Davies and Allison, *Saint Matthew:*
W. D. Davies and D. C. Allison, Jr., *The Gospel According to Saint Matthew,* International Critical Commentary, 1, 2, Edinburgh: T. & T. Clark, 1988, 1991.

Donaldson, *Jesus on the Mountain:*
T. L. Donaldson, *Jesus on the Mountain: A Study in Matthean Theology,* JSNTsup 8, Sheffield: JSOT, 1985.

France, *Matthew:*
R. T. France, *Matthew,* Tyndale New Testament Commentary, Grand Rapids: Eerdmans, 1985.

France, *Evangelist and Teacher:*
R. T. France, *Matthew: Evangelist and Teacher,* Grand Rapids: Zondervan, 1989.

Gnilka, *Matthäusevangelium:*
J. Gnilka, *Das Matthäusevangelium,* Herders theologischer Kommentar zum Neuen Testament I/1,2, Freiburg/Basel/Vienna: Herder, 1986, 1988.

Green, *Matthew:*
H. B. Green, *The Gospel according to Matthew,* Oxford: Clarendon, 1975.

Gundry, *Matthew:*
R. H. Gundry, *Matthew: A Commentary on His Literary and Theological Art,* Grand Rapids: Eerdmans, 1982.

Heil, *Jesus Walking on the Sea:*
J. P. Heil, *Jesus Walking on the Sea : The Meaning and Functions of Matt 14:22–33, Mark 6:45–52 and John 6:15b–21,* AnBib 87, Rome: Pontifical Biblical Institute, 1981.

Held, "Matthew as Interpreter of the Miracle Stories":
H. J. Held, "Matthew as Interpreter of the Miracle Stories," *Tradition and Interpretation in Matthew,* Philadelphia: Westminster, 1963.

Hengel, *Charismatic Leader:*
M. Hengel, *The Charismatic Leader and His Followers,* Edinburgh: T. & T. Clark, 1981.

Horsley, *New Documents:*
G. H. R. Horsley, *New Documents Illustrating Early Christianity,* Sydney: Macquarie University, 1983, 1987.

Hull, *Hellenistic Magic:*
J. M. Hull, *Hellenistic Magic and the Synoptic Tradition,* SBT 28, London: SCM: 1974.

Llewellyn, *New Documents:*
S. R. Llewellyn, *New Documents Illustrating Early Christianity,* Sydney: Macquarie University, 1992.

Limbeck: *Matthäus-Evangelium:*
M. Limbeck, *Matthäus-Evangelium,* Stuttgart: Katholisches Bibelwerk, 1986.

Luz, *Matthew 1–7:*
    U. Luz, *Matthew 1–7: A Commentary,* Minneapolis: Augsburg, 1989.
Luz, *Matthäus (Mt 8–17):*
    U. Luz, *Das Evangelium nach Matthäus (Mt 8–17),* Zurich: Benziger/
    Neukirchener, 1990.
Manson, *Sayings:*
    T. W. Manson, *The Sayings of Jesus,* London: SCM, 1949.
Meier, *Matthew:*
    J. P. Meier, *Matthew,* New Testament Message 3, Wilmington: Michael
    Glazier, 1981.
Meier, *Vision:*
    J. P. Meier, *The Vision of Matthew,* New York: Paulist, 1979.
Sabourin, *Matthew:*
    L. Sabourin, *The Gospel according to St. Matthew,* Bombay: St. Paul, 1983.
Sand, *Matthäus:*
    A. Sand, *Das Evangelium nach Matthäus,* Regensburger Neues Testa-
    ment, Regensburg: Friedrich Pustet, 1986.
Sanders, "Psalm 118":
    J. A. Sanders, "A New Testament Hermeneutic Fabric: Psalm 118 in the
    Entrance Narrative," *Early Jewish and Christian Exegesis: Studies in Mem-
    ory of William Hugh Brownlee,* ed. C. A. Evans and W. F. Stinespring,
    Atlanta: Scholars, 1987.
Senior, *The Passion of Jesus:*
    D. P. Senior, *The Passion of Jesus in the Gospel of Matthew,* Wilmington:
    Glazier, 1985.
Senior, *The Passion Narrative:*
    D. P. Senior, *The Passion Narrative according to Matthew: A Redactional
    Study,* Bibliotheca ephemeridum theologicarum lovaniensium 39, Leuven:
    Leuven University Press, 1975.
Strecker, *The Sermon on the Mount:*
    G. Strecker, *The Sermon on the Mount: An Exegetical Commentary,*
    Edinburgh: T. & T. Clark, 1988.
Syreeni, *The Making of the Sermon on the Mount:*
    K. Syreeni, *The Making of the Sermon on the Mount: A Procedural
    Analysis of Matthew's Redactional Activity. Part 1: Method and Compo-
    sitional Analysis,* Annales Academiae Scientarum Fennicae Dissertationes
    Humanarum Litterarum 44, Helsinki: Suomalainen Tiedeakatemia, 1987.
Talbert, *Reading Luke:*
    C. Talbert, *Reading Luke: A Literary and Theological Commentary on
    the Third Gospel,* New York: Crossroad, 1982.
Tannehill, *The Sword of His Mouth:*
    R. Tannehill, *The Sword of His Mouth,* Philadelphia: Fortress, 1975

INTRODUCTION

The author of this Gospel hides behind the anonymity of the community of faith in which he taught as a scribe "instructed in the truths of the kingdom" (13:52), but he has long been associated with the name of Matthew. Whether he was the Matthew who left his tax office to follow Jesus as a disciple (9:9; 10:3) is questionable. What can be said with more confidence about the one who penned this Gospel is that he belonged to a Hellenized Jewish culture, was able to write in good Greek, and was well versed in the Scriptures.

The earliest testimony that explicitly mentions Matthew is a citation found in Eusebius from Papias, the bishop of Hieropolis (*ca.* 110–25 c.e.) that, if it refers to our Gospel, highlights its Jewish orientation. Papias is said to have written: "Matthew made an ordered arrangement of oracles [*logia*] of the Lord in the Hebrew dialect [*dialektos*], and each one interpreted them as he was able" (*Ecclesiastical History* 3.39.16). Rather than referring to an Aramaic composition, J. Kürzinger argues that Papias was referring instead to its Jewish manner of presentation. The word *dialektos* was a "technical term of rhetorical technique"; and, in this case, it refers to the Gospel's rhetorical style ("Das Papiaszeugnis und die Erstgestalt des Matthäusevangeliums," *BZ* 4 [1960]: 20–23). The context of the quote suggests that Papias was contrasting Matthew's arrangement with the unordered arrangement of Mark:

> Mark, having become the interpreter of Peter, wrote down accurately whatever he remembered of the things said and done by the Lord, but not however in order. For neither did he hear the Lord, nor did he follow him, but afterward, as I said, Peter, who adapted his teachings to the needs of his hearers, but not as though he were drawing up a connected account of the Lord's oracles. So then Mark made no mistake in thus recording some things just as he remembered them. For he took forethought for one thing, not to omit any of the things that he had heard nor to state them falsely. (*Ecclesiastical History* 3.39.15)

1

Papias seems to be arguing that while Mark may be less accomplished rhetorically, it is nonetheless a dependable record of Peter's preaching. Matthew, on the other hand, reflects a Semitic rhetorical form.

While Papias's statement is enigmatic, Matthew's Jewish bent of mind is readily apparent even to the casual reader. He leaves unexplained many Jewish terms and customs such as handwashing (15:1; compare Mark 7:3), the nature of the two didrachma (=the temple tax, 17:24-27), the seat of Moses (23:2), phylacteries and fringes (23:5), and flight on the sabbath (24:20), assuming that his reader had some notion about what is being talked about. He goes to some lengths to demonstrate that Jesus was the son of David, a title highlighted in Matthew, and that he met all the qualifications to be the messiah of Israel. He illuminates the mission and destiny of Jesus throughout his Gospel with a creative rereading of the Scripture. He alone emphasizes that during Jesus' earthly ministry he was sent only to the lost sheep of the house of Israel (10:5-6; 15:24) and that he was not only perfectly obedient to the law, which has enduring validity, he was its fulfillment (5:17-20).

One should not conclude too quickly, however, that Matthew was written primarily for Jews. The Gospel contains significant material that smacks of an anti-Jewish bias (see 21:43; 23:32-33, 35; 27:25), and it also reflects an interest in the inclusion of gentiles into the church (8:11-12; 12:21). Jesus' final command ordains that disciples come from all the nations (28:19). Matthew's church has apparently split from its parent, Judaism. Matthew's church gathers around the name of Jesus, not the Torah (18:20). It confesses Jesus to be the son of God, God's promised messiah, because it has received divine revelation (11:25-27; 13:11-12; 16:17). Its members regard themselves as "sons" who are free from obligations associated with the Jewish sacrificial cult because of their relationship to Jesus (17:24-27). Salvation is to be found only in Jesus' church (16:18; 18:17), which has its own peculiar rituals: baptism in Jesus' name (28:19) and the supper that commemorates his death for the forgiveness of sins (26:26-29). Matthew's church also understands itself as divinely obligated to be obedient to the commands of its Lord (28:19). The self-awareness of Matthew's church is also evident in that it sees itself over against others who claim to be Israel. The kingdom of God has been taken away from the former tenants and given to "others," a "nation" that will produce its fruits in due season (21:41, 43). The invective hurled at Jewish leaders and teachers throughout the Gospel hints that the rupture was less than amicable. The synagogue is the arena of hypocrites (6:2; 23:6) and is clearly a foreign entity. Matthew consistently refers to "their synagogues" (4:23; 9:35; 10:17; 12:9; 13:54; see also "your synagogues," 23:34; and "their scribes," 7:29). The church, which believes in the resurrection of Jesus, is also considered to be distinct from those who do not who are designated as "the Jews" (28:15). Matthew apparently does not consider that term to be applicable to Christians.

Unfortunately, the exact historical setting in which this Gospel was composed and its date will probably never be known for certain. The majority of scholars surmise that it was composed some time after the disastrous Jewish rebellion against Rome when Jerusalem and the temple were ravaged and before the beginning of the second century. An array of possibilities for its origin have been proposed: Palestine, Edessa, Caesarea Maritima, Phoenicia, Syria, Antioch, Alexandria, east of the Jordan (perhaps Pella in the Decapolis; see 4:15, 25; 19:1). The best conjecture seems to be that it was written somewhere in Syria. Matthew 4:24 records that Jesus' fame "spread throughout all Syria" (contrast the parallel in Mark 1:28, which mentions only Galilee). If one needs to be more precise, the city of Antioch has been a traditional contender. According to Acts 11:19–26, it had one of the earliest Christian communities outside of Palestine, founded by Jewish Christians from the Hellenist group who began a circumcision-free mission. As a predominantly Greek-speaking city, it would have been a natural site for a Gospel written in Greek. Antioch also had a large Jewish population, which might explain the Jewish tone, interests, and mode of argument of the Gospel; but it was also the scene of violent anti-Jewish riots in 40 and 66–70 C.E., which might explain some of the negative attitudes toward the Jews in the Gospel. The origin in Antioch might also explain the prominence of Peter in this Gospel, since Paul places Peter in Antioch as an influential figure (Gal 2:11–14). All of these "mights" are only conjecture, and the evidence is far from compelling.

This commentator accepts the predominant view that Matthew made use of the Gospel of Mark and a collection of Jesus' sayings, commonly identified as Q. This introduction is not the place for the technical arguments pro and con. Suffice it to say that while a debate on this issue rages on, this hypothesis provides the least complicated explanation of the evidence and has served as a productive tool for the investigation of Matthew. Proponents of Matthean priority have also never satisfactorily answered the question of why, if one has Matthew and Luke, would one create a Gospel like Mark? The acceptance of the two-source hypothesis, however, is not allowed to get in the way of reading the text in the commentary. It is unnecessary to identify the sources to be able to read Matthew, but it will be helpful at points to read it side by side with Mark and Luke so that the reader can see its distinctive emphases. As with paint, one need not know what base color or tints were used to make a certain shade to be able to appreciate it. But a paint swatch does help one to see how the color "pearl white" differs from "icicle mist" and "ivory hue." Other ancient literature will also be read side by side with the Gospel to show how Matthew may be different or similar.

The question of Matthew's use of sources does impinge on the purpose behind its composition. Approximately 90 percent of Mark is found in Matthew, but it has been fundamentally transformed. Why? J. D. Kingsbury answers that Mark was no longer adequate to meet the needs of Matthew's church, and so it was revised to include more material with a different organizational pattern and to address differently issues of christology, ecclesiology, and the history of salvation (*Matthew*, 2d ed. [Philadelphia: Fortress, 1986], 15). Others have made quite specific proposals about Matthew's purpose: (a) Matthew was arranged after the fashion of Mosaic Pentateuch with a fivefold structure to provide a new law for the Christian community that was beset by lawlessness or libertinism. (b) Matthew was composed as a revised Gospel lectionary conveniently incorporating Mark and other traditions to provide a united whole that provided regular readings for Christian worship. (c) Matthew was a converted Rabbi who systematically arranged his Gospel so that it might become a handbook to serve catechetical needs in the church. (d) Matthew wrote from a Jewish standpoint to defend Christianity to Jewish Christian readers and to influence Jews away from the leadership of the Pharisees who controlled the "synagogue across the street." (e) Matthew wrote to portray the church as the true Israel, which has replaced the false Israel represented by the majority of Jewish unbelievers who have forfeited their place in the history of salvation as God's chosen people. (f) Matthew wrote after the debacle of the Jewish War against Rome to defend to a Torah-obedient Jewish Christianity the decision to turn from its failed mission to Israel to a gentile mission. These varied proposals suggest that the primary purpose of this Gospel is either not immediately obvious, or that it is in the eyes of the beholder, or that a variety of purposes were in mind that cannot be reduced to a few summary sentences.

Since the text contains so little unambiguous information that helps to specify its setting and date, one needs to be cautious in deciding what occasion may or may not have generated its production. One should not spin off some hypothetical context and then read it into the interpretation of the text or assume that the Gospel was drafted solely to address burning issues for a limited group. It is conceivable, if not likely, that Matthew was intended for broad circulation in a variety of Christian communities with a variety of needs and issues and that it was motivated simply by "a general desire to tell others about Jesus, who he was, what he did and what happened to him in the end" (R. A. Burridge, *What Are the Gospels? A Comparison with Graeco-Roman Biography*, SNTSMS 70 [Cambridge: Cambridge University Press, 1992], 214). The assumptions that Matthew used Mark and Q and that the Gospel belongs in the overall genre of "lives" – both of which are debated – would support this more general conclusion about why it was penned.

(1) K. Syreeni contends that the basic characteristic of Matthew is the combination of Mark and Q to produce "a new unified gospel" that included a fuller account of Jesus' teaching (*The Making of the Sermon on the Mount*, 110). He writes: "Matthew's *basic plan* was to produce a 'double' gospel with the complete story of Jesus and the whole of Jesus' authoritative teaching" (113). This aim was achieved by integrating Mark and Q with limited rearrangements, "by following their guidance if possible, and especially by elaborating on their speech sections in order to form representative discourses" (95). The discourses (chaps. 5-7; 10; 13; 18; [23] 24-25) were placed in ready-to-order Markan scenes in the main story of the Gospel and connected to the narrative through the use of a fivefold refrain ("And it happened when Jesus had finished . . . ," 7:28; 11:1; 13:53; 19:1; 26:1), which places emphasis on Jesus' authoritative words (7:24, 28-29). The discourses tend to coalesce around certain themes. The first discourse (5:1-8:1) deals with basic issues of discipleship ethics; the second (10:1-42), with missionary duties; the third (13:1-52), with the response to Jesus' ministry and the understanding of the disciples. The fourth (18:1-35) addresses internal strife within the community, and the last ([23:1-39] 24:1-25:46) concerns the destruction of the temple and preparation for the parousia and the final judgment. The result of the inclusion of these discourses is that Matthew provides us with a rich store of Jesus' teaching, which is the church's only secure foundation (7:24-27), and connects it to the narrative of his life and death.

(2) A second clue for understanding the Gospel's purpose is that it belongs to the overall genre of "lives," "a highly selective, often anecdotal account of an individual's life with everything chosen to illuminate

his essential being" (C. Talbert, "Once Again: Gospel Genre," *Semeia* 43 [1988]: 56). R. A. Burridge has most recently sought to demonstrate that the Gospels share a number of features with other "lives" that were used in groups or philosophical schools for teaching about the beliefs of their founder and for attack and defense in debate with others (*What Are the Gospels? A Comparison with Graeco-Roman Biography,* SNTSMS 70 [Cambridge: Cambridge University Press, 1992]). From his general observations, the following apply to Matthew.

(a) To tell the story of Jesus. This Gospel is about Jesus' life and teaching, not about the fate of Israel, the disciples, the Jewish leaders, or the community, even if all of these figure into the telling of the story. Matthew records words and deeds of one he proclaims to be the long-promised messiah who was conceived by the Holy Spirit (1:18), who was perfectly obedient to God's will, who taught (5:21–54; 7:29; 21:23) and performed miracles (8–9) with divine authority, and who prevailed over the rule of Satan and his demons. Following him is more urgent than fulfilling filial obligations to one's parent (8:22). Jesus was sent to save his people from their sins (1:21). He has authority to pronounce the forgiveness of sins (9:6), and his death brings atonement for sins that makes the animal sacrifices of the temple obsolete (20:28; 26:28). His humiliating death on the cross is vindicated by God through his resurrection, and God has given to him all authority over heaven and earth (28:18). The ultimate destiny of the world, Jew and gentile, depends on its giving its allegiance to the one who alone has broken the bonds of death. The promise of God being with his people (Zech 8:23; *Jubilees* 1:26) has been fulfilled. For Matthew, Jesus' story is the story of God with us (1:23; 28:20) and the coming of the reign of heaven on earth. Who Jesus is therefore cannot be captured by the various titles ascribed to him, son of David, son of God, son of man, Lord, wisdom. Only the complete story of Jesus' preaching and deeds, his death and resurrection, will convey the whole truth about who he is.

(b) To bolster faith. Tertullian wrote that no one comes to Christian literature for guidance "unless he is already a Christian" (*The Soul's Testimony* 1). The implied readers of this Gospel are assumed to be already acquainted with the story about Jesus and believe and confess that he is the son of God (14:33; 16:17; 27:54). In the opening chapter, Matthew feels no need to argue it or even proclaim it; it is simply assumed (D. Verseput, *The Rejection of the Humble Messianic King* [Frankfurt: Peter Lang, 1986], 31). Matthew was written therefore to buttress faith (see 6:30; 8:26; 14:31; 16:8; 17:20; 21:21; 28:17), to enable deeper reflection on the story (13:23, 51; 16:12; 17:13), and to help establish the identity of the church by reinterpreting the revered tradition of the Scripture as fulfilled in Christ (5:17; 26:54).

(c) To convince and refute. The Gospel defends its tradition by refuting those from Jewish circles who have apparently not allowed the faith of Christians to go unchallenged. Justin's *Dialogue* may include some of the Jewish aspersions on the Christian faith as "empty fables" that Matthew also had to contend with. Justin's partner in debate, Rabbi Trypho, accuses him of following a "man of no account," forsaking God and placing his "hope on a man," and ignoring God's law (8:3-4). He dismisses Justin's conviction that Jesus was the messiah by arguing:

> But Messiah, if indeed He has ever been and now exists anywhere, is unknown and does not even know Himself at all nor has any power, until Elijah shall have come and anointed Him, and shall have made Him Manifest to all. But you people, by receiving a worthless rumour, shape a kind of Messiah for yourselves, and for His sake are now blindly perishing. (8.4)

Matthew's Gospel counters such charges by verifying Jesus' credentials as the messiah, his lineage, birthplace, and field of operations. Matthew's frequent appeal to the fulfillment of Scripture is an attempt to show that Jesus' life and death conforms to a divine blueprint. Those who do not recognize this fact simply misread the Scripture.

Matthew also clarifies Jesus' relation to the law. He did not transgress the law and did not come to destroy the law or the prophets but to fulfill them (5:17-20). Whenever an incident in the story has to do with the law, Matthew always includes some explanation as to why Jesus may counter it, an appeal to a higher law, or God's original intention. As M. Hooker states the matter,

> [the] contrast is not between the Law given on Sinai and a new Law given by Jesus, but between the partial understanding of the divine will which came through Moses and the fuller understanding which is now given by Jesus. It is not a question of two different laws, but of one reality – the will of God – witnessed to by the Law and the prophets, but now made plain in Jesus. The Law given in Sinai was not wrong – but it was incomplete, and now its completion is here. (*Continuity and Discontinuity* [London: Epworth, 1986], 31)

The Gospel counters in addition any charges that Jesus' exorcisms were achieved through magic or because he himself was possessed by the prince of demons (9:34; 10:25; 12:24, 27). They were the work of the Spirit of God that was routing the domain of Satan through Jesus. Matthew also explains the earthly degradation of the messiah who many assumed would appear in a blaze of glory and judgment. Jesus seems to be powerless; but, at his arrest, Matthew makes it clear that he had access to a legion of angels and submitted to his captors solely because he was completely obedient to the divine plan laid out in the Scripture. He will appear in power and glory only at the end of the age when he comes to judge the world (25:31). The Gospel furthermore debunks tales that have spread about Jesus' resurrection. The rumors about his body being stolen were malicious lies spread by unprincipled enemies. It is they, not Jesus, who are the deceivers of the people (27:63; 28:11–15).

(d) To explain present circumstances. The Gospel attempts to reconcile theology with reality. Jerusalem and its holy temple lay in ruins, and the majority of the Jews did not accept Jesus as the messiah. Matthew seeks to explain how this has come about. Jesus was faithful to Israel; it was Israel that rejected both its messiah and the one who sent him. Matthew gives three reasons for this repudiation of Jesus. They are like stubborn chicks who willfully refused to be gathered under his wings (23:37; 11:20–24; 22:3). They have false leaders whose false teaching has led them astray (15:13–14; 16:6–12; 23:13; 28:15). They are in the clutch of Satan (12:43–45; 13:19). The Gospel therefore makes it clear that because Jesus fulfilled the promises made to Israel and imparted the true understanding and interpretation of God's will to his disciples they have become the true heirs of the covenant and the true teachers. They stand over against Pharisaic teachers and their followers who are thoroughly discredited.

(e) To exhort. The Gospel not only tells Christians who they are but shows how that is integrally related to how they are to behave. It was written to spur believers to steadfast obedience to Jesus' commands, and Matthew has no qualms about holding the threat of a grisly judgment over their heads. According to D. Marguerat (*Le jugement dans l'Évangile de Matthieu* [Geneva: Labor et Fides, 1981], 13), the theme of judgment appears in 60 of 148 pericopes in Matthew compared with 10 out of 92 in Mark and 28 out of 92 in Luke. Disciples are warned lest they be found wanting on the day of judgment and will be cast out into the outer darkness and the fires of hell. The prominence of this theme makes Matthew less appealing to many modern readers for whom the peril of an eventual judgment has lost its power in their imaginations.

(f) To arm for mission. The disciples of Jesus have acquired both Israel's promises and its job. The disciples are to be a light to all the world (5:14) and must go out to those who will hate them (10:22; 24:9). They must be fully confident in the divine authority and power of Jesus, who sends them out on mission until the end of the age (28:20).

The final introductory issue concerns the structure of this Gospel. A fivefold division of the Gospel that takes the refrain at the conclusion of the discourses ("when Jesus finished . . . ") as the structural key has long been the dominant view. The problems with this framework are many. It makes the birth and the passion and resurrection of Jesus simply prologue and epilogue, which hardly does justice to their significance. The refrain does not separate discourse from narrative but connects the two. The summaries in 4:23 and 9:35, for example, mark an inclusio of this section of discourse and narrative that are separated in this particular outline. The lack of any clear decisive beginnings for the discourses also creates a problem for using them to define the structure of the Gospel.

J. D. Kingsbury has promoted the argument for a threefold structure to the Gospel that makes the phrase "from that time Jesus began . . . " in 4:17 and 16:21 a key structural marker (*Matthew: Structure, Christology, Kingdom* [Philadelphia: Fortress, 1975], 7–25). This refrain marks a turning point in the life of Jesus that begins a new stage: "From that time Jesus began to preach and to say, 'Repent, for the kingdom of heaven is at hand!' " (4:17); "From that time Jesus began to show his disciples that he must go to Jerusalem and suffer many things . . . " (16:21). Kingsbury outlines the Gospel as follows:

> 1:1–4:16 The Presentation of the Person of Jesus Christ, Son of David, Son of Abraham, Son of God
>
> 4:17–16:20 The Presentation of Jesus in Terms of His Public Proclamation
>
> 16:21–28:20 The Presentation of Jesus in Terms of His Passion and Resurrection

While Matthew has a clear predilection to present things in triads, it must be admitted, given the number of competing structures that have been proposed for the Gospel, that Matthew may not have had some "broad overall structure" in mind at all (G. Stanton, "The Origin and Purpose of Matthew's Gospel: Matthean Scholarship from 1945–1980," *ANRW* II.25.3 [1985]: 1905). The search for some comprehensive blueprint may therefore be in vain. But this threefold structure commends itself because it allows the narrative about Jesus Messiah, son of God, to dominate the reading and rereading of Matthew. The story of Jesus is of primary importance, and this way of structuring the Gospel brings out the christological focus that this commentator considers to be crucial.

Matthew 1:1–4:16

INTRODUCING JESUS THE MESSIAH, THE SON OF GOD

INTRODUCTION

The first division of Matthew's Gospel (1:1–4:16) introduces the reader to its subject, Jesus Christ, son of God. It falls into four major sections. (1) The first section (1:1–25) introduces Jesus as the legitimate heir to the throne of David. The curtain raiser, a lengthy genealogy, is less than enticing to the modern reader, who tends to skip hastily over lists of descendants with their unpronounceable names to get to the good part, the action. But Matthew assumes that his readers are familiar with biblical genealogies and appreciate their significance, and he wants them to pause and reflect on the lineage of Jesus as a way of retracing biblical history to this point and as a means of evaluating Jesus. Matthew does not first introduce Jesus to the reader as the son of God (see Mark 1:1) but as the long-awaited messiah of the Jews, and he promptly establishes his messianic credentials as the son of David. The genealogy also sketches the contours of salvation history and highlights the fact that the time of Israel inaugurated by Abraham (1:2) has reached its fulfillment with the birth of Jesus, the one called Christ (1:16–17). (2) The second section (2:1–23) traces the movements of the born king of the Jews and demonstrates from the Scripture that they conform to a messianic pattern directed by God. Being from Nazareth in Galilee does not disqualify Jesus from being Israel's messiah. (3) The third section (3:1–4:11) shows Jesus in the wilderness as God's obedient son. He fulfills all righteousness in passing through the waters of John's baptism with the faithful of Israel, and he triumphs over the wiles of Satan, who tries in vain to subvert his complete submission to God's will. Unlike the generation of Israel that succumbed to temptation in the wilderness and turned away from the path of obedience, Jesus remains faithful. (4) The last section (4:12–16) presents Jesus returning to Galilee of the gentiles prepared to begin his ministry to Israel.

THE BIRTH OF THE MESSIAH: THE FULFILLMENT OF GOD'S PROMISES

Matthew 1:1-25

The opening section of the Gospel introduces the pedigree of Jesus Messiah and his birth to a virgin. It consists of two parts: (1) the genealogy of the messiah (1:1-17), and (2) Jesus' conception by the Holy Spirit and adoption by Joseph, which resolves a genealogical problem (1:18-25). The first part (1:1-17) begins with the phrase "the book of the genealogy [*genesis*] of Jesus Christ." Some argue that since this same phrase appears in Genesis 2:4 (LXX) to introduce the generations of the heavens and the earth, and in 5:1 (LXX) to introduce the generations of humans it should be taken as the introduction to the entire Gospel. It is best, however, to read it as the introduction to the genealogy in 1:1-17. "Ancient writings either begin with a formal dedication describing the purpose of the book (like Luke-Acts) or with a sentence marking the first subject treated" (H. Koester, *Ancient Christian Gospels: Their History and Development* [London: SCM, 1990], 14). The three names in the opening verse, Christ, Abraham, and David, reappear in 1:16-17 and form an inclusio for this first part that traces Jesus' royal lineage from Abraham to Joseph. A concluding summary in 1:17 affirms that all this genealogical history has been leading up to the birth of Jesus.

The second part (1:18-25) repeats the noun *genesis* from 1:1 and clears up a problem for the genealogy of the messiah. The Davidic ancestry is traced through Joseph, son of David (1:20); but the reader learns in 1:18 that Jesus is not the biological son of Joseph. Matthew therefore must clarify how it came to pass that someone born of a virgin could be the son of David.

(1) The Gospel opens with a genealogy (1:1-17). Other ancient biographers also included genealogies (cf. Plutarch, *Parallel Lives;* Suetonius, *Lives of the Caesars;* Josephus, *Life* 6; *Against Apion* 1:7).

14

Quintilian contends that in celebrating the deeds of a man it is helpful to provide information about his family background:

> In the first place there is a distinction to be made as regards time between the period in which the objects of our praise lived and the time preceding their birth; and further, in the case of the dead, we must also distinguish the period following their death. With regard to things preceding a man's birth, there are his country, his parents and his ancestors, a theme which may be handled in two ways. For either it will be creditable to the objects of our praise not to have fallen short of the fair fame of their country and of their sires or to have ennobled a humble origin by the glory of their achievements. (*Institutio Oratoria* III 7, 10; cited by G. Mussies, "Parallels to Matthew's Version of the Pedigree of Jesus," *NovT* 28 [1986]: 33)

Far from being an archive of Jesus' ancestors, the genealogy reviews what has happened in the story of God's people before Jesus' birth and tells the reader how to evaluate Jesus. It is therefore important to know something of the story behind the names in this registry because it also tells the reader something about what the God of Israel has done and has promised to do. The genealogy discloses more than that Jesus belongs to the legitimate line of the king of Israel. It reveals that his roots go deep into Israel's sacred history, which God has been guiding, even in the blackest of moments, to its culmination. All biblical history has been leading up to the birth of the messiah.

By introducing Jesus immediately as the son of David and the son of Abraham, Matthew links Jesus to God's two great promises to Israel. (a) "Son of David" recalls God's promise to raise up David's offspring and to establish the kingdom of his throne forever (2 Sam 7:12-16; 1 Chron 17:11-14; Ps 89:3; 132:11; Isa 11:1-5, 10; Jer 23:5-6; 30:9; 33:14-18; Ezek 34:23-24; 37:24; Sir 47:11; 1 Macc 2:57). This promise was seemingly frustrated by the deportation to Babylon and the political upheaval after the exile, but the hope was not lost. In the benedictions prayed three times a day by pious Jews, the fifteenth beseeches God: "Cause the Shoot of David to shoot forth quickly, and raise up his horn by thy salvation. For we wait on thy salvation all the day. Blessed art Thou, O Lord, who causest the horn of salvation to shoot forth." The author of the *Psalms of Solomon* voiced the same longing:

> [21]See, Lord, and raise up for them their king, the son of David, to rule over your servant Israel in the time known to you, O God.
> [22]Undergird him with the strength to destroy the unrighteous

rulers, to purge Jerusalem from gentiles who trample her to destruction; [23]in wisdom and in righteousness to drive out the sinners from the inheritance; to smash the arrogance of sinners like a potter's jar; [24]To shatter all their substance with an iron rod; to destroy the unlawful nations with the word of his mouth; [25]At his warning the nations will flee from his presence; and he will condemn sinners by the thoughts of their hearts. (17:21-25)

According to Matthew, the time of salvation known only to God has arrived with the advent of Jesus. But as the story unfolds, the reader learns that Jesus, son of David, will not reign over a kingdom in Israel but will have all authority in heaven and earth (28:18). His eternal throne of glory will be an inglorious cross. He will take away the sins of his people, not drive away sinners (1:21; 8:17); and his kingdom shall include, not subjugate, men and women from the unlawful nations (28:20).

(b) Identifying Jesus also as "son of Abraham" may not seem at first glance to provide any vital information about him except that he was a Jew, since all Jews were considered to be sons of Abraham (see 3:9). It is intended, however, to recall God's promise to Abraham that by his seed all the nations of the earth shall gain blessing (Gen 22:18). Jesus Christ is that seed (see Gal 3:16) in whose name the gentiles will find hope (12:21). The genealogy contains names that hint of the universality of salvation that will be offered in Jesus. When he is born, gentiles from the East come to worship him (2:1-12). The final fulfillment quotation of the first major division of the Gospel draws attention to Galilee of the gentiles receiving a great light (4:14-16), and the Gospel will end with Jesus sending his disciples to all the nations (28:19).

(c) Both David and Abraham were promised a son. The birth of Isaac, miraculous as it was (Gen 22:7), and the birth of Solomon, beloved of the Lord (2 Sam 12:24-25), are superseded by the birth of Jesus, whose conception is even more miraculous and who is beloved as God's own son.

To unlock the theological significance of the genealogy itself, one can focus on the four points where it deviates from convention and the basic pattern of "X the father of Y." (a) First, we note that this genealogy is unusual in that it begins with the last entry, Jesus Christ, instead of the first person, who started the family. The reason is that Matthew understands Jesus to be the fulfillment of God's promises to Israel who therefore overshadows all those who came before him. While Abraham marks the emergence of Israel and David stands at the royal pinnacle of its history, it is Jesus who is the completion of Israel's national heritage and hopes. The promise of a great nation and the promise of an eternal kingship find their fulfillment in Jesus.

(b) The pattern, X the father of Y, is broken with the reference to "Judah and his brothers" (1:2) and "Jechoniah and his brothers" (1:11). Perhaps the reference to the brothers of Judah at the beginning of the first generation of fourteen and to the brothers of Jechoniah (never mentioned in the Scripture) at the end of the second generation of fourteen is meant to underscore the fact that the genealogical history of Jesus Christ encompasses the experience of all Israel: from the inception of the twelve tribes to their scattering in the exile. No brothers are mentioned, however, in the third generation of fourteen. In the Gospel, the disciples of Jesus fill this role (12:49-50; 28:10). They will mark a new dimension in the sweep of Israel's history.

(c) The pattern, X the father of Y, is broken again by the unexpected mention of the mothers (Tamar, 1:4; Rahab and Ruth, 1:5; the wife of Uriah, 1:6; and Mary, 1:16). Women were not normally included in a genealogy unless there was an irregularity of pedigree or some noteworthy association (B. M. Nolan, *The Royal Son of God: The Christology of Mt 1-2,* OBO 23 [Göttingen: Vandenhoeck & Ruprecht, 1979], 62). No woman, not even Mary, appears in the genealogy of Jesus recorded in Luke 3:23-38. What is even more surprising is the fact that these particular women are not the great matriarchs of Israel even though they lived at important phases in Israel's history: Tamar in the time of the patriarchs, Rahab in the time of the conquest, Ruth in the time of the judges, and Bathsheba in the time of the monarchy. They are never listed together in any other known Jewish text, perhaps because of their spotted histories.

When Judah failed to provide a husband to Tamar in accordance with the Israelite custom of levirate marriage, she took matters into her own hands. Posing as a prostitute, she lured Judah and conceived twin sons (Gen 38). According to *Jubilees* 41:1, she was an Aramean (see also *Testament of Judah* 10:1; Philo, *On the Virtues* 221). Rahab, on the other hand, did not pose as a prostitute; she was one (although Josephus covers up this distinction by referring to her simply as an "innkeeper," *Antiquities* 5.1.1 §9-15). Rahab acquired biblical favor, however, by sheltering the spies sent out by Joshua (Josh 2:1-21; 6:25); but the Bible makes no mention of her marriage. Ruth was from the cursed race of Moab stemming from Lot's incest with his firstborn daughter (Gen 19:30-38). Moses decreed that no Ammonite or Moabite may enter the

assembly of Israel (Deut 23:3). The mother of Solomon is identified only
as wife of Uriah. The name of Uriah, a Hittite, dredges up the tawdry
story of David's adultery and death-dealing (2 Sam 11-12).

Of this group of women, four were gentiles or associated with gentiles, and three would hardly win accolades for virtue. Is there some
common denominator that explains their inclusion in the genealogy
of the messiah? Many have contended that it is the shocking nature of
the stories behind these names that foreshadows that redemption will
be offered to sinners such as these – the unrighteous and the disrep-
utable. Jesus was born to save a sinful people, not a perfect race. But
this explanation of the women's presence in the genealogy should be
dismissed because they come off quite well in later Jewish discussions
of them. Each was venerated for advancing in some way the cause of
the nation of Israel. This standard explanation also ignores the fact that
the men in the list committed far worse sins. Manasseh, for example,
was reckoned as the most evil of the kings (2 Kgs 21:1-18). Why single
out the women as examples of a sinful race? If anything, the women
might represent that redemption will be offered to the helpless and
oppressed, although Tamar, Ruth, and Bathsheba moved aggressively
to secure their future.

It is more likely that the inclusion of these women foreshadows
that God's offer of salvation will be universal. All of them were of gentile stock. Ruth, in particular, was identified as "the Moabitess" (Ruth
4:5); and the later Rabbis felt compelled to defend vigorously this blem-
ish in David's bloodline (see *Babylonian Talmud Yebamot* 76b–77a;
Sanhedrin 110a; *Midraš Psalms* 4:9; 116:9; *Ruth Rabba* 8:1). The inclusion of these women reveals that even the family tree of the messiah
transcends national limits. Gentiles have been grafted into the Davidic
line. But these are not just any gentiles. Their stories reveal that they
were pious gentiles. Judah must confess in the end that Tamar is more
righteous than he (Gen 38:26). Rahab trusted the pledge of the spies
to protect her and her family (Heb 11:31; Jas 2:25; 1 Clem 12:1-8),
and her faithfulness contrasts with the Israelites who "broke faith in
regard to the devoted things" (Josh 7:1). Ruth looked for a husband in
accordance with the Jewish custom of levirate marriage and sought to
provide for her Jewish mother-in-law (Ruth 3:10–11). Uriah, the Hittite, refused to violate the taboos regarding those consecrated for war
(2 Sam 11:11) and was more righteous than King David, who committed adultery with Uriah's wife, plied him with drink to try to get him
to break his vow, and finally orchestrated his death on the battlefield.

The stories behind these names prepare us for the kind of tenacious faith we will see in the gentile centurion (8:5-13) and the Canaanite woman (15:21-28) – a faith that surpasses that found even in Israel. Their stories also make clear that the inclusion of gentiles did not damage the cause of Israel but benefited Israel and moved things along their divinely appointed course.

(d) The names of these women also prepare us for the fifth mother on the list, although she is neither a foreigner nor unchaste (Brown, *Birth,* 73-74). Yet another break in the pattern, X the father of Y, occurs in 1:16. Joseph is identified as the husband of Mary rather than Mary as the wife of Joseph, and the passive voice is used for the first time: "of whom Jesus was begotten." The story behind the other breaks in the pattern can be filled in by the Scripture, and each case betrays some violation of religious convention – incest, prostitution, exogamy, and adultery. None of these women were the "right" marriage partner. The story behind the change in the pattern in 1:16, however, cannot be filled in from Scripture. It is only from what the Evangelist tells us in 1:18-25 that we learn that Mary became pregnant from the Holy Spirit prior to the consummation of her marriage to Joseph. Joseph decides on his own that Mary cannot be the "right" woman for a righteous man to marry (1:19). But God's purpose overrides. As the four women in the genealogy are vehicles of God's messianic plan in spite of their irregular circumstances, so is Mary. The previous aberrations prepare one for the holy aberration of the virginal conception and point to the mysterious workings of God in salvation history. "God's way is often a detour through which his promise is nevertheless fulfilled" (E. Lohmeyer, *Das Evangelium des Matthäus,* 2d ed. [Göttingen: Vandenhoeck & Ruprecht, 1958], 5). One can therefore expect the unexpected when dealing with God.

The conclusion to the genealogy organizes the history of Israel until the birth of Jesus into fourteen generations, repeating the key names from the opening verse: Abraham, David, and Christ. When the biblical historians schematized generations they declared their faith that "history is the sphere in which God works out his purpose" (Milton, "The Structure of the Prologue to Matthew," *JBL* 81 [1962]: 176). Apocalyptic writers, however, arranged history into epochs to assess the present age and the future (see *2 [Syriac] Apocalypse of Baruch* 53-74). The question in 4 Ezra 6:7 is typical of apocalyptic writings: "When will the end of the first age and the beginning of the second age be?" Matthew knows the answer to that question after the fact and fashions the table of genealogy to demonstrate that Jesus inaugurates the new age. At the appointed time (see Gal 4:4), God has stepped in with the birth of his son. W. D. Davies concludes: "The genealogy is an impressive witness to Matthew's conviction that the birth of Jesus was no unpremeditated accident but occurred in the fullness of time and in the providence of God, who overruled the generations to this end, to inaugurate in Jesus a new order, the time of fulfillment" (*Setting,* 73). The genealogy is not the record of one birth after another. It discloses that God has been working within history to achieve foreordained purposes and that Jesus, the last person of the last epoch, is the fulfillment of God's plan for Israel and the beginning of a new messianic age.

(2) The second part of this introductory section of the Gospel (1:18–25) is frequently entitled "birth narrative," but this is a misnomer. It implies that what follows will tell us about how Jesus was born. But no details of the birth are forthcoming even in 1:25. It is not a story to be read by the fire on Christmas eve. We have no trip to Bethlehem, no manger, no angels rejoicing, no shepherds looking for a babe in swaddling clothes, nothing to dramatize on Christmas cards. The best texts also do not read "birth" in 1:18 but "genealogy," the same word that introduces the genealogy in 1:1. No verb such as "took place" (NRSV) is present. Verse 18 reads literally: "And the genealogy [*genesis*] of Jesus Messiah was in this way."

This second part is not "some new and unrelated story of the way Jesus came to be born, but rather an extension or explanation of the genealogy" (L. Cantwell, "The Parentage of Jesus: Mt 1:18–21," *NovT* 24 [1982]: 304). The series of begats in the genealogy leads the reader to expect at the climax "and Joseph begat Jesus." Instead, we have noted the marked change in the pattern: "Joseph was the husband of Mary of whom Jesus was born" (1:16). The careful reader is prompted to ask, Why this change in the pattern? Is Joseph the father of Jesus or not? What happened? It also raises the question, Why bother to trace the lineage of Jesus through Joseph if he did not beget Jesus?

The introduction to this second part (1:18) provides the reader with the explanation for the use of the passive voice in 1:16. Joseph did not beget Jesus as Jacob, his father, begot him; Jesus was conceived by the Holy Spirit. But what must be explained, from Matthew's point of view, is not how something so extraordinary could come to pass but how Jesus, who had no physical, human father, could be the son of David. The object of 1:18–25 is not to prove that Jesus was born of a virgin. The virginal conception is something that is taken for granted by Matthew and dealt with as a problem for Jesus' lineage that is surmounted only by direct angelic intervention. If one looks for the aim of a unit from what is stressed at its conclusion, one finds that the emphasis falls not on the birth of the son but on the naming of the son by Joseph (1:25) in obedience to the instructions of the angel (1:21).

This section reveals how Jesus, who was not the biological son of Joseph because he was conceived by the Holy Spirit, became Joseph's legal son and was grafted into David's line. The object then is not to spotlight the virginal conception so much as to narrate how Jesus is the son of David *in spite of* the virginal conception.

The explanation begins by disclosing that Mary was betrothed to Joseph. Betrothal was not a promise to marry but the first stage of marriage. For girls, it could take place as early as twelve years of age (*Babylonian Talmud Yebamot* 62b). The betrothed couple did not live together until the marriage ceremony when they entered the wedding canopy and the marriage blessings were recited, and a year might pass before the woman moved to her husband's home (*Mishna Ketubot; Nedarim* 10:5; *Babylonian Talmud Ketubot* 57b). The betrothal could only be canceled by an official bill of divorce (*Mishna Ketubot* 8:1). After introducing Mary as betrothed to Joseph and pregnant by the Holy Spirit, the Evangelist tells us why Joseph completed the marriage procedure with Mary and made Jesus his legal son by naming him.

The explanation contains five theological themes important to Matthew. (a) The first has to do with Jesus' dual paternity as son of God and son of David. Dual paternity at the divine and human levels was common for deified rulers in the Near East from the Bronze Age to Roman times (C. H. Gordon, "Paternity at Two Levels," *JBL* 96 [1977]: 101). Gordon cites Odysseus as an example. He was said to be sired by Zeus but is heir to the throne of Ithaca because of his father, Laërtes (Homer, *Iliad* 10:144). His royal station in society derived from his mother's human husband, not from divine conception.

The same is true for Jesus. His royal station as the messiah of the people is certified by his adoption by Joseph, his mother's husband. The section ends with Joseph naming the child as the angel commanded (1:21, 25). It is the acknowledgement of a child by the father that officially makes the child his son (often cited is *Mishna Baba Batra* 8:6: "If a man said, 'This is my son,' he may be believed"). Jesus, born of the virgin Mary, is thereby grafted into the Davidic line through Joseph's juridical recognition of him as his own son (see 13:55).

Jesus' conception by the Holy Spirit affirms his divine sonship, which certifies the presence of God with the people. It makes clear that the salvation that is offered in Jesus does not come from human potentiality. The progress of salvation history revealed in the genealogy does not hinge on human procreation. It comes from the creative power of God's Spirit alone. This account furnishes the answer to the question that stumps the Pharisees in 21:45-46: how is it that Jesus is David's Lord and David's son?

(b) A second theological theme has to do with what it means to be righteous. Joseph is described as "a righteous man" (1:19), which classifies him as a faithful observer of the law (see Luke 1:6, Zechariah and Elizabeth). He responds conscientiously to news that his betrothed has become pregnant by planning to divorce her. He knew that he was not the father of the child, which meant that either Mary had been seduced (Deut 22:23-24) or violated (Deut 22:25-27). As a righteous man, he could not take Mary as his wife, for to do so, according to the law, was to tolerate evil in your midst. But his plan to divorce Mary "quietly" (1:19) reveals that as a righteous man he was also concerned about mercy. He is the model of the law-observant Jew who blends submission to the law with compassion for others (see 9:13; 12:7). He could have insisted on a public trial to determine whether or not Mary had prostituted herself (Deut 22:13-19), was seduced (Deut 22:23-24), or was raped (Deut 22:25-27) and would have saved himself the obligation of paying out the amount of money he had pledged to her if she were divorced (*ketuba*). Instead, he chose not to expose her to public disgrace.

Throughout Matthew's infancy narrative, God directs persons in dreams (1:20; 2:12, 13, 19, 22; see also 27:19). Joseph's righteous intentions ordained by the law are vetoed by no less an authority than an angel of the Lord who appears to him in a dream. While Joseph knew that Mary was pregnant, he could only know that it was by the Holy Spirit through special revelation. The dream removes all suspicion of impropriety surrounding Mary's pregnancy and makes her permissible to Joseph within the law. But to others not privy to this revelation or not inclined to believe it, the marriage may still be construed as shocking. The righteous person, however, is not one who simply conforms to conventional expectations but one who is obedient to God's revelation no matter how scandalous it might appear to others.

(c) The third theological theme has to do with the names chosen by God for the child that draw out the significance of his vocation — "Jesus" and "Immanuel." These names anticipate his future career and reveal that God has taken the initiative to do more than provide Israel with a messiah who will produce military victories. With the conception of this child, God has acted to redeem humankind.

The name Jesus, which in popular etymology meant "Yahweh saves," captures his role: "he will save his people from their sins" (compare Sir 46:1; Philo, *On the Change of Names* 12:121). In Psalm 130:8, God promises to redeem Israel from all its iniquities. The angel ascribes that task now to Jesus. Matthew adds the interpretation of the name Immanuel in Isaiah 7:14, "God with us," to underline the fact that salvation comes from God who acts in and through this Jesus conceived by the Holy Spirit. For Matthew, the birth of Jesus is the fruition of God's promise through the ages to be with and to save God's people.

(d) A fourth theological theme is Matthew's conviction that Jesus fulfills the promise of Scripture and that Scripture, properly interpreted, illumines who Jesus is. In this passage, the angel and the Scripture work in tandem in revealing God's purpose. Isaiah 7:14 provides the scriptural assurance that Joseph should abandon his plan to divorce Mary and should assume paternity of the child by naming him. Matthew or his source was able to draw the connection to Jesus from Isaiah 7:13, where the prophet does not address King Ahaz by name but says: "Hear then, O house of David!" The text that follows about a virgin conceiving therefore has to do with the house of David; and for the Evangelist, it is not simply "a virgin" as in the LXX, but *the* virgin (see Rabbi Trypho's objections to this interpretation in Justin Martyr, *Dialogue* 67:1–2). The text from Isaiah reads: "she shall call his name Emmanuel." But the mother will not name Jesus; Joseph will, which is the point at issue. Consequently, Matthew renders it: "they shall call his name Immanuel," as if to say, what the Scripture really meant to say was this.

(e) A final theological theme relates to Jesus' conception by the Holy Spirit. The Holy Spirit is not only the source of creation and life (Gen 1:2) but also the initiator of the messianic age (Isa 61:1). Jesus' conception is therefore understood by Matthew to be an eschatological event of a new creation. It sets it off as a radical disruption of what preceded it in the genealogy in 1:2–16. Human genealogical possibilities have been completed and exhausted. God now steps in. This divine intervention marks a new beginning; and while there is continuity with the past, there is also an unmistakable discontinuity. "With Christianity religious identity is fundamentally detached from nation, family and sex" (K. F. Plum, "Genealogy as Theology," *SJOT* 3 [1989]: 90). The virginal conception of Jesus indicates that membership in the family of God or becoming a brother or sister of Jesus is not based on physical descent from a common ancestor, as with old Israel. It will depend only on one's obedience to God's will, which creates a greater, more inclusive, and closer family (see 12:48-50).

FROM JUDEA OF DAVID
TO THE GALILEE
OF THE GENTILES

2:1-23

The second section of the first large division of the Gospel also consists of two parts. (1) The first part (2:1-12) has to do with the search of the magi for the born king of the Jews, which meets with the nervous reaction of Herod and all Jerusalem. It is bracketed by the reference to Herod (2:1, 12) and the worship of the magi (2:2, 11) and can be divided into two segments: 2:1-8 and 2:9-12. Each of these segments begins with the magi on a journey and the mention of the star that had attracted their notice at its rising (2:2, 2:9). (2) The second part (2:13-23) has to do with the migration of Joseph and his family to evade the threat from Herod and is bracketed by references to Joseph's dreams and the verb "to depart" (2:13, 14, 22).

(1) The next stage in the introduction of Jesus (2:1-12) begins with the announcement of his birth in Bethlehem of Judea during the reign of Herod and the sudden arrival of magi from the East in Jerusalem. The term "magi" could have positive or negative shades of meaning in the ancient world. It could refer to wise men who possessed mystical knowledge, to practitioners of the black arts (see Acts 8:9, 11), to astrologers, or to beguiling frauds (Acts 13:6, 8). In Matthew's account, the magi are no sorcerers but pious gentiles like those encountered in the genealogy (the phrase "king of the Jews" appears only on the lips of gentiles in the Gospel, 27:11, 29, 37; contrast "king of Israel" on the lips of the chief priests and scribes, 27:42). They come to pay homage to Jesus, the born king of the Jews; and they heed the divine forewarning to evade the evil Herod. The magi therefore represent the best of pagan lore and religious perception, and they seek Jesus through the best of pagan science (Brown, *Birth*, 168).

These students of the heavens spotted the star of Jesus "at its rising," not, as in some translations, "in the East." The word for "East" and "rising" is the same in Greek, but it means "East" in 2:1, 8:11, and 24:27 when it is in the plural and used with the preposition "from." The word in 2:2 has a definite article, and since the points of the compass never take the definite article, it serves to function as a weak possessive pronoun (BDF §253.5). The magi connected the rise of the star with the birth of the king of the Jews and came to the Jewish nerve center, Jerusalem, for more information.

The appearance of the magi with gifts befitting a king sounds two biblical themes. First, it accords with the expectation that nations would come to Israel in the latter days in recognition of God's reign (Ps 72:10-11; Isa 2:1-4; 43:5-10; 60:3-6; Mic 4:1; *Psalm of Solomon* 17:31; *Sibylline Oracles* 3:702-19, 772-73, 785-88). Second, the magi serve as an antitype for Balaam, a diviner who came from the mountains of the East (Num 22:5; 23:7; Philo, *Moses* 1.276, dubbed Balaam a *magos*), acclaimed Israel's king and kingdom (Num 24:7), and prophesied that a star would arise from Jacob (Num 24:17). One Jewish tradition goes so far as to identify Balaam as a prophet like Moses among the nations (*Sipre Deuteronomy* §357). The story of the magi also sounds two themes found in Matthew's Gospel: (a) the indifference of his own people to the born king (2:2-8), and (b) worship as the proper reaction to Jesus (2:9-12).

(a) The gentiles' diligent search for the born king of the Jews and their exceeding joy on finding him contrasts markedly with the uneasiness of Herod and all Jerusalem at the news of the birth. Since Herod was an Edomite who was appointed king by the Romans (Josephus *Antiquities* 14.14.4-5 §381-89; 14.15.1 §403), he would have been understandably threatened by any inquiry about a "born king of the Jews." Omens from the stars also were nothing to be brushed aside. The appearance of comets, for example, were assumed to portend the birth or the death of someone of great consequence. Suetonius tells us that when a comet appeared over Rome for several nights, Nero took the precaution of having several Roman noblemen executed, so that it would have augured their deaths and not his (*Nero* 36).

Herod's vexation does not startle anyone familiar with his paranoid concern to preserve his throne and power at all costs. What is surprising, however, is the report that "all Jerusalem" is troubled with him (2:3). One might have expected that all Jerusalem would erupt in great rejoicing at news of the birth of a born king. Perhaps it is the case that when this psychopathic king is troubled, it is time for everyone else to be troubled as well. But later in the story, when Jesus arrives on the outskirts of Jerusalem, the city is again shaken (21:10-11). Troubled Jerusalem therefore forms a united front with Herod against Jesus, and this reaction is an ominous foreboding of what is to come. Herod's ruthless stealth in trying to eliminate this child competitor (2:7) foreshadows the malevolent cunning of the Sanhedrin in Jerusalem who also will furtively plot the death of Jesus (26:3-5).

That Herod would summon high priests and scribes to inquire about the whereabouts of the messiah's birth is most unusual (2:4). According to Josephus, Herod began his reign with a massacre of the members of the Sanhedrin and kept their influence to a bare minimum (*Antiquities* 14.9.1 §175; see *Babylonian Talmud Baba Batra* 3b). The gathering of "all the high priests and scribes of the people" serves to emphasize the complete indifference of official Judaism to the birth of the messiah. Although the priests and scribes would also believe in the portents of stars (if Josephus is any indication, *Jewish War* 6.5.3 §289), they were not expecting nor even looking for the star of the messiah. Unwittingly, however, they confirm Jesus' messianic credentials by providing the scriptural confirmation that the messiah is to be born in Bethlehem. Their mastery of the Scriptures, however, does not lead them to obedience. It is the magi, outsiders with only their unholy science of astrology (see Isa 47:13-14; Jer 10:2; *Jubilees* 12:16-18; *Sibylline Oracles* 3:227-29), who are the first to learn of and to search for the born king. The scribes and the high priests provide only fine-tuning adjustments to their search. It turns out, however, that the magi do not need their directions; God grants them a miraculous star to guide them to the place.

(b) The theme of worship emerges in the second segment (2:9-12). Matthew's story begins with gentiles coming to pay homage to a king (2:2, 11) and ends with the disciples worshiping the resurrected Jesus on the mountain (28:17). In between a leper (8:2), a ruler (9:18), the disciples (14:33), a Canaanite woman (15:25), the mother of James and John (20:20), an anonymous woman (26:6-13), and the women at the tomb (28:9) all worship him. The story will reveal that Jesus is not only worthy of reverence as a king but is due the same adoration that previously was reserved only for God.

(2) The second part of this section (2:13-23) focuses on messianic topography. In their only speaking part, the magi raise the question, "Where is the born king of the Jews?" (2:2). It is echoed by Herod: "Where is the.Christ to be born?" (2:4). The answer is that the Christ is

to be born in Bethlehem (see John 7:42), and Jesus meets this requirement. But this section also records Jesus' journey from Judea (2:1) to Egypt (2:13-14), back to the land of Israel (2:21), and on to Nazareth in Galilee (2:22-23). As the first section answers the question, How can one born of a virgin be the son of David? the second section solves a similar problem: How is Jesus really the messiah if he is called the Nazarean and is associated almost entirely with Galilee? (Green, *Matthew,* 56). The problem for Matthew is voiced explicitly in the Fourth Gospel. Nathaniel asks, "Can anything good be from Nazareth?" (John 1:46); and the crowds inquire skeptically, "The Christ does not come from Galilee, does he?" (John 7:41). Matthew describes how Jesus, who was born in Bethlehem (2:1), eventually wound up in Nazareth and shows that each move was a fulfillment of Scripture.

The three names in the quotations from the Scripture – Bethlehem, the city of David (2:6); Egypt, the land of Exodus (2:15); and Ramah, the mourning place of the exile (2:18; see Jer 40:1) – evoke decisive moments in the history of the people of Israel (Brown, *Birth,* 217). As the first section (1:1-25) demonstrates that Jesus is the fulfillment of Jewish hopes, the second section shows Jesus recapitulating the major events in the story of Israel; but it is with some irony. Jesus, the son of David, is rejected in the land of Judah and therefore must find a refuge in Egypt, the symbol of bondage. When he returns to "the land of Israel" (2:20, 21, the only time this phrase occurs in the New Testament), he cannot stay there but must retreat to Galilee (2:22), which is later identified as the Galilee of the gentiles (4:15). Had he remained in Judea, he would have been killed. When he finally returns to Judea, he *is* killed. "Judea" and "the land of Israel" come to represent the place of unbelief, and refuge is to be found only beyond their borders.

A distinctive characteristic of Matthew's infancy narrative and his Gospel is the inclusion of fulfillment quotations that freeze the action and explain its significance. There are forty-two explicit citations of the Old Testament in Matthew compared to nineteen in Mark and Luke and fourteen in John. One quarter of these citations are introduced by a formula with the passive voice of the verb "fulfill." They particularly dominate the second part of this section (2:16, 18, 23).

Why this recurring appeal to the Scripture? First of all, "It was imperative that Matthew argue the case of Christ in terms of the scriptural authority available and compelling to him, in the Law and the Prophets" (J. A. Sanders, "*Nazoraios* in Matt 2:23," *JBL* 84 [1965]: 172). It is the Scripture that authoritatively clarifies who Jesus is, and therefore Matthew turns to it to explain the biblical import of the events he narrates. Second, the Scripture citations create a set of resonances for the reader. J. A. Sanders warns modern readers against ascribing "their possible ignorance of Scripture, that is the Scripture of the first century church, to either the New Testament writers or their congregants," and argues "that common to all programs of instruction upon conversion in the early churches was assiduous reading of Scripture, what we call Old Testament, as well as Jesus traditions" ("Psalm 118," 178). The citations would have evoked for the early readers a bundle of associations connected with the context in the same way that the theme songs from TV shows or movies do for the modern reader. Third, the appeal to Scripture demonstrates that the things that Jesus did and that happened to him were predetermined components of an agelong design of God. This conviction reassures the reader of God's ultimate control over events, then and now.

What is particularly interesting about Matthew's use of Scripture is the way he seems to taper it to fit the context of his account. The quotation about Bethlehem (2:6) is a conflation of Micah 5:1 and 2 Samuel 5:2. Matthew has "land of Judah" instead of Ephrathah (Hebrew), which heightens the associations with the root of David and his kingship (see Rev 5:5; Gen 49:10). He also completely alters the meaning of Micah 5:1 by writing, "by no means least among the governors of Judah," instead of "who are little to be among the clans [the LXX reads "thousands"] of Judah." The verb form of "governors" is used of David in 2 Samuel 5:2–3 (LXX), and it may have influenced Matthew's variation. The "for" in the next clause calls attention to the dramatic alteration of Bethlehem's role in Israel's history from an inconsequential hamlet to the birthplace of the long-awaited messiah, and Matthew modifies the Scripture accordingly. The conclusion of Micah 5:2, "whose origin is from old, from ancient of days," is omitted in favor of a quotation from 2 Samuel 5:2 (1 Chron 11:2) that contains God's promise to David, "you shall shepherd my people Israel" (see 9:36; 10:6; 15:24).

Danger brews when the news of Jesus' birth reaches the royal court in Jerusalem. The holy family does not escape by means of a miracle but by flight, as the church will also not escape its persecution by miracle but by flight (10:23; 24:16). Like a perfect disciple, Joseph obeys the command from God to retreat to Egypt without asking how long he will have to stay or what will happen to him there. Jesus starts life as a refugee, and the self-exile in Egypt is said to fulfill Hosea 11:1 (2:15). The fulfillment citation is unlike others in Matthew in that it refers to an event before it has been narrated ("out of Egypt I will call my son"). The reason is perhaps due to the primary interest in the reference to Egypt as the place of refuge (1 Kgs 11:40; 2 Kgs 25:26; Jer 41:16–18; Jer 26:21; 41:17; 43:1–7; Josephus, *Antiquities* 12.9.7 §387; 14.2.1 §21; 15.3.2 §46; *Jewish War* 7.10.1 §410; 7.10.2 §423). The phrase "my son" in Hosea 11:1 refers to Israel; but Matthew takes it to refer to Jesus because he understands Jesus to embody true, obedient Israel as the son of God. Jesus will reenact a new exodus.

The authority of a tyrant can be exerted only through the use of deceit and terror. Herod intends to annihilate the newborn king through wholesale carnage, much the way Pharaoh tried to destroy the child who would be born to the Israelites and would abase the sovereignty of the Egyptians (according to Josephus, *Antiquities* 2.9.2 §205). Consequently, no one sings in Matthew's infancy narrative as they do in Luke's; instead they weep. The contrast between what the born king of Israel will do and what the one who arrogated the throne to himself does is stark. Jesus has come to save his people (1:21), to shepherd them (2:6), and to give his life on behalf of others (20:28). Herod only exploits the people for his own ends and kills others to save himself. Matthew tells us, however, that the massacre of infants fulfilled the Scripture; but does Scripture sanction such brutal slaughter?

The fulfillment quotations are normally introduced with "in order that" (see 1:22, 2:15; 2:23; in 2:6, the formula would be inappropriate on the lips of the scribes and is therefore omitted). The "in order that" is absent in 2:17. The murder of the children did not take place *in order that* the word spoken through the prophet might be fulfilled. Instead, the prophecy is introduced by "*then* was fulfilled. . . . " It simply records the brute fact of what happened, which had nothing to do with the gracious will of God. God does not will evil or death. Note Matthew's laconic report of Herod's death in 2:19. He does not go into any of the gory details of his final suffering that Josephus itemizes and interprets as just punishment for his sins (*Antiquities* 17.6.5 §168–71). The bloodshed in Bethlehem was the result of the evil designs of Herod, who sought to preserve his rule at all costs. Because of Herod's wickedness, a cry was uttered in Ramah. For God's part, it was heard.

The "then" introduces only one other fulfillment quotation in Matthew: after the suicide of Judas (27:9). Jeremiah is the prophet cited in both instances, and in both instances deaths occur that are not God's will. Nevertheless, God is able to overcome the sins of humans to accomplish his plan for their salvation. God rescues his son from this first danger as God will rescue him at the end from death. In the first instance, Jesus escapes and others die; in the second, Jesus dies and another escapes, Barabbas. Jesus' death, however, is a ransom for many (20:28; 26:28). On one level, his death meant a reprieve for Barabbas; on another level, it means a pardon for all who believe.

The conclusion to the second section is similar to the first in that it calls attention to Jesus' name: "he called his name Jesus" (1:25); "he shall be called a Nazarean" (2:23). This last name was not a term of respect but comparable to being called a country bumpkin or a hick since Nazareth was scorned by the Jerusalem urban elite as a unimportant backwater town. This name would have been particularly significant for Matthew's first readers since Nazareans had become a byname for Christians, who were as rejected and despised as their Lord (Acts 24:5, the sect of the Nazarenes).

Nazareth is never mentioned in the Old Testament, which gives some indication of its insignificance, and what passage is fulfilled by Jesus' association with Nazareth (2:23) is difficult to discern. In other introductory formulas to fulfillment quotations, Matthew writes, "this happened in order to fulfill the word of the prophet, saying." In this introduction, he refers to "the prophets" and omits the verb "saying." This omission may suggest that in this particular case Matthew intends to allude to a passage or passages not quoted exactly. A number of suggestions have been made to identify which passage might be in mind. The most likely is that Matthew is making a play on the word "nazirite," and the reference is to Judges 13:5, 7 (which was numbered among the former prophets). Jesus would be likened to Samson, who was made holy to God from his mother's womb (Judg 16:17, LXX) and was to save Israel from its enemies (Judg 13:5, LXX). Like Samson, Jesus is a specially consecrated person who will save his people. Like Samson, Jesus will save his people through his own death.

GETTING READY:
GOD'S SON IN THE WILDERNESS

3:1–4:11

The first two sections of the first large division of the Gospel have introduced Jesus to the reader as the long-promised messiah, the son of David. In contrast to Herod, Jesus is the born king of the Jews. The inevitable question is, What kind of king is he going to be?

The Roman philosopher Musonius Rufus set forth his convictions about what the ideal king was supposed to be and do (C. E. Lutz, *Musonius Rufus* [New Haven: Yale University Press, 1947], viii). The first duty of the king is to protect and benefit his people; therefore he needs to know what is good and bad, what is helpful and harmful, what is advantageous and disadvantageous. He must arbitrate justice between subjects and therefore must himself be just and understand the nature of justice. He must exercise self-control and demand self-control of his subjects. Wantonness must be eliminated. He must be above pleasure and greed, must admire thrift and avoid extravagance, and must be able to control his tongue and have self-command. He must also possess courage and be invincible in reason to prevail in debate. Of greatest importance is the requirement to be faultless and perfect in word and action, "a living law," suppressing lawlessness and dissension. What follows in Matthew reveals that Jesus possesses all of the qualities of the ideal king. But these qualities are his because he is God's son.

The next two sections are more explicit in introducing Jesus as the son of God and reveal what kind of son he is. (1) The first presents Jesus as God's son who fulfills all righteousness (3:1–17). (2) The second (4:1–11) presents him as the obedient son of God who triumphs over Satan in the wilderness.

32

God's Son Who Fulfills All Righteousness
(3:1-17)

Matthew skips some thirty years and shifts the scene to the wilderness of Judea where John the Baptist comes preaching "in those days." This section (3:1-17) can be divided into three parts: (1) the introduction of John the Baptist (3:1-4), (2) the coming of the people to him and the warning to the Pharisees and Sadducees (3:5-12), and (3) the coming of Jesus from Galilee to be baptized by John (3:13-17).

The opening phrase, "in those days," is laden with eschatological import (Zech 8:23; *1 Enoch* 99:10). For Matthew, it marks the time of the messiah. John sounds the alarm that the kingdom of heaven has drawn near and that now is time to repent before it is too late. Unlike a Hellenistic philosopher who first surveyed human beings around him and then scolded them for their wickedness, wealth, or debauchery, John's message was based on what God is about to do in ushering in a new age (G. Friedrich, *"keryx...," TDNT* 3:692-94). The philosophical preacher aimed at changing people into healthier human beings whose virtues outnumbered their vices; John's preaching required a radical renewal if his hearers were to escape the wrath to come.

(1) The Evangelist is interested in John only because of his importance for Israel and for Jesus, and therefore no background information about his origins or ministry is forthcoming in 3:1-4. For Matthew, John is the one of whom the prophet Isaiah spoke (Isa 40:3, LXX) who is now crying out in the wilderness for the people to prepare the way of the Lord. He is the forerunner. The description of John's clothing hints that he is an Elijah figure because it matches that worn by Elijah the Tishbite (2 Kgs 1:8; see Zech 13:4). Later in the Gospel, Jesus will unambiguously identify John as Elijah (11:10, 14, 17:11-13).

(2) John seems to have interpreted his baptism as preparation for the new exodus to be led by the messiah (3:5-12). That is why he retired to the desert where he expected the new exodus to begin. John's baptism symbolically implied "a new passage through the Red Sea, whereby Israel is again cleansed from its heathen ways of life and from it sins, and its people become the true sons of Abraham, worthy of receiving the Messiah on His arrival" (Harald Sahlin, "The New Exodus of Salvation according to St. Paul," *The Root of the Vine,* ed. A. Fridrichsen [London: Dacre, 1953], 88-89; see 1 Cor 10:2). Whether or not this view is correct, the announcement of the beginning of "those days" takes place in the wilderness where others ventured out to await God's

deliverance (see Acts 21:38; Josephus, *Jewish War* 2.13.4 §259; 2.13.5 §261). The renewal of Israel does not begin in its hallowed center of political and religious power. John makes no appearance in Jerusalem or the temple; instead, Jerusalem, all Judea, and the region across the Jordan must come out to him. Even many of the Pharisees and Sadducees came to him to be baptized.

The Pharisees and Sadducees in Matthew represent branches of Jewish piety (see 5:20) and theology (Sand, *Matthäus,* 67) who will join in common cause against Jesus. They are first introduced as coming together for John's baptism in hopes of eluding the judgment to come. Later, they both demand to see some authenticating sign from heaven to confirm who Jesus is (16:1), and Jesus lumps them together as having a leavenlike teaching that is to be shunned by his disciples (16:6, 11, 12). In 22:15–46, the Sadducees follow close upon the heels of the Pharisees in firing antagonistic questions at Jesus designed to trap or to humiliate him. In Matthew, the Pharisees and the Sadducees are associated with Jewish theological agenda and are not distinguished as the leaders of the Jews. The leaders are the chief priests, the elders (of the people), and/or scribes who figure prominently in the passion predictions (16:21; 20:18). It is they who control the temple and who orchestrate Jesus' death (21:15, 23, 45; 26:3, 14, 47, 51, 57, 58, 59, 62, 63, 65; 27:1, 3, 6, 12, 20, 41, 62 [and Pharisees]; 28:11–15).

The Pharisees and Sadducees are presented to the reader from the perspective of John the Baptist, a messenger of God accredited by Scripture who claims to know their minds. He immediately pronounces them to be a brood of vipers, unworthy of his baptism (3:7–10). John thunders warnings against them and any others who might presume to be a part of God's special people. Baptism is not a magical rite that will preserve them from the judgment if they have not first turned in obedience to God. The ax is laid at the root of the trees that were supposed to bear fruit (Isa 27:6). Pointedly, he says that they will not be pruned but will be cut down and thrown in the fire. Divine retribution therefore does not threaten only heathens but also the respected exponents of Jewish piety and theology, and John does not hold out much hope that they will repent from their entrenched resistance to God's will. This wholesale rejection of both Pharisees and Sadducees by the prophet from God conveys that the Judaism represented by them is fatally flawed. It must change, or it will be judged.

John also warns them against appealing to Abraham as their father.

This reference is related to the concept of the merit of the fathers, which was considered to be a key component of divine grace (see Exod 32:13–14; *Pesiqta Rabbati* 205.7: "When will you mention before me the merits of the fathers and be acquitted in law? On *Roš Haššana* in the seventh month"). One can find traditions in Rabbinic literature that claim that even the fire of Gehenna has no power over the transgressors of Israel because Father Abraham will bring them up and receive them (*Babylonian Talmud 'Erubin* 19a; see *Mishna Sanhedrin* 10:1: "All Israelites have a share in the world to come"). This conviction was challenged by those who feared too much dependence on the merits of the fathers (*'Abot de Rabbi Nathan* B 27 and *Sipre Deuteronomy* §329: "Fathers cannot save their children; Abraham cannot save Ishmael, nor can Isaac save Esau"). Matthew has John the Baptist score that point: acceptance by God has nothing to do with lineage or heritage, only repentance (see *Mishna 'Abot* 4:11). There is no collective security (Limbeck, *Matthäus-Evangelium,* 60). For John, one's future with God will be determined by whether or not one bears fruit. For Matthew, the fruit that matters grows out of a fundamental disposition of the heart that is submissive to God's reign, and it is expressed in spontaneous, charactcristic acts of obedience. One's character is not a matter of race but of internal existence. This basic assumption levels the playing field and makes it possible for non-Israelites to belong to God's people. The jibe that God can raise up children to Abraham from these rocks implies three things: (a) God is free to create a new people if God wants, and those in Israel who do not bear fruit will be cut off (Hos 9:16–17). (b) The barrenness of Sarah was nothing compared to the spiritual barrenness of the Pharisees and Sadducees. (c) The church gathered around Jesus that will produce the required fruits of the kingdom (21:43) is not something other than Israel. They are children of Abraham (Gal 3:29).

(3) John also warns them of a mightier one who is coming and who will vanquish the enemies of God with a fiery Spirit baptism and uses an image that depicts the wheat and the chaff as already separated and lying on the threshing floor (3:13–17). This impending figure will come with a shovel to clean it thoroughly, heaping the grain into piles to be moved into the granary and the chaff into piles to be burned with unquenchable fire. The implication is that John's ministry of baptism has "in effect, already 'winnowed' the wheat, from the chaff" (R. L. Webb, "The Activity of John the Baptist's Expected Figure at the Threshing

Floor [Matthew 3:12=Luke 3:17]," *JSNT* 43 [1991]: 109). The mighty one comes to execute the final separation of the repentant from the unrepentant, and John expresses his unworthiness even to offer him the service of a slave (*Babylonian Talmud Ketubot* 96a; *Qiddušin* 22b). If Pharisees and Sadducees are unworthy to be baptized by one who is unworthy even to serve the one who comes after him, they are clearly chaff that has been winnowed out and will be burned with an unquenchable fire (compare the image of evildoers who do not repent and wash themselves "in perennial rivers" being consumed by fire and their cities turned to smoking dust in *Sibylline Oracles* 4:162–78).

Matthew presents Jesus as the unnamed stronger one who comes after John (see the "from then" in 4:17). When Jesus comes from Galilee to be baptized, John knows him as he knew the Pharisees and Sadducees. This time he protests that he is unworthy to baptize him (3:13–15). The implication is clear: How can he who is to baptize with the Holy Spirit receive the inferior baptism of water? John wants to receive from Jesus the eschatological baptism of all baptisms that he predicted was coming.

That Jesus submitted to John's baptism has caused theological consternation because it seems to imply that Jesus is subordinate to John or in some way in need of repentance (see Justin Martyr, *Dialogue* 88). Matthew's handling of this ticklish issue is significant. His description of John's baptism differs from that in Mark 1:4 in four ways: (a) In Matthew, John's baptism is not a baptism of repentance but a call to repentance, "Repent!" (Matt 3:2 / Mark 1:4, Luke 3:3). The imperative comes first; then, in 3:11, John the Baptist asserts that he baptizes on the basis of repentance. (b) Matthew does not mention the forgiveness of sins in connection with John's baptism. For Matthew, that is accomplished only by the death of Jesus (26:28). The reason for John's call to repentance is the nearness of the kingdom of God, not the forgiveness of sins (3:2). (c) Matthew alone includes John's protest of unworthiness and the detail that he relents only when Jesus commands him to let it be so "for now" (3:14). The implication is that the baptism of the Spirit is not yet. For now, John has been commissioned by God to prepare Israel by making it pass through the waters. In Matthew's scheme of things, submitting to this baptism does not mean that Jesus was an evildoer who was now reforming his ways. He undergoes John's baptism because he is faithful to Israel. (d) Jesus sets aside the question of whether he or John has the greater role to focus on a more important question, How must John and Jesus fulfill all righteousness?

"Righteousness" refers to conduct in accord with God's will. It is doing that which is pleasing to God (B. Pzrybylski, *Righteousness in Matthew and His World of Thought,* SNTSMS 41 [Cambridge: Cambridge University Press, 1980], 94). The first word that Jesus speaks in the Gospel is, "It is fitting for us to fulfill all righteousness" (see 5:20). It is simply the right thing to do. In his baptism, Jesus is shown to be one who binds himself to the destiny of Israel and who is intent on doing what God requires. The contrast between Jesus and the Pharisees and Sadducees who will not repent and do what God requires could not be clearer.

When Jesus arises from the water, the heavens open, the Spirit of God descends upon him, and a voice from heaven speaks, "This is my beloved son in whom I am well pleased" (a combination of Ps 2:7 and Isa 42:1). The audience for this revelation is neither the crowds, who have faded from view, nor John, who already recognizes Jesus' significance, nor Jesus, who, in Matthew's account, does not need to be informed about his identity and therefore does not respond. The voice from heaven is a narrative aside directed to the reader. To this point, the divine sonship of Jesus has only been implied by his conception through the Holy Spirit (1:18, 20), his name, Immanuel (1:23), and the Scripture referring to "my son" that is linked to Jesus (2:15). Now we have an unambiguous pronouncement direct from heaven. Jesus is God's son who is endowed with God's Spirit. According to Matthew, Isaiah's prayer, "O that you would tear open the heavens and come down" (Isa 64:1), has been answered by the arrival of Jesus, who will do "awesome deeds that we did not expect" (Isa 64:3).

God's Son Who Vanquishes Satan (4:1–11)

Jesus, conceived by the Spirit and endowed with the Spirit, is now led by the Spirit into the wilderness to be tested by the devil. Matthew alone states that testing was the purpose of this forty-day stint. The wilderness was traditionally a place of testing (see Exod 16–20; 24; 33–35) and was presumed to be haunted by demons and things that go bump in the night (see 12:43; Deut 8:15). When Jesus is faint and weary from his forty-day fast, the devil deferentially approaches him to try to preempt the Spirit as the one who will direct him.

The testing narrative reflects a chiastic structure:

a   Wilderness: Stones into bread to satisfy his hunger

    b   Jerusalem temple: Jumping from the pinnacle to test God's promises that the angels will save him

        c   High Mountain: The offer of the kingdoms of the world and the dismissal of the devil

        c′   The devil left him

    b′   The angels came

a′   His needs are served

There are three ways of explaining the testing episode. (a) The testing establishes how Jesus will pursue his messianic ministry. It forces him to ponder three questions. Will he be a messiah who brings only bread by means of magical powers? Will he strive to gain a following through dramatic demonstrations? Will he seek after worldly kingdoms by worldly means (compare Nero's declaration to Tiridates, king of Armenia, that he has "the power to take away kingdoms and to bestow them," Dio Cassius, *Roman History* 62.5.3)?

(b) Jesus' obedient submission to the will of God when tested after his baptism provides a model for the newly baptized disciple who can also expect trials (see Tertullian, *On Baptism* 20). Jesus faces down the enemy that torments all of us and who vies with God's will through lying words that sound religious. He overcomes the temptation to be self-serving and to seek instant gratification (bread with no plowing, planting, harvesting, or baking). He refuses to put God to the test to see if he, as one who is special to God, is immune from physical danger. He spurns the devil's offer of worldly power on easy terms. It can all be his if he would only worship the devil – no need to follow the hard road of obedience that will lead to the cross.

(c) While these first two options for understanding the testing are possible, it is more likely that a third was primary for Matthew. Jesus has been proclaimed son of God by a voice from heaven at his baptism; he is then sent into the wilderness to probe his fidelity and filial obedience (cf. Deut 13:3). Jesus recapitulates the history of God's covenant son, Israel; but he proves true at the very points where Israel failed: hunger (Exod 16), testing God's faithfulness (Exod 17), and idolatry (Exod 32). Matthew's interpretation of Hosea 11:1 in 2:15 makes it clear that, for him, Jesus is Israel, God's son, who is called out of Egypt (see Exod

4:22–23; Deut 1:31; Jer 31:9). Jesus passes through the waters and is taken up into the wilderness for forty days and nights (the verb "taken up" is used in the LXX, Num 20:5, 1 Kgs 12:6, and Ps 80:1, for Israel's ordeal). The number forty alludes to the period of Israel's wilderness sojourn. Forty days is equated with the forty years in Numbers 14:34 and Ezekiel 4:6. Jesus' rejoinders to Satan come from the section in Deuteronomy 6–8 that recall Israel's disobedience in the wilderness and explain why God allowed his "son," Israel, to wander forty years in the desert (4:4=Deut 8:3; 4:7=Deut 6:16; 4:10=Deut 6:13).

The devil bids the son to do for himself what the Father did for the children of Israel in the wilderness when they were weak from hunger: "Speak that these stones become loaves!" Jesus responds that it is not his word but God's that sustains life (Deut 8:6; see Wis 16:26). The devil then shifts Jesus to the temple and cites a psalm of assurance that no evil will befall the faithful (Ps 91:11–12; see Wis 2:16–20). The temple is the place where God's protection is particularly effective as God's shelter, refuge, and fortress (Ps 91:1–2); and the devil invites Jesus to see if he will find safety under God's wing: "Jump, the angels will catch you!" The temptation challenges Jesus to test God as Israel did. Even though the wilderness generation had been spared the plagues, delivered through the divided sea, led by a cloud by day and a fire by night, and given the bread of angels to eat, they still demanded that God provide them with certified proof of his presence among them (see Deut 29:2–6; Exod 17:2, 7; Num 14:22; Deut 6:16; Pss 78; 95). Jesus will not impugn God's power or faithfulness by putting them to the test. Finally, the devil sheds all pretense of piety when he escorts Jesus to a high mountain to view all the kingdoms of the world and their glory and demands to be worshiped. Moses was taken to Mount Pisgah and shown the promised land that the people would eventually enter (Deut 3:27; 34:1–4; see also *2 [Syriac] Apocalypse of Baruch* 76:3), and he warned the people that when they enter the land they are not to turn to other gods. That is exactly what transpired (Deut 31:20; 32:15–17; Ps 106:35–37). Jesus, however, will not submit to false gods and forcefully dismisses the devil. The angels then appear without Jesus having done anything to compel their coming (26:53–54; see *Testament of Naphtali* 8:4). Their arrival is another token of God's approval of his son.

The testing episode serves two theological purposes for Matthew. (a) Jesus' triumph over the devil settles the question about who can claim to be true Israel, the representative of God's people. "Jesus was called to live out in his own experience the Sonship that was to have

characterized Israel – a relationship with God which invites dependence on him for provision of needs, trust in his presence without
the need for demonstration, and acceptance of sovereignty only on his
terms" (Donaldson, *Jesus on the Mountain,* 92). He alone has proved
himself to be the true son of God who lives by God's word, and only
those who are joined to him as his brothers and sisters (12:50) may
understand themselves to be God's people.

(b) Jesus is able to confront and vanquish Satan. The stronger one
that John looked for has come, and Satan's domain will be eroded as
Jesus sweeps through Israel casting out demons (4:24; 8:16, 28–33;
9:32–34; 12:22, 29; 15:22–28; 17:14–20). But others hostile to Jesus'
ministry will spring up to test him (16:1; 19:3; 22:18, 35), and still
others who mistakenly assume that suffering and sonship are incompatible will try to impose their will on him (Peter, 16:21–23; the onlookers
at the cross, 27:40, 43). The reader knows from this incident, however,
that any further attempts to deflect Jesus from the path of obedience
will fail.

On the mountain at the beginning of the story, Satan pledges to give
Jesus "all the kingdoms of the world" if only he would bow down and
worship him (4:8–10). Jesus grasps after nothing and will receive much
more through his faithful obedience to his heavenly Father. On the
mountain at the end of the story, Jesus announces to his disciples that
he has been given authority over all that is visible and invisible (28:18).
That comes about only after he has obediently gone to the cross.

DISPELLING THE DARKNESS
IN GALILEE

4:12-16

The imprisonment of John is recorded by Matthew as the divinely appointed signal that Jesus' public activity should begin. Galilee is to be the starting point of his mission to Israel as it will be the starting point of the church's mission to the nations (28:16-20). The seventh and last fulfillment quotation (4:15-16 from Isa 8:23-9:1) in this first major division of the Gospel provides the biblical warrant for his return to Galilee. Capernaum is known to be Jesus' own city (9:1), and once again Matthew looks to the Scripture to confirm that this Galilean sea village was a valid messianic venue. The quotation from Isaiah also links the messiah with the gentiles (8:23-9:1). It is the reviled Galilee of the gentiles (see 1 Macc 5:15) where the light of the messiah has risen. The star that the magi saw at its rising (the verb in 4:16 and the noun in 2:2 are related) has now become a light that shines upon those sitting in spiritual darkness (*1 Enoch* 48:4: the son of man "is a light of the gentiles and he will become the hope of those who are sick in their hearts").

This first division of the Gospel has introduced Jesus as the messiah of Israel and the son of God empowered with God's Spirit who is perfectly obedient to God's will. It has dropped broad hints that the salvation offered in Jesus Christ will extend beyond Israel, according to the flesh, to include gentiles. But Jesus has been sent to shepherd the lost sheep of the house of Israel (2:6), and they are the primary concern of his ministry. The second major division of the Gospel (4:17-16:20) presents Jesus in his ministry to Israel. This first division, however, has also indicated that not all will gladly receive him. Resistance can be expected from the malevolent powers that be and from recalcitrant teachers whose power and authority are threatened by his presence.

41

Matthew 4:17–16:20

JESUS' MINISTRY TO ISRAEL

Part 1

Teaching, Healing, and Calling Lost Sheep
4:17–11:1

The phrase "From then Jesus began to preach and to say: repent, the kingdom of heaven is at hand" is the heading of the second major division of the Gospel, which presents Jesus' public ministry to Israel (4:17–16:20). This large division can be broken into two major blocks (4:17–10:42; 11:1–16:20). In the first half, Matthew introduces Jesus announcing the advent of the kingdom, presenting its demands (5:1–7:28), performing miracles of healing (8:1–9:35), calling disciples, and sending them on mission to the lost sheep of the house of Israel with the warning that they will meet with bitter hostility and abuse (9:36–10:42). In the second half, Jesus himself encounters doubt (11:2–6; 12:46–50), censure (12:24–32; 15:12–14), and rebuff (11:16–24; 13:53–58; 16:1–5). A fissure between Jesus and this generation of Israel widens into a chasm in spite of his unmatched authority in word and deed. The explanation for this growing estrangement is provided by the parables in chapter 13 (13:10–17, 34–35). The disciples, on the other hand, grow closer to their Lord. They receive private instruction (13:36), understand the parables (13:52), confess Jesus as the son of God (14:33; 16:16), and thereby reveal themselves to be the worthy recipients of special revelation (11:25–27; 13:11; 16:17). The foundation is laid for the establishment of Jesus' church, but it has become clear that many in Israel will not be included.

The first half of this large division can be outlined as a chiasm:

4:17 The Proclamation of the Kingdom

A   4:18-22 The calling of disciples (to fish for people)

   B   4:23-25 Summary of Jesus' ministry to Israel

      C   5:1-7:29 Illustration of Jesus mighty in word (teaching as one clothed with divine authority)

      C′ 8:1-9:34 Illustration of Jesus mighty in deed (working as one clothed with divine authority)

   B′ 9:35 Summary of Jesus' ministry to Israel

A′ 9:36-11:1 The calling of disciples (to be harvesters) for the mission to Israel and an in depth explanation of what discipleship and mission will mean.

JESUS' DEBUT:
AUTHORITY AND COMPASSION

4:17-25

The presentation of the beginning of Jesus' ministry falls into three parts: (1) Jesus' proclamation of the kingdom of heaven (4:17); (2) the calling of disciples to be fishers for people (4:18-22); (3) a summary of Jesus' ministry in Galilee (4:23-25).

(1) Jesus' preaching in 4:17 echoes John's summons in 3:2: "Repent for the kingdom of heaven is at hand." Jesus will also echo John in using the same rebuke, "brood of vipers" (12:34, 23:33=3:7), issuing the same threat about trees being uprooted (7:19, 15:13=3:10), and giving the same warning about the judgment of unquenchable fire (13:40-42, 50=3:12). But Jesus does not baptize to prepare the people for a coming one. He is the one that John announced would come after him, and his preaching, teaching, and healing inaugurate the presence of the kingdom of heaven.

Matthew's preference for the phrase "kingdom of heaven" (thirty-two occurrences in his Gospel and none in the other Gospels) is not simply due to a pious aversion of using the name of God (see 21:25). The "kingdom of God" appears four times in the Gospel (12:28; 19:24; 21:31, 43). The kingdom of heaven is favored because it is a way of referring to God's transcendent work and lordship that is coming down from heaven (H. Traub, *"ouranos," TDNT* 5:522). It is never defined or discussed in detail in the Gospel except in parable (13:24, 31, 33, 44, 45, 47; 18:23; 20:1; 22:2; 25:1) but serves as an image for God's sovereignty as Lord of heaven (11:25) who will make all things right on earth. It is described as something that is coming and, in fact, is close at hand (3:2; 4:17; 10:7; 12:28; 6:10). It is to be preached to the whole world (24:14) as something that comes both as a gift (5:3, 10; 21:43; 25:34, including its mysteries, 13:11) and as a demand. One is to enter the kingdom of heaven (5:20; 7:21; 18:3; 19:23-24; 21:31; 23:13). To enter or to be in the kingdom of heaven (5:19; 8:11; 13:43; 18:1,

47

4; 26:29), one must submit to God's kingly power and join in God's redemptive action in the world.

(2) Before any public response to Jesus' preaching regarding repentance and the advent kingdom of heaven is reported, he calls four disciples (4:18–22). The sharp command, "Follow me!" with no narrative preparation (contrast Luke 4:38–39; 5:1–11; John 1:35–42) perhaps surprises. The instant response of the fishermen, however, illustrates what the call to repentance is all about. Repentance is not simply remorse and a desire to turn over a new leaf. It is the readiness to heed Jesus' call "immediately" and to leave everything to follow him (4:20, 22; see 19:27; 8:21–22). It requires a total reordering of priorities in life and unreserved commitment to Jesus.

The master-disciple relationship between Jesus and his disciples that is portrayed in Matthew is markedly different from that relationship as it is reflected, for example, in Rabbinic literature. In Rabbinic literature, a disciple was to choose his own master (*Mishna 'Abot* 1:6); and his first commitment was to the law. Consequently, he could transfer from one master to another to acquire more knowledge of the law. By contrast, Jesus does not wait for volunteers but selects his own disciples and confronts them with an unconditional demand. He requires absolute allegiance to himself, not merely respectful service. He does not call them to be his apprentices in the intellectual probing of Torah or to rehearse venerable religious traditions. He calls fishermen to a new kind of fishing: they are "to fish for people." The parable of the net that gathers fish of every kind connects the image of fishing to the mission enterprise (13:47–48). The task of mission that is central to the disciples' role in this Gospel is therefore introduced as soon as they are. The image of harvest in 9:36–10:42 links the appointment of the twelve with their mission, and this concluding unit of the first block will clarify more thoroughly what it means to follow Jesus and the interrelationship between discipleship and mission.

(3) Matthew 4:23–25 provides an overview of Jesus' activity: teaching, preaching, and healing. A sampling of the preaching of the kingdom can be found in the Sermon on the Mount in the beatitudes (5:3–11) and the warnings to enter the narrow gate and to build on a solid foundation (7:13–27); and an example of his teaching is found in 5:13–7:12. But Jesus is more than a teacher and preacher; he comes with power and heals every disease and every malady among the people (4:23, 24; see Deut 7:14–15a; Isa 29:18–19; 35:5–6). The healing of the demon-possessed, the moon-struck (epileptics), and the paralyzed are

highlighted in 4:24 because they were widespread, not helped by medical therapy, and associated with demonic powers. They represent the desperate human situation that can be overcome by God alone (Sand, *Matthäus*, 88). The miracles recorded in chaps 8-9 provide concise illustrations of Jesus' healing ministry and signal that he is God with us who has come with divine power to relieve human distress.

The summary also tells us that people came to Jesus in Galilee from far and wide, but the list of areas from which they came takes in the four corners of the kingdom of Israel as it existed in the glory days of David: NW Galilee; NE Decapolis; SW Judea; SE Perea, beyond the Jordan, with Jerusalem in the center. Samaria is omitted as a heathen land. They come from all over to Jesus who is in Galilee. These same crowds whose sick are healed comprise the audience from Israel that Jesus challenges in what follows (7:28-29; see G. Lohfink, "Wem gilt die Bergpredigt? Eine redaktionskritische Untersuchung von Mt 4, 23-25 und 7,28f," *TQ* 163 [1983]: 274-76). The summary of their healing is therefore vital as the prelude to the Sermon on the Mount. Before the people can obey his radical demands, they must be healed. One can easily get the impression that this Gospel emphasizes works almost to the exclusion of grace (see 7:21; 16:27; 21:28-32), but the narrative sequence conveys a doctrine of grace that lies behind these moral demands:

> Having done nothing, nothing at all, they are benefited. So grace comes before the task, succor before the demand, healing before the imperative. The first act of the Messiah is not the imposition of commandments but the giving of himself. Today's command presupposes yesterday's gift. (Davies and Allison, *Saint Matthew*, 1:427)

MAGISTERIAL TEACHING:
A CHARTER FOR DISCIPLESHIP

5:1–8:1

When one responds to Jesus' call to follow him, what then? How is one to live? The Sermon on the Mount provides the answer. The fact that it reflects Matthean vocabulary, compositional techniques, and themes makes it likely that it was composed by the first evangelist from different sayings of Jesus. John Calvin recognized this fact years ago in describing the Sermon on the Mount as "a brief summary of the doctrine of Christ... collected out of his many and various discourses" (*Commentary on a Harmony of the Gospels,* repr. [Grand Rapids: Eerdmans, 1956], 1:258–59). Matthew wove these sayings into a tapestry that reflects central themes in the teaching of Jesus as well as his Gospel. Various interpretations of the sermon have been proposed through the years that tailor loopholes for the reader to escape its awesome demands. But Matthew understands it to be the unconditioned expression of God's will and the charter of conduct for disciples. Obedience is obligatory for any who would enter the kingdom of heaven (5:20), but obedience is a response to the gracious activity of God that has already been experienced (4:23–25). With the offer of grace comes a demand. After the beatitudes that pronounce God's blessing, the emphasis falls on hearing and doing (5:19; 7:24–27), on works (5:16), on righteousness (5:20; 6:1, 33), and on bearing fruit (7:15–23). The Evangelist knows that this teaching presents a narrow gate and a road less traveled (7:13–14), but the question of its practicality did not arise for him – only for later Christians. Paul's concept of human enslavement to sin and the consequent incapacity to do God's will until liberated is unknown to Matthew. The assumption is that these commands not only can be done, they must be done. The disciples' ultimate destinies depend not only on their relationship to Jesus (7:21–23) but also on their obedience to his words (7:24–27). Obedience is rewarded by inclusion in the kingdom of heaven (5:20); disobedi-

50

ence will meet with final punishment (5:22, 25–26, 29–30; 7:13, 19, 23, 27).

The sermon may be outlined as follows:

5:1–2   Jesus Ascends the Mountain

5:3–12   Pronouncements of God's Blessing

5:13–16   The Disciples' Vocation and Role in the World

5:17–48   Jesus and the Law: the Greater Righteousness

6:1–18   Directions on Piety

6:19–34   Directions on Money

7:1–12   Directions on Social Relations

7:13–27   Pronouncements of Warning

7:28–8:1   The Reaction of the Crowds and Jesus' Descent from the Mountain

A New Moses?
(5:1–2)

Moses' words "The Lord your God will raise up for you a prophet like me from among your own people; you shall heed such a prophet" (Deut 18:15) led many in Matthew's day to assume that the messiah would be like the redeemers of Israel who had come before. A later Rabbinic tradition (*Qoheleth Rabba* 1:9) reveals that this belief continued to persist in Judaism and also reveals a prevalent way of reading the Scripture that may strike a modern reader as quite odd:

> R. Berekiah said in the name of R. Isaac: As the first redeemer was, so shall the latter Redeemer be. What is stated of the former Redeemer? "And Moses took his wife and his sons, and set them upon an ass" (Exod 4:20). Similarly it will be with the latter Redeemer, as it is stated, "Lowly and riding upon an ass" (Zech 9:9). As the former redeemer caused manna to descend, as it is stated, "Behold, I will cause to rain bread from heaven for you" (Exod 16:4), so will the latter Redeemer cause manna to descend, as it is stated, "May he be as rich as a cornfield in the land" (Ps 72:16). As the former redeemer made a well to rise (Num 21:17–18), so the latter Redeemer brings up water, as it is stated, "And a fountain shall come forth of the house of the Lord, and shall water the valley of Shittim" (Joel 4:18).

Given these expectations, Matthew must show not only that Jesus is the son of David if he is the messiah but also that Jesus is like the first redeemer if he is indeed the latter Redeemer.

The parallels with Moses are readily apparent in the events surrounding Jesus' birth: a dream about the child's birth (Josephus, *Antiquities* 2.9.3 §210-16; Pseudo Philo, *Biblical Antiquities* 9, 10); a king informed of the birth of a liberator by scribes and wisemen (Josephus, *Antiquities* 2.9.2 §205-9, 2.9.7 §234; astrologers in *Exodus Rabba* 1:22); the slaughter of male children by a tyrant (Exod 1:15-22); and the narrow escape of the infant (Exod 2:1-10). Moses also was forced to flee into exile (Exod 2:15) and returned only when he was told, "all those seeking your life are dead" (Exod 4:19=Matt 2:20). The beginning of Jesus' ministry recalls the Exodus: he passes through the waters and is led into the wilderness to be tested. As Moses fasted for forty days and nights (Exod 34:28; Deut 9:9, 18), so does Jesus. Now, in 5:1, Jesus ascends a mountain as Moses did (Exod 19:3; 24:16-17; Deut 9:9; *Babylonian Talmud Megilla* 21a; *Soṭa* 49a).

These parallels between Jesus and Moses should not be overdrawn, however. There are also major differences: (a) Moses ascended the mountain to be taught by God, to be given succor, and to worship. Jesus ascends (or descends) a mountain to teach others the definitive intention of God's will, to give aid to others (14:23-33; 15:29-31), and to commission his disciples (28:16-20). Jesus is the one who is worshiped on the mountain by his disciples (28:17). (b) While Moses' face shone from his encounter with God on the mountain (Exod 34:29-35), Jesus is completely transfigured; and after Moses and Elijah fade from view, a voice from a cloud proclaims, "This is my beloved son, listen to him!" (17:1-9). (c) Moses is a solitary figure on the mountain, and the people were threatened with death for coming near it (Exod 19:12-13, 23-24). Jesus is not alone on the mountain as both crowds and disciples come to him (5:1; 15:29-30; 17:1; 28:16). (d) Unlike Moses, who spoke in the name of God, Jesus speaks in his own name (5:21-48) and recovers the will of God that had been diluted by Moses to accommodate human hardness of heart (19:7-8). While Matthew presents Jesus as Moses-like, he does not depict him as a new Moses but as the Lord, the son of God.

Congratulations Are in Order
(5:3-12)

The makarism (from the Greek word for "blessed") was a familiar ascription in the Greek world. It was used to congratulate persons who were judged in some way to share the privileged estate of the gods who were free from earthly toils and to extol the wise (Menander, *Fragments* 114K: "Blessed is the man who has both mind and money for he employs the latter for what he should"). Those applauded possessed the things that were thought to make for happiness: a lovely bride, excellent children, moral rectitude, wisdom, knowledge, wealth, honor, and fame. The beatitudes in the Old Testament congratulated persons for their commendable piety. Those who are blessed are those who have God as Lord (Ps 144:15), who fear God (Pss 112:1–3; 128:1–4; Prov 84:12), who trust in God (Ps 84:12), who dwell or take refuge in God (Pss 2:12; 84:4), who prudently obey God (Ps 119:1–2; Prov 8:32–34; Isa 56:2), and who heed the counsels of the wise (Sir 50:28). They are to be saluted because they are in the enviable position of having divine approval. In the Wisdom literature, the beatitude takes on a distinctly moralizing tone. It was assumed that God rewards trust in him with worldly well-being, and the beatitudes imply that one should emulate virtuous conduct to join the ranks of the happy (Pss 1:1–2; 84:12; Job 29:10–11; Sir 26:1; 31:8; 4Q525). Only rarely is a beatitude associated with any eschatological hope (Isa 30:18; Dan 12:12).

The thrust of the beatitudes in Jewish literature from the intertestamental period marks a distinct change of emphasis from how to be happy in this life to how to be happy in the life to come (see Tob 13:14–16; *Psalms of Solomon* 4:23; 6:1; 17:44; 18:6; *1 Enoch* 58:2; 81:4; 82:4; 99:10; *2 Enoch* 42:6–14; 52:1–16). The assumption now is that happiness is not to be found in the external circumstances of this present evil age but only in the sphere of God – in the life to come, or after God has intervened to bring the new age. Those congratulated live in the future day of salvation (see Luke 14:15; Rev 19:9; 20:6). The beatitude promises consolation to those living in the midst of despair and oppression (see R. A. Guelich, "The Matthean Beatitudes: 'Entrance Requirements' or Eschatological Blessings?" *JBL* 95 [1976]: 417).

Jesus' beatitudes herald the near approach of the kingdom of heaven when all will be put right. Sirach looked back to a golden past and considered those blessed who saw Elijah (48:11). The author of the *Psalms of Solomon* looked forward to a magnificent future and ascribed blessing on those who will be born in the days of the messiah and see the good fortune of Israel and the good things of the Lord (17:44; 18:6). In Matthew, Jesus declares that Elijah has already come in the person of John the Baptist (17:12) and that the kingdom of God is at hand. Jesus directly addresses his disciples as blessed because they are able to see and hear what the prophets and the righteous longed to see (13:16–17).

The long-awaited blessings of the future age have come near for the poor in spirit, the weeping, the lowly, the hungry, the reviled, and the perse-cuted. "Poverty, humility or suffering" would never have been "morally recommended in classical culture" (Horsley, *New Documents,* 4:170). A world that prizes only earthly well-being would hardly consider such as these worthy of notice, let alone plaudits. Jesus' beatitudes, however, look at things from God's point of view (see *Babylonian Talmud Pe-sahim* 50a: "people who are honored in this world, but will be lightly esteemed in the next world"). He congratulates those who are open to the gracious activity of God to save his people. Fortunate external circumstances are irrelevant, and the pursuit of such things will only doom one to be excluded from God's future.

The Matthean beatitudes can be divided into two stanzas of four beatitudes (5:3-6, 7-10), which are framed by the promise "theirs is the kingdom of heaven" (5:3, 10). The term "righteousness" appears in the fourth and the eighth beatitudes ("those who hunger and thirst for righteousness," 5:6; "those who are persecuted for righteousness' sake," 5:10). The first four also begin with alliterative p-sounds in Greek that can be rendered: "Blessed are the poor in spirit, the plaintive, the powerless, and those who pine for righteousness." The first group pertains to one's disposition toward God, while the second group has to do with one's demeanor toward others: showing mercy, being pure in heart, peacemaking, and being persecuted for righteousness. The structure and wording may have been regulated by word count since each group contains thirty-six words for a total of seventy-two (A. A. Di Lella, "The Structure and Composition of the Matthean Beatitudes," *To Touch the Text,* ed. M. P. Horgan and P. J. Kobelski [New York: Crossroad, 1989]: 237-42). The much longer ninth beatitude (5:11-12) marks a transition. It repeats the key word "persecute" from 5:10 and switches from the third person to the second person plural.

(1) The dispositions toward God (5:3-6)

"Congratulations to the poor in spirit." In both the Gospels of Matthew and Luke, the first recorded sermon of Jesus opens with good news for the poor (Luke 4:17-19). In the Greek world, the term "poor" referred simply to material poverty. But in the Old Testament the term took on religious connotations as well as referring to the needy (Ps 40:17; 86:1). It came to denote the humble pious who were beloved by God (Isa 61:1-2; see Jas 2:5, "the poor in this world, rich in faith"). T. W. Manson

(*Sayings*, 47) notes that in *Psalm of Solomon* 10:6 ("And the devout shall give thanks in the assembly of the people, and God will be merciful to the poor to the joy of Israel") the "devout" and the "poor" stand in synonymous parallelism. He contends that this understanding of the poor as saints goes back to the days of the Seleucid rule of Palestine when the wealthy upper classes were enticed to betray their religious heritage by the attractions of heathenism while the poor remained loyal to it. Poverty did not allow the poor the arrogance or aggressiveness of the wealthy. Their vulnerability forced the poor to look to God for everything. They quietly endured earthly suffering, waiting patiently upon God, for that is all that they could do. The term "rich" came to refer to the "worldly" and "impious" while the "poor" referred to the opposite, the "godly" and "pious."

In contrast to Luke's "blessed are the poor" (6:20), Matthew has "the poor in spirit" (see 1QS 4:3; 1QM 14:7; 1QH 14:2; 18:14–15). The Evangelist prevents a strictly economic interpretation of the phrase by referring to the quality of the inner life, because poverty is not something that is blessed in itself, nor does it necessarily create greater spiritual depth. The "long in spirit" are those who are patient, the "high in spirit" are the proud (*Babylonian Talmud Berakot* 57b: "Three things increase a man's self-esteem [literally, enlarge his spirit]: a beautiful dwelling, a beautiful wife, and beautiful clothes"). The poor in spirit are those who live in humble acknowledgement of the their impoverishment before God and who lift up hopeful prayers (*Psalm of Solomon* 18:2). The only good that they can hope for in their lives comes from the God who "raises the poor from the dust and lifts the needy from the ash heap" (Ps 113:7). The New English Bible aptly translates it as "those who know their need of God." Jesus proclaims that the more one is aware of the need for God, the more one is going to be receptive to the reign of God that is dawning in his ministry of healing and teaching. The proud, who bask in their reputations, learning, and titles (23:5–8), will shut themselves from the kingdom of heaven (23:13). The forlorn, however, will throw pride and caution to the wind in desperate appeals for help (8:1–4, 5–13; 8:14–25; 15:21–28; 20:29–34), and they will be saved.

"Congratulations to those who mourn." Not all who mourn are blessed, and not all sorrow finds comfort. The second beatitude refers to those who "see this suffering aeon as it is" (R. Bultmann, *"pentheō,"* *TDNT* 6:43) and are not duped by the world's charms like the ones who laugh (Luke 6:25). The mourners are those who grieve over Satanic tyranny and the apparent eclipse of God's purpose on earth (see Ezek 9:4), and it sets them apart from those who are at home with war and injustice. Their penitent distress over their own sins and the sins of the world generates their yearning for God to act to make things right (see Isa 66:2, 13; Rev 21:4).

"Congratulations to the meek." The meek are the powerless (Ps 37:11; Isa 11:4; 29:19; 57:15; 61:1). They are fortunate because they are more likely to welcome God's sovereignty, while those who run the present kingdoms of this earth are little interested in a coming kingdom that promises to topple them from their thrones. The meek acknowledge their complete dependence on God and do not exalt their own pitiful sufficiency.

The Psalmist declares: "The meek shall possess the land, they shall delight in abounding peace" (Ps 37:11; the LXX, 36:11, has "the meek shall inherit land"; see Isa 57:13; 60:21; 65:9). The promise refers to a radically renewed land. At Qumran, this psalm was applied to the end-time vindication of the community: they will possess the high mountain of Israel (4QpPs37[a]; see Isa 57:13). For Matthew, the land is spiritualized to refer to God's new world. The land does not come as a result of violent conquest but as a legacy, a gift.

"Congratulations to those who hunger and thirst after righteousness." Philo applauded those "who hunger and thirst after nobility of character" (*On Flight and Finding* 139). Jesus' beatitude has nothing to do with simply wanting to be a better person. Righteousness refers to what God requires, and those who hunger and thirst know that they lack what is vital to sustain life. Those who hunger and thirst after righteousness have a gnawing desire to see God's will accomplished in their lives (see Amos 8:11). An escape-hungry society that craves all the wrong things will never be satisfied. Only those whose deepest longings are for fellowship with God will know the comfort that can be supplied only by God.

(2) The demeanor toward others (5:7–10)

"Congratulations to the merciful." Mercy is not simply an inward sentiment but action that leads one to spare or to help another. As God is bound by the covenant of mercy with the people (Deut 30:3), so the people are bound to act mercifully to the oppressed, alien, orphan, and widow. The poor in spirit appreciate the fact that they live by God's mercy, and they realize that they cannot withhold it from others. It is one of the besetting sins of the scribes and Pharisees in Matthew's story that they fail to grasp the significance of the mandate to be merciful (9:13; 12:7; 23:23). Two parables in Matthew single out mercy or the lack of it as the criterion that will decide one's ultimate fate (18:23–35; 25:31–46). A merciful spirit is the outstretched hand by which one grasps God's mercy. When that hand is closed tightly into a fist, it gives nothing but also can receive nothing.

"Congratulations to the pure in heart." This beatitude is inspired by Psalm 24:3–4 (see Ps 73:1; 4Q525). The heart was considered to be more than the seat of the emotions; it was the center of a person's innermost being. It was the place where decisions are made (15:18–20, "what comes from the heart"; 18:35, "forgiving the brother from the heart"). The heart shapes a person's life (6:21) and governs a person's speech (12:34). The condition of the heart therefore determines one's actions. Jesus' teaching on anger (5:21–2), lust (5:27–28), and acts of piety (6:1–6, 16–18) all go beyond the external act to the heart of the matter, the source of those actions. At issue is moral purity (15:19). The pure in heart contrast with those who fix their attention only on such things as the purification of cups while ignoring the greed and filth within themselves (23:25–26).

The reward of the pure in heart is to see God. This biblical idiom was associated with coming before God in the temple worship (Pss 11:7; 17:15; 24:3; 42:2; Isa 6:5). The beatitude assumes that communion with God depends on purity of heart, not purity of cups (see 23:25–26; Heb 12:14). The poor in spirit recognize, however, that only God can create purity of heart (Ps 51:10).

"Congratulations to the peacemakers." The Romans had brought about the pacification of nations through the use of force, and their emperors were hailed as bringers of peace. But the peacemakers in this beatitude are those who bring an end to strife between individuals. Peacemaking is a cardinal virtue in Rabbinic literature: Rabbi Hillel said: "Be of the disciples of Aaron loving peace and pursuing it" (*Mishna 'Abot* 1:12; see *Sipre Numbers* §42). "The ways of peace" is the hermeneutical principle behind many enactments that were designed to foster peace and reduce friction. It is also a major concern in Matthew (see also Rom 12:18; Jas 3:18). Examples of peacemakers are those who would leave the altar to seek reconciliation with one who has been offended (5:23–24; see 17:24–27; 18:15–18), those who love their enemies and pray for them (5:43–44), and those who go to those who hate them with a message of God's love because they are followers of the prince of peace. The poor in spirit, however, recognize that God alone is the creator of true peace.

"Congratulations to the those persecuted for righteousness' sake." There were many martyrs for the cause of righteousness in the recent history of Israel, and they were accounted as saints (2 Macc 6:18–7:42). Josephus tells the story of two revered scholars who incited their younger disciples to avenge God's honor by tearing down the golden eagle that Herod had erected in the temple. They spurred them on with these words: "It was a noble deed to die for the laws of one's country; for the souls of those who came to an end attained immortality and an eternally abiding sense of felicity" (*Jewish War* 1.23.2–4 §648-55). The attempt failed, and Herod had the perpetrators burned alive. The persecution under the Emperor Hadrian led Rabbi Nathan to apply Exodus 20:6, "of them that love me and keep my commandments," to those who dwelt in the land of Israel and risked their lives for the sake of the commandments:

> "Why are you being led out to be decapitated?" "Because I circumcised my son to be an Israelite." "Why are you being led out to be burned?" "Because I read the Torah?" "Why are you being led out to be crucified?" "Because I ate the unleavened bread." "Why are you getting the one hundred lashes?" "Because I performed the ceremony of the Lulab." And it says: "Those with which I was wounded in the house of my friends" (Zech 13:6). These wounds caused me to be beloved of My father in heaven." (*Mekilta Baḥodesh* 6 to Exod 20:6)

It is one thing to pronounce blessed those who are persecuted because of righteousness or devotion to the law (2 Macc 7:9, 11, 23, 37; 4 Macc 6:24–30); it is something else to pronounce blessed those who are persecuted because of their relationship to Jesus, "for my sake" (see also 10:18, 39; 16:25; 19:29). This beatitude reflects the high christology of the Gospel.

(3) The situation of the church (5:11–12)

"Congratulations to you when people revile you and utter all kinds of evil against on my account." The ninth beatitude also embraces a high christology, because it assumes that persecution as a result of one's ties to Jesus will reap as great a reward in heaven as persecution for devotion to righteousness, what God requires. The switch from the third to the second person directly addresses a Christian community that has been the target of harassment, public scorn, and libel. They are congratulated because they share the same fate as the prophets. The hearers were conditioned by the belief that: (a) God's agents will be rejected by humans but will be vindicated by God; (b) all of God's prophets were rejected (see 23:29–31; 2 Chron 36:16; Acts 7:52; Heb 11:37; *Martyrdom of Isaiah* 5; *Lives of the Prophets,* 34–35); (c) truly honorable persons are those who are treated like prophets with persecution and dishonor; (d) true honor is something that is hidden and revealed only to the truly wise (B. Malina and J. Neyrey, *Calling Jesus Names* [Sonoma, Calif.: Polebridge, 1988], 117).

Changing the World
(5:13–16)

If the disciples are likened to prophets, it implies that they too have a divine mission to fulfill as the prophets did (Strecker, *The Sermon on the Mount,* 47). The images of salt, light, and a city on a hill clarify the disciples' vocation in the world. The salt metaphor is not self-evident, however. It may reflect proverbial wisdom about the necessity and usefulness of salt (as a seasoning [Job 6:6; Col 4:6]; a preservative; a fire catalyst; or as fertilizer), or it may draw on a literary image from Judaism. Only in Matthew is it coupled with two brief parables. A city set on a mountain cannot be hidden. No one lights a lamp only to extinguish it at once by putting it under a basket. Their meaning should help in ascertaining the connotation of salt in this context.

The city set on a mountain is a transparent metaphor for Jerusalem on Mount Zion. Isaiah 2:2–3 forms the backdrop:

> [2]In the days to come the mountain of the Lord's house shall be established as the highest of the mountains, and shall be raised above the hills; all the nations shall stream to it. [3]Many peoples shall come and say, "Come let us go out to the mountain of the Lord, to the house of Jacob; that he may teach us his ways and that we may walk in his paths." For out of Zion shall go forth instruction, and the word of the Lord from Jerusalem. (NRSV; see also Deut 26:18–19; Ezek 5:5)

The image of the city echoes the ancient apocalyptic hope sounded by Isaiah and refers to "the eschatological congregation of the faithful" (G. Von Rad, "The City on the Hill," *The Problem of the Hexateuch and Other Essays* [Edinburgh: T. & T. Clark, 1966], 242). In using this image, Jesus identifies his disciples as the new community of Zion (K. M. Campbell, "The New Jerusalem in Matthew 5:14," *SJT* 31 [1978]: 362-63).

The emphatic "you are the light" implies that the disciples are set over against someone or something else that others would presume to be the light (H. Weder, *Die "Rede der Reden,"* 2d ed. [Zurich: Theologischer Verlag, 1987], 85-86). Israel was called to be a light to the nations, a beacon that would draw those in darkness to God and to God's city set on Mount Zion. Again, Isaiah provides the setting:

> Is it too light a thing that you should be my servant to raise up the tribes of Jacob and to restore the survivors of Israel; I will give you as a light to the nations, that my salvation may reach to the end of the earth." (Isa 49:6, NRSV; see 42:6; Ps 18:29; Rom 2:19; *Pseudo-Philo, Biblical Antiquities* 11:1)

Jesus' parable does not urge that one *should* not hide one's light under a basket but assumes that one *does* not do this. The point of comparison is that God does not do such things either. God does not provide a lamp to enlighten the world only to snuff it out with a basket. God sends light to enlighten, and the disciples now have the function, assigned to Israel, to be the light for the world that otherwise will end up being cast into the outer darkness at the judgment (8:12; 22:13; 25:30).

Since it is combined with two images from Scripture, the salt metaphor is more likely to be a literary symbol than a piece of proverbial wisdom. In the Hebrew Scriptures, salt was used in the binding of covenants to suggest their permanence and was likened to the covenant (Exod 30:35-36; Lev 2:13; Num 18:19; 2 Chron 13:5; 11QTemple 20:13-14). Jesus' saying poses this question: If salt becomes useless, what is there to salt the earth? It begins, however, with the answer: "You are the salt of the earth." God will not be without covenant witnesses in the world. But it is Jesus' church that preserves the covenant calling of Israel. Following the beatitude for the persecuted and reviled, the salt saying affirms that the disciples are in prophetic succession to the covenant witnesses of old who were persecuted and reviled. As salt, the disciples guarantee the continuation of Israel's appointment as a light to the gentiles (W. G. Dumbrell, "The Logic of the Role of the Law in Matthew v. 1-20," *NovT* 23 [1981]: 1-21).

The disciples are to make an impression on the earth as salt, which may entail suffering and sacrifice, and on the world as light, which means going where it is dark. They are also to make an impression upon humanity as doers of good works that will lead others to glorify the source, the Father. The disciples' mission to the world is again in view. The light that dawned in Galilee (4:16) will spread to the entire world that lives in darkness.

The Fulfillment of the Law
(5:17–19)

In the Hebrew Scriptures God declares: "You shall not add to the word which I command you, nor take from it; that you may keep the commandments of the Lord your God which I command you" (Deut 4:2). Any prophet who presumes to speak what God has not commanded shall die (Deut 18:20; see *Babylonian Talmud Sanhedrin* 90a: "if one prophesies so as to eradicate a law of the Torah, he is liable [to death]"). Josephus boasts about the law:

> For, although such long ages have now passed, no one has ventured either to add, or to remove, or to alter a syllable; and it is an instinct with every Jew, from the day of his birth, to regard them as the decrees of God, to abide by them, and, if need be, cheerfully to die for them. Time and again ere now the sight has been witnessed of prisoners enduring tortures and death in every form in the theatres, rather than utter a single word against the Laws and the allied documents. (*Against Apion* 1:42–43)

Philo claims that the law is "immortal as long as the sun and moon and heaven and the whole heaven and universe exist" (*Moses* 2.3). Baruch 4:1 refers to "the Law that endures for ever"; and Wisdom 18:4, to "the imperishable light of the Law." Other pious Jews proclaim the permanent glory of the law: it does not perish but remains in its glory (4 Ezra 9:37); even when humankind disappears, the law will abide (*2 [Syriac] Apocalypse of Baruch* 77:15). Later Rabbis have God pronounce that Solomon and a thousand like him shall be obliterated before one word of the Torah will be (*Jerusalem Talmud Sanhedrin* 2:6, 20c).

Before any example of Jesus' interpretation of the law is given, the auditors are warned that they are not to conclude that he annuls or contradicts it. Given the prevailing belief in the sanctity of the law, it was obviously important for Matthew to fend off any allegation that Jesus was a false prophet who led Israel astray (Deut 13) or that his followers are a "godless and lawless sect" (Justin, *Dialogue* 108:2). In 5:18–19, Jesus affirms that the law and the prophets faithfully express

God's will and that what he does and teaches complies with them. The phrase "I have come," however, accords Jesus a special status as one who comes with a particular mission. The reader is already aware that the Scriptures bear witness to him (1:22-23; 2:6, 15, 17-18; 23; 4:14-15), and now Jesus openly declares that he has come to fulfill them. Moses prophesied that God would speak anew through a prophet like himself (Deut 18:15-20), and Matthew presents Jesus as that promised prophet who fulfills the long-awaited promise of the Scriptures. But fulfillment also implies transcendence. When Jesus appears as God with us (1:23), the center of gravity shifts to him. The law and the prophets remain valid, but Jesus is the canon by which to gauge obedience to the Scripture and is its sole interpretive guide. The so-called antitheses that follow in 5:21-48 make it clear that Jesus is the key for unlocking meaning of the law and the prophets.

Restoring God's Intention in the Law
(5:20-48)

Jesus' interpretation of the law is prefaced by this statement: "Unless your righteousness exceed that of the scribes and Pharisees, you will not enter into the kingdom of heaven" (5:20). One can easily get the impression from reading Matthew that the scribes and Pharisees were monstrous hypocrites, but their righteousness, based on their meticulous interpretation of the law, must have been popularly regarded as exceptional for this statement to pack any punch (see Josephus, *Jewish War* 1.5.2 §110; Phil 3:5-6). Even the proverbial righteousness of the scribes and Pharisees is deficient for entry into the kingdom of heaven. It flunks the test because it does not go far enough and because a different kind of righteousness is required. The demand for a greater righteousness announces the theme of what follows. The question "What are you doing that is more than others?" (5:47) and the insistence that "you must be perfect" (5:48) conclude this unit (the verb "to exceed" [*periseuein,* 5:20] and the adverb "more" [*perisson,* 5:47] bracket it). The "more" that Jesus requires has to do with both quantity and quality. In 5:21-48, Jesus offers examples of what is to set the disciples apart from others in their attitudes, words, and actions. Much of what is taught here reflects ethical ideals found in Judaism; in Jesus' teaching, however, the ideal becomes an imperative.

The challenge that follows can be divided into two parts, 5:21-31 and 5:33-48. (1) The first series begins with the phrase "You have heard that it was said *to those of ancient times*" (5:21) and deals with laws from Exodus and Deuteronomy: murder (Exod 20:13; Deut 5:17), adultery (Exod 20:14; Deut 5:18), and divorce (Deut 24:1). (2) The second series begins, "*Again* you have heard that it was said *to those of ancient times*" (5:33), and deals with laws from Leviticus: oaths (Lev 19:12), retaliation (Lev 24:20), and love of enemies (Lev 19:18).

Some scholars consider Jesus to have abrogated the law in these so-called antitheses, but one must heed the warning of 5:17-19. Rather than abrogating the law, challenging its authority, giving a new law, or interpreting it "in a higher key" (Davies, *Setting*, 102), Jesus restores its original intention. He does not add more laws nor raise the standards of what is right. Instead, he recovers what God has always required in the law — much like those who removed the accumulation of grime that collected over the years on Michelangelo's paintings in the Sistine chapel in order to restore them to their full glory.

What constitutes an assault on the law is in the eye of the beholder. It is always one's opponents who are labeled as the false prophets and who make a mockery of God's commandments, while one's own interpretations are believed to uphold the law (see Rom 3:31). K. Snodgrass ("Matthew and the Law," *SBLSP* [1988]: 549) points out, for example, that no one accuses the Rabbis of nullifying the law when they modified its literal sense. They substituted financial penalties for the law of exact retaliation. They reduced the requirement of a ritual bath and the setting of the sun for cleansing to the washing of hands. Rabbi Hillel is credited with instituting the *prozbul* that circumvented the mandate to remit loans in the seventh year (Deut 15:2). A debtor could then sign an agreement before a court of law that the debt was still payable regardless of the sabbatical year. This expedient was designed to make the rich less likely to refrain from loaning to the poor prior to a sabbatical year (*Mishna Šebi'it* 10:3-4; Deut 15:9 is cited as the grounds for this change). Rabbi Joḥanan ben Zakkai is said to have abolished the trial of the suspected adulteress decreed in Numbers 5 (*Numbers Rabba* 19:8). The later Rabbis certainly did not consider these changes in the tradition an abrogation of the law (contrast Jesus' view in 15:3), and the alterations to the law in 11QTemple indicate that the same process of adjustment was occurring at Qumran.

By the same token, Matthew does not consider Jesus to have rendered the law and the prophets null and void by his greater stringency: requiring strict truth so as to make oaths superfluous, forbidding divorce so as to make the law about the certificate of divorce and the prohibition of remarrying the divorced wife unnecessary. But the translations that render these sayings as antitheses, "You have heard it said..., but I say to you," do give the impression that Jesus deliberately set himself over against the law. The translation of the Greek word *de* as "but" makes the contrast too strong. It is better translated, "and I say to you," which makes it akin to a Talmudic phrase that was used to introduce an elucidation of the Torah, never a contradiction. The phrase "you have heard that it was said" means: "you have understood a scriptural passage in the following way," and is followed by a quotation of the literal sense, the current exegesis, or the opinion of an opponent (P. Lapide, *The Sermon on the Mount: Utopia or Program for Action?* [Maryknoll, N.Y.: Orbis, 1986], 44). The second phrase, "and I say to you," presents the new explanation that departs from the customary interpretation (see also E. Lohse, "Ich aber sage euch," *Festschrift für Joachim Jeremias* [Göttingen: Vandenhoeck & Ruprecht, 1970], 196).

While the form of these sayings may be parallel to Rabbinic phraseology, the content is unique. For the later Rabbis, the interpretation of the law is a process that never concludes. Jesus closes the issue; the law means this and only this. Jesus also does not justify his rejection of a certain interpretation by citing other Scriptures according to the accepted rules of interpretation as the later Rabbis did. He makes no appeal to any external authority, a passage from Scripture, a renowned teacher, or knowledge derived from a heavenly vision, to give weight to his pronouncements. The authority for his interpretation is located solely in his own person (H. Weder, " 'But I Say to You...': Concerning the Foundations of Jesus' Interpretation of the Law in the 'Sermon on the Mount," *Text and Logos,* ed. T. W. Jennings, Jr. [Atlanta: Scholars, 1990], 214, 222). Matthew underscores this fact by capping the sermon with the astonished reaction of the crowds: "he was teaching as one having authority and not as their scribes" (7:29).

In Matthew's Gospel, one is to listen only to Jesus (17:5). He is the one teacher (23:8), and the disciples are to make other disciples from the nations by teaching them to observe all things that Jesus has commanded. A. Ginsberg wrote: "Israel cannot accept with religious enthusiasm as the Word of God, the utterances of a man who speaks in his own name — not 'thus saith the Lord' but 'I say unto you.' This 'I' is in itself sufficient to drive Judaism away from the Gospel forever" (*Ten Essays on Zionism and Judaism* [London, 1922], 232). In Matthew's story, we first detect this same revulsion among the scribes and Pharisees who label Jesus a blasphemer and sorcerer, and they will attempt to deter the crowds from being swayed by him.

(1) Anger (5:21-26). Jesus forges beyond the command against murder given by Moses (Exod 20:13; Deut 5:17). While the law of Moses deals with the punishment of the violent act (Gen 9:6; Exod 21:12-14; Lev 24:17; Num 35:12, 16-21; Deut 17:8-13), Jesus deals with the prevention of it. In the process, he redefines murder by addressing its root cause. If one refrains from murdering another, one may escape the judgment of human courts, but one is not exonerated before God. Murder begins in the seething heart that is not cooled (see Gen 4:6-7). Later Rabbis would not disagree: "Whoever hates his neighbor is to be counted among those who shed his blood" (*Babylonian Talmud Qiddušin* 28; see also 1 John 3:15). If one has aimed looks that could kill, one must face the eschatological judgment of God.

Jesus offers one example of anger that is expressed improperly, name calling, something that humiliates another (*Babylonian Talmud Baba Meṣi'a* 58b: "A teacher of *Mishna* taught before Rab Naḥman ben Isaac: 'If anyone makes the face of a companion pale before a crowd, it is as if he shed blood' "). He then gives two examples of what to do when anger comes between two people.

The primary concern about name calling is not just that it is an inappropriate way to vent anger but that it triggers anger in others. Jesus commands us not only to check our own anger but also not to provoke it in others. He does not imagine that we live in a Utopia, because the next illustrations provide examples of what to do when we have aroused anger in another. The first illustration pictures someone at the altar preparing to sacrifice. The altar is the place where one goes to become reconciled with God; but if one remembers that a person has something against one (implying that one has offended the person, see Rev 2:4, 14; 20), Jesus says to abort the sacrifice and first be reconciled with that person. The assumption behind this teaching is that one approaches God through one's neighbor (see Sir 28:1-7; *Mishna Yoma* 8:8-9), and Jesus uses hyperbole to make that point. It would be inconceivable for Galileans, for example, to halt sacrificial proceedings, to return to Galilee, to search out the offended person and do whatever is necessary to bring about reconciliation, and then to return to the temple in Jerusalem and pick up the sacrifice where they had left off. The teaching makes it clear, however, that religious rituals that seek atonement with God are profitless if one disregards making amends for one's offenses against others. The second illustration pictures someone being hauled before a judge by an antagonist, and Jesus advises doing all in one's power to assuage the other's anger before the inquiry. These two illustrations indicate that what is of primary importance is not the punishment of the murderer or the angry person but the reconciliation of one with another.

(2) Adultery (5:27–30). The law defines adultery as carnal intercourse between a man and a woman married or betrothed to another Israelite (Exod 20:14; Lev 20:10; Deut 22:22–27) and requires unconditional respect for the rights of the (male) neighbor. Consequently, a man guilty of intercourse with another's wife does not violate his own marriage or commit adultery against his wife; he violates the marriage of another married Israelite.

A double standard was created by the fact that unconditional fidelity was specifically required only of the wife (see Gen 38:24–26). The bitter water ceremony in Numbers 5 applies only to the suspected adulteress; there were no procedures to probe the suspected adulterer. The double standard could be far worse among gentiles. Cato pontificates: "If you should take your wife in adultery, you may with impunity put her to death without a trial; but if you should commit adultery or indecency, she must not presume to lay a finger on you, nor does the law allow it" (Gellius, *Attic Nights,* X.23.5). The ritual of the bitter water at least provided some protection for a wife from being killed by a husband in a fit of jealousy.

Jesus redefines adultery and again goes to the heart of the matter. Adultery is not limited to the physical act. It is the look that begins in the heart. It is insufficient simply to refrain from the physical act while harboring lust. Adultery of the eyes is just as grievous a sin, and many others concurred (see also Job 31:1, 9; *Jubilees* 20:4; *Psalm of Solomon* 4:4–5; *Testament of Issachar* 7:2; Epictetus, *Discourses* II.xviii.5–17; Sextus, *Sentences* 233: "Know that you are an adulterer even if you merely think of committing adultery"). But Jesus denies the male's right to sexual freedom on the basis that the woman, whether she is someone's wife or not, is a person who is on the same level and possesses the same dignity as the male. Adulterous looks are sins against her, not just her husband.

The later Rabbis were no less concerned about the problem of lust than Jesus, and women were regarded as known occasions of sins and a danger to the devout male. The story of the daughter of the notoriously harsh Rabbi Jose provides an extreme example of a tendency to blame the victim (*Babylonian Talmud Ta'anit* 24a). He was said to have had a beautiful daughter, and one day he caught a man boring a hole in the fence to catch a glimpse of her. When Rabbi Jose challenged the intruder, he answered: "Master, if I am not worthy enough to marry her, may I not at least be worthy to catch a glimpse of her?" Rabbi Jose then turned on his daughter and exclaimed, "You are a source of trouble to mankind; return to the dust so that men may not sin because of you." This kind of attitude has been shared by the church. Tertullian insisted that even natural beauty ought to be obliterated by concealment and neglect, "since it is dangerous to those who look at it" (*On the Apparel of Women* ii.2). This outlook locates the problem not in the male's lust, which is viewed as uncontrollable, but in the woman who is the occasion of male lust. The solution was therefore to avoid women, to segregate them, and to cover them up (Sir 9:9: "With a married woman dine not, recline not at table to drink by her side, lest your heart be drawn to her and you go down in blood to the grave"; *Mishna 'Abot,* "Talk not much with womenkind . . . "; *Babylonian Talmud 'Erubin* 18b [=*Berakot* 61a]: "It is taught: No man should walk on a road behind a woman, even if she is his own wife. If she happened [to be in front of] him on a bridge, he should leave her on one side; and whosoever crosses a river behind a woman has no share in the life to come").

By contrast, Jesus does not warn his disciples about women but about themselves. Jesus accepted women in his group of followers because he expected his disciples to control their desires (J. Jeremias, *New Testament Theology* [New York: Scribners, 1972], 227). He does not say do not look, but do not look with lust. The solution to lust is for one to purge one's own heart so that one is able to see a person and not an object for self-gratification.

(3) Divorce (5:31–32). Most Jews in Jesus' day were of the opinion that husbands had an inalienable right to put away their wives, although the scholars may have differed over the permissible grounds for doing so and when the wife forfeited her rights to the money pledged to her (*ketuba*) if she were divorced. The lone protest of Malachi against divorce, "I hate divorce, says the Lord, the God of Israel" (Mal 2:13–16), had little effect on its general acceptance. *Targum Jonathan,* for example, radically refashions Malachi 2:16 by rendering it: "If you hate her, divorce her." The pious who cared about such things therefore did not believe that God hated divorce but that God wanted it to be controlled by due process as outlined in Deuteronomy 24:1–4. The law requires the husband who puts away his wife to give her a bill of divorce and forbids him from ever remarrying her after she becomes the wife

of another man who later divorces her or dies. The abomination is not divorce but remarrying the first wife, and the law aims at preventing this abomination from occurring in Israel.

One must remember in interpreting this passage that Jesus is not engaged in pastoral care in this section of the sermon but is setting forth what God requires (see further, D. E. and D. S. R. Garland, *Beyond Companionship: Christians in Marriage* [Philadelphia: Westminster, 1986], 151–72). Jesus argues that the husband is not to divorce his wife because it makes her an adulteress (assuming that she will remarry) and makes the one who marries her an adulterer. This statement would have stupefied the original hearers because the essential words in a bill of divorce were: "Behold thou art permitted to any man" (*Mishna Gittin* 9:3). The whole point of the procedure was to avoid the charge of adultery on anyone's part when the wife remarries. Jesus' pronouncement, however, assumes that no action a husband might take against his wife can ever sunder the marriage relationship in the eyes of God. The rationale for this conviction will be given in 19:3–9. Here, this extraordinary judgment serves to emphasize the permanence and sanctity of marriage that disciples are expected to uphold.

Only Matthew includes an exception in Jesus' comments about divorce. Matthew 5:32 reads, "everyone who puts away his wife except on the ground of *porneia* [*parektos logou porneias*] causes her to commit adultery, and whoever marries a woman who has been put away commits adultery," and 19:9 reads "whoever puts away his wife except for *porneia* [*mē epi porneias*] and marries another commits adultery." This exception has been the occasion of much debate and many explanations have been offered.

It is probable that Matthew, without the modern conventions of printing such as italics, footnotes, brackets, or parentheses to identify his explanations or comments, added the exception as a parenthetical remark to make explicit what would have been assumed by Jesus — namely, that adultery broke the marriage bond. If the wife has already violated the marriage, she cannot be made an adulteress if she is divorced and remarries.

According to Jewish tradition, adultery was not only sufficient grounds for divorce but something that necessitated it. It was considered improper to remain with a wife who has been defiled by another man (see Matt 1:18–19; Deut 22:20–22; *Mishna Yebamot* 2:8; *Sota* 5:1; *Babylonian Talmud Gittin* 90b; *Numbers Rabba* 9:12) and was widely disdained in the Greco-Roman world as well. According to Demosthenes, a citizen who failed to divorce a wife taken in adultery was deprived of his civil rights (*Against Neara* 115). According to the Julian law in Rome, a man who failed to divorce his wife caught in adultery was guilty of the offense of condoning (P. Corbett, *The Roman Law of Marriage* [Oxford: Clarendon, 1930], 133–46). The Shepherd of Hermas deals with the very question of whether or not it is sinful to live with a wife who has committed adultery. The answer is that the husband is not guilty as long as he does not know about it, but he must put her away if he is aware of it and she does not repent of her sin. The husband is then to remain single and be prepared to take her back if she repents (*Mandates* 4.1.4–10).

One other possible interpretation of the exception clause is worthy of mention. Jesus may have disallowed divorce for any reason, including adultery. The surprised reaction of the disciples in Matthew 19:10, "if such is the case of a man with his wife, it is expedient not to marry," would suggest that the disciples understood Jesus to forbid divorce, period. The exception seems to run counter to Jesus' argument that God intended for the marital union between husband and wife to be permanent. It seems to say that the bond is permanent only until *the wife* does something to break that permanence, and it allows divorce on demand for the husband (only) as long as the wife has committed some sexual sin. One should note that the husband is no less guilty if he commits adultery with his eyes (5:28), and that Jesus expects his disciples to love and forgive without limit (see Matt 6:14–15, 18:21–35). There is no reason to exclude the adulterous spouse from this mandate.

An increasing number of scholars have therefore argued that the Greek word *porneia* can refer to sexual sins in general and does not mean "unchastity" in this instance. It refers instead to marriage within the forbidden degrees of kinship (Lev 18:6–18, 20:11–12, 14, 17, 19–21; Deut 22:30, 27:20, 22–23). The marriage of Herod Antipas to Herodias, the former wife of his brother, would have been such an unlawful union (it was not a levirate marriage since she had a child by her former husband, who was also still alive; Deut 25:5–10); and it prompted John the Baptist's bitter attack against them (14:3–4). The word that specifies adultery (*moicheia,* verb forms, *moicheuō, moicheaomai*) is used in 5:27–28, 32, but not in the exception clause. The two words are distinguished from one another by the Evangelist, since they appear together in the same list of vices in Matthew 15:19 (see also 1 Cor 6:9, Heb 14:4). No special technical term for incest was current in Greek before the Byzantine era, and the word *porneia* could serve to refer to it. Paul expresses his shock that a man was living with his father's wife and calls it *porneia* (1 Cor 5:1; see Lev 18:6–8; *Testament of Reuben* 1:6, 4:8; *Testament of Judah* 13:3; *Jubilees* 16:5, 20:5). The Jerusalem Council ruled that if gentile converts wanted to have fellowship with Jewish Christians, they need not become circumcised but must abstain from "pollution of idols, what is strangled, blood and *porneia*" (Acts 15:29; also 21:25). *Porneia* is usually translated "unchastity," but why specify that gentiles need to refrain from unchastity as a minimal requirement for fellowship with Jewish Christians? Chastity was not something that was or is optional for Christians. Since the other requirements in the list refer to restrictions found in the Holiness code in Leviticus 17–18 (meat offered to idols, 17:8–9; blood, 17:10–12; strangled meat, 17:15), it would seem likely that *porneia* refers to sexual contact with a partner prohibited in Leviticus 18:6–18.

If *porneia* refers to what a Jew would consider to be a forbidden union, then Matthew may have added this exception because the infusion of gentile converts within the Christian community posed a practical dilemma. The predicament was this: if a gentile Christian was married, and in the eyes of Jewish Christians the relationship was incestuous (see Paul's vehement reaction in 1 Cor 5:1), what was to be done? The answer: divorce was required. Why? Because God could not possibly have joined together two who were forbidden to one another. God could never have recognized this marriage. Therefore, Matthew's church, in a mission setting quite different from that of Jesus, adapted Jesus' repudiation of divorce to make clear that this did not apply to a situation that they believed required divorce. Jesus' prohibition of divorce applies only to valid marriages, and the exception clause applies only to quite exceptional cases – marriage within forbidden degrees of kinship – and does not provide an escape hatch for those husbands whose wives have committed adultery.

Whether the first or the second explanation for the exception clause is correct is difficult to decide. The first, however, is the simplest solution and does not require a presupposed mission setting for the Gospel.

(4) On Swearing Oaths (5:33–37). Oath taking was a prevalent practice that was open to abuse. In the Hebrew Scriptures, one was enjoined to swear by the name of God (Deut 6:13; 10:20) as a sign of allegiance to the Lord rather than to idols. What is forbidden are false oaths because they are a profanation of the name of God. Jesus' reference to oaths and vows reflects a combination of texts (Lev 19:12; Num 30:2;

Deut 23:22; Ps 50:14; Zech 8:17) that were intended to safeguard the sanctity of God's name. Jesus, however, prohibits all oaths. The plain sense of "at all" allows no exception.

Jesus was not alone in his opposition to oaths (see Sir 23:9–11). Josephus says of the Essenes: "Any word of theirs has more force than an oath; swearing they avoid, regarding it as worse than perjury for they say that one who is not believed without an appeal to God stands condemned already" (*Jewish War* 2.8.6 §135). This stance was rooted in a pious abhorrence of using the name of God in an oath (CD 15:1–5; 1QS 6:27), and Philo viewed it as a testimony of their love for God (*Every Good Man Is Free* 84). On entrance into their society, however, new members were "made to swear tremendous oaths" regarding the practice of piety and secrets of the sect (*Jewish War* 2.8.7 §139–42; see CD 15:5–6; 1QS 5:7–8). The Essenes also permitted swearing a judicial oath (CD 9:9–12), but one could only swear by the curses of the Covenant and thereby not become liable to death for profaning the name by breaking the oath (CD 15:1–5).

Philo also disdained oaths, but his reasoning was that it best suited "a rational life which has been taught to speak the truth so well on each occasion that its words are regarded as oaths." To swear truly was only second best, he wrote, "because the mere fact of swearing casts suspicion on the trustworthiness of the man" (*On the Decalogue* 84; see *On the Special Laws* II.1–8). He roundly condemned taking oaths to disguise the truth because it is the height of profanity to implicate God in knavery, and he criticized the habit of many to fill up the gaps in their talk with oaths (*On the Decalogue* 92; see also *On the Special Laws* II.6; and Sir 23:9–11).

Rabbinic literature devotes significant attention to oaths and vows. The *Mishna* tractate *Šebu'ot* addresses the issue of what constitutes valid oaths, and *Nedarim* does the same with vows and their annulment. The Rabbis carefully distinguished between oaths and vows. In a vow, a person pledges before God that some item or act is forbidden to him or another. Oaths are of two kinds (*Mishna Sebu'ot* 1:1; 3:1, 5). In an assertive oath, one swears that one has or has not done something, usually in a judicial context to substantiate or reject testimony. A voluntary oath is similar to a vow in that one swears that one will or will not do something. This kind of oath was a prominent element of everyday life. The development of divine circumlocutions and ersatz oaths, the subject of 5:34b–36 and 23:16–22, probably arose from a desire to avoid profaning the holy name (Exod 20:7). Because of a pious fear of real oaths (see Deut 23:23; Eccl 5:4; *Sipre Deuteronomy* §265), substitute oaths were in vogue among the populace. Unschooled in the fine points, the masses tended to confuse the distinctions between oaths and vows, to regard substitute oaths as valid, and to use them on all occasions. While some later Rabbis acquiesced to the widespread practice of the masses, others protested against the use of invalid oaths. The latter stressed that valid oaths were sacred and not to be transgressed but taught that some oaths were not binding. The later Rabbis were no less concerned than Jesus to make clear that an oath was no substitute for habitual veracity, and it is not legitimate to infer from Jesus' attack in 23:16–22 that the scribes and Pharisees employed their knowledge about valid and invalid oaths for dishonest advantage. They were primarily concerned about the legal niceties of oaths and vows.

While many may have lamented the abuse of oaths, Jesus differed from all others by rejecting them entirely. He scorns the pious effort to skirt round the name of God in oaths by using circumlocutions for God. An oath is an oath regardless of how oblique the reference to God. He condemns swearing by one's head (or life) because it usurps God's jurisdiction over one's life. While others advocated total honesty, Jesus demands it and insists that honesty needs nothing to prop it up. This is the meaning of "let your yes be yes, and your no, no." Disciples are to speak the truth as a matter of course because they are inwardly pure in heart, not because it has been imposed upon them by the use of an oath. Jesus' demand assumes that humans are bound to God in all of life, not just when they call upon God as a witness; and they will be accountable for every idle word (12:34–37). The call for God to notarize one's fallible utterances is an infringement on God's majesty and reduces God to an object of human manipulation. In forbidding oaths, Jesus ignores the practical problems this demand creates for his disciples in a society that required oaths in all manner of disputes. With the advent of the reign of God, all such concerns have been superseded.

(5) An eye for an eye (5:38–42). The law of the tooth (Exod 21:23–25; Lev 24:19–20; Deut 19:21) served to rein in unrestricted blood vengeance such as Lamech's boast to his wives, "if Cain is avenged seven fold, Lamech seventy fold" (Gen 4:23–24). It mandates responsibility for damages, equality of justice, and a just proportion between the crime and the punishment. Jesus, however, prohibits even measured retaliation (see Prov 20:22; 24:29; Isa 50:6; Rom 12:19–21; 1 Thess 5:15; 1 Pet 2:23). This word does not encourage complete surrender when one is confronted by the evil person. That is how kings and oppressors

would prefer it to be interpreted. What Jesus renounces is the violent response: "Do not resist [violently] the evil one." The fact that the opponent is designated as evil implies that God will deal with this one in due time, but that is the prerogative of God, not humans. Jesus then offers three illustrations of the proper response to mistreatment (when one is struck, sued, and coerced) and one of how to respond to another victim who asks for help.

(a) Striking another on the cheek is a way of humiliating that person (Job 16:10; Lam 3:3). Aristotle contended that it is not always an outrage if a man strikes another, only if he intends "to bring disrepute upon the other or to please himself" (*Rhetoric* 1.13.10). To be struck on the *right* cheek implies that a person has been slapped with the back of the hand. Jesus is therefore not simply urging his disciples to turn the other cheek when someone aims a blow at them but when someone assaults them with insulting violence. Such a calculated indignity is considered to be at least four times as injurious in a Mishnaic discussion on indemnities for violence:

> If a man cuffed his fellow he must pay him a *sela* [four *zuz*; a *zuz* was approximately a day's wage]. R. Judah says in the name of R. Jose the Galilean: One hundred *zuz*. If he slapped him he must pay 200 *zuz*. If [he struck him] with the back of his hand he must pay him 400 *zuz*. (*Mishna Baba Qamma* 8:6)

Jesus demands that we overcome the initial impulse to requite violence with violence, but does turning the other cheek simply mean humble submission?

Others encouraged nonresistance to oppression. According to Josephus, Herod Agrippa tried to dissuade the crowds from rebelling against Rome by saying: "There is nothing to check blows like submission, and the resignation of the wronged victim puts the wrongdoer to confusion (or turns him aside; *Jewish War* 2.16.4 §351). Musonius Rufus was said to teach that the wise and sensible philosopher would never prosecute anyone for personal injury or disgrace. He should be immune to insults, malignant glances, and the jeering slap in the face and should meekly submit because "this befits one whose purpose is noble minded." "To accept injury not in a spirit of savage resentment and to show ourselves not implacable toward those who wrong us, but rather to be a source of good hope to them is characteristic of a benevolent and civilized way of life" (C. E. Lutz, *Musonius Rufus* [New Haven: Yale University Press, 1947], x). The Rabbis also praised restraint from seeking retribution (*Babylonian Talmud Šabbat* 88b; *Yoma* 23a; *Giṭṭin* 36b). But the first statement comes from a client king of the oppressors who would like nothing better than to keep the people docile. The second comes from one who has the power to sue others for injury in courts of law. The last comes from those who had suffered enough from two ruinous revolts against Rome.

W. Wink argues that the issue for Jesus is not simply resistance or surrender but what kind of resistance. He claims that turning the other cheek is a third way, which he labels "nonviolent direct action," a "practical, strategic measure for empowering the oppressed." By turning the other cheek, for example, the victim "robs the oppressor of the power to humiliate." The oppressor must decide whether or not to slap the person again, but this time not as one would slap a slave with the back of the hand but as one would an equal. Wink contends that turning the cheek "seizes the initiative from the oppressor, overcomes fear, and reclaims the power of choice, all the while maintaining the humanity of the oppressor" (W. Wink, "We Have Met the Enemy," *Sojourners* 15, no. 11 [1986]: 15; see also "Beyond Just War and Pacifism: Jesus' Nonviolent Way," *RevExp* 89 [1992]: 197–214).

(b) The second illustration refers to being sued. If someone wants to take your tunic in litigation, Jesus says, let the person have your outer garment as well. The law, however, specifically forbids a plaintiff from claiming the cloak that covered one's nakedness and kept the poor warm in the evening (Exod 22:25–27; Deut 24:10–13, 17). This word addresses the poorest of the poor, who have only their garments to give as collateral for a loan. Jesus says, in effect, if someone sues you for your cloak, let the person have the shirt off your back.

To respond in this way means that one would literally become naked. The situation envisioned is that of a destitute peasant hounded by a merciless creditor. The peasant is seemingly powerless. He is not well connected and cannot appeal to civil rulers for justice. Again, the counsel to give the creditor all your clothes completely changes the power initiative and opens up the nemesis to ridicule. To understand this, one must picture the small Palestinian village. A man seizes another and demands his tunic. The debtor proceeds not only to give him the cloak but offers him all his clothing. The result will be a poor person standing naked before his creditor and all the village onlookers (see the taboos associated with seeing or causing another's nakedness, Gen 9:20–27). In a shame/honor society, the creditor would be humiliated before others as a cruel and harsh person. Whether he is honorable or dishonorable, he would be likely to urge the other to stop undressing. This response to an antagonist empowers the victim, restores a sense of dignity, and provides a strategy that lovingly confronts the antagonist to face up to the evil in an age when the powerless had no other recourse but to rely on malicious magic or prayers of revenge to redress the wrongs done to them.

(c) This interpretation of these sayings is confirmed in the third illustration about going the extra mile. The word "compel" translates a technical word for being impressed into service (Simon of Cyrene is "compelled" to carry Jesus' crossbar, 27:32). It was a hated form of Roman exploitation (note that "mile" is a Latin loan word of a Roman measurement). Epictetus advises, if a soldier commandeers your donkey, "let it go, do not resist nor grumble. If you do, you will get a beating and lose your little donkey just the same" (*Discourses* IV.i.79). A graphic example of the truth of this statement is provided by Apuleius (*Metamorphoses* [*The Golden Ass*] 9.39–42).

This teaching of Jesus has unfortunately been domesticated into "going the extra mile," which may mean anything from giving 110 percent in work to being especially kind. Jesus applies his teaching, however, to the hated enemy who had occupied one's country. Wink writes: "The rules are Caesar's, but how one responds to the rules belongs to God, and Caesar has no power over that" ("The Third Way: Reclaiming Jesus' Nonviolent Alternative," *Sojourners* 15, no. 11 [1986]: 31). The soldier is used to coercing others; he would be thrown off by one who volunteers to carry his pack to the next mile marker. The victim may find himself in the unusual situation of having the soldier demanding the return of his pack after the first mile (see the discussion of the historical setting in Wink, "Beyond Just War and Pacifism: Jesus' Nonviolent Way," 202–5).

(d) In the fourth illustration, Jesus instructs disciples to give without restrictions to one who asks. Giving was most often used as a means of establishing power over recipients and as a means of self-glorification (6:2). The benefactor becomes a patron, and the recipient becomes a client who must reciprocate in some way (see Sir 12:1–7; *Pseudo Phocylides* 80). Jesus says the true benefactor is one who gives without expecting any return from the person who receives.

Some contend that this saying does not fit the present context of sayings about revenge and love of enemies. The disciple is now no longer a victim but one with means to lend to others. But one must understand this saying in light of Jesus' Galilean context. The rich wanted to invest their wealth in land, but since the land was part of one's ancestral heritage it was not put up for sale (Lev 25:23-24, 34; 1 Kgs 21:6). The only way to acquire it was when peasant farmers defaulted on loans. The strategy of the rich was to pick off one farm at a time as farmers fell into a whirlpool of debt. It is telling that one of the first acts of the rebels in their revolt against Rome was to seize and burn the debt records in Jerusalem (Josephus, *Jewish War* 2.17.1 §426-27). The rich became richer by dividing and conquering insolvent debtors. Jesus' advice about giving to those who asked was a realistic way of empowering peasants by encouraging them to band together to fend off being caught in the tentacles of debt.

Matthew's community was possibly located in an urban social context. Nevertheless, the Evangelist faithfully preserves the teaching of Jesus that was relevant for a rural peasant setting. The teaching is therefore understood to be illustrative of how the principle of directive nonviolence works. Disciples will continually have to create new ways that enable victims to retain their human dignity in the face of intimidation while, at the same time, confronting oppressors with the evil of their conduct. There will be situations, however, when it is more prudent for the victims simply to flee (10:23; 24:16).

(6) Loving Enemies (5:43-48). It was not uncommon in the ancient world for a farmer to pray to the gods for the protection of his own animal and for the animal of his rival to break its leg. The Hebrew Scriptures, however, enjoin loving the neighbor. The neighbor is carefully defined as the fellow Israelite, although it is also extended to the resident alien (Lev 19:18, 33-34; see Deut 10:18-19). Nowhere does the Scripture explicitly say that one is to hate one's enemy, although it might be inferred from some passages (see Deut 7:2; 20:13-18; 25:17-19; Pss 137:8-9; 139:19-22). Explicit commands to hate the enemy, the sons of darkness, do appear in the Qumran Literature (1QS 1:3-4, 9-10; 10:17b-18; 1QM 9:21; 11QTemple 61:12-14); and one should not ignore the impressions of outsiders about Jews. Some believed that hatred of everyone but Jews was part of their religion (see Tacitus, *Histories* 5.5; Juvenal, *Satires* 14.102).

"Love" and "hatred" in this saying do not refer to emotions. To love means "to favor, prefer, or select"; to hate means "to disfavor, neglect." Simply put, loving the neighbor and hating the enemy is to place the neighbor first and the enemy second (O. Linton, "St. Matthew 5,43," *ST* 18 [1964]: 70). An example of this common attitude is found in a Rabbinic interpretation of Exodus 22:25 ("if you lend money to any of my people"): "If an Israelite and a gentile stand before you to borrow, 'any of My people' should be given preference" (*Mekilta Kaspa* 1 to Exod 22:25). The principle that the one who is nearer to you should be given preference is used to conclude that one should give aid to the poor supplicant over the rich, relatives over nonrelatives, and residents of your own city over residents of another place. This premise governs most human relations, but Jesus says that both enemy and neighbor (the far and the near) are to be treated in the same way. He rejects conventional wisdom by demanding the love of the enemy.

The statement in Didache 1:3, "If you love those who hate you, you will have no enemy," is naive (see Diogenes Laertius, *Lives of Eminent Philosophers* 8.1.23: "Your good behavior will turn enemies into friends"). The enemy may not be changed by a loving response. On the contrary, it may bring out the worst in the other person instead of the best; but this ethic is not to be practiced for ulterior motives. Only here does Jesus provide the reasoning behind his teaching. (a) He points out that it is God's way to shine the sun and rain the rain indiscriminately on both good and evil (see *Mekilta Amalek* 3 to Exod 18:12). The children of God disclose their parentage by doing as God does, loving inclusively. (b) Disciples are expected to do more than pagans and tax collectors whose every action is calculated on a cost-benefit ratio — what will it get them in return. (c) Disciples are to be perfect like God. The perfection that is required is not moral flawlessness but the perfection of love that reaches out to one and all, neighbor and enemy, indiscriminately (Davies and Allison, *Saint Matthew,* 1:563). "As God is unrestricted in His goodness [pouring out blessings on evil and unrighteous, v. 45] so ... the disciples of Jesus should be 'total' in their love, bringing even their enemies within its compass" (G. Delling, *telos, TDNT* 8:74).

Anger, adultery, divorce, false statements, retaliation, and hatred are destructive behaviors that fragment individuals and society. God's redemptive purpose as expressed in Jesus' interpretation of the law is to restore harmony, create community, and elevate humanity.

Acts of Devotion: For Applause or for God?
(6:1–18)

This next unit in the sermon deals with two issues: (1) the proper motives behind acts of piety; and (2) how to pray. (1) The first issue is addressed in 6:1–6, 16–18. According to 5:16, the disciples are supposed to let their light shine so that others might see their good works and glorify God. The danger is that they may wish to be glorified as well, and Jesus now warns against doing righteousness before others for the sake of being observed and praised by them as the hypocrites do (6:1). Three perfectly balanced sayings follow (6:2–4, 5–6, and 16–18), which provide examples of primary expressions of piety in the time of Jesus: almsgiving, prayer, and fasting (see Tob 12:8: "Prayer is good when accompanied by fasting, almsgiving and righteousness . . . "). Deuteronomy 6:4 commands loving God with all one's heart, and Jesus addresses the disposition of the heart when one does what God requires.

These sayings address the bane of all religions: hypocrisy, the discrepancy between outer appearance and inner reality. Hypocrisy can take two forms: (a) A hypocrite may be a play actor who consciously feigns piety to cloak an inner godlessness (see *Psalm of Solomon* 4:1–6). In this case, the hypocrite is more aware of the hypocrisy than anyone else. (b) Or the hypocrite may be self-deceived, and the discrepancy is not between what others think about a person and the inner reality but what the hypocrite thinks of himself or herself and what God thinks. This form of hypocrisy is the most insidious because there is nothing easier to prove to oneself than one's own sincerity. In this case, others are sometimes more aware of hypocrisy than the hypocrite.

The hypocrites who are pilloried in these sayings may be sincere or insincere in their show of piety. The problem is that it has become a show. Religious posturing that seeks to win the applause of an audience whether to deceive others or not (see Sir 31:11, "the assembly will relate his acts of charity") is not serving God. Jesus later condemns the scribes and Pharisees for parading their piety to reap human plaudits (23:5). If the goal of religiosity is to earn the admiration others, one can easily succeed; but it cancels out any hope of a reward from the Father. If one seeks credit from others, one cannot expect extra credit from God. The voucher already has been cashed in.

Jesus does not say give alms, pray, and fast with perfectly pure motives, however. Instead, he offers practical steps to keep impure motives from tarnishing one's devotion to God. If one is tempted to give, pray, or fast to show off, Jesus says, do it in secret. This advice provides clear evidence that Jesus intended what he taught to be lived. He is not calling us to some impossible ideal but offering realistic ways of living out our piety.

(2) The second issue concerns prayer. The segment in 6:7–15 breaks up the careful parallelism of the three sayings on acts of piety, but Matthew is more interested in providing directions on prayer than

in maintaining the structural symmetry. The warning not to pray like the pagans immediately precedes the Lord's Prayer. The pagans mistakenly believed that it was the squeaky wheel that would get the grease, and so they plied the diffident gods with lengthy invocations, names, surnames, and descriptive predicates to solicit their attention and to get them to draw near to hear their requests. In Philostratus's *Life of Apollonius of Tyana,* a man is imprisoned by the emperor Domitian because at a public sacrifice he omitted to mention that Domitian was the son of Athene (a virgin goddess, 7.24). This pettiness, many people feared, was typical of deities. One had to invoke the gods with meticulous care so as not to offend them; but since the gods had completely different functions and domains of power under different names, one had to be sure to utter the right name to get the response one wanted. An example of pagan invocation in prayer is found in Apuleius's *Metamorphoses* (*The Golden Ass*) 11.2. Lucius appeals to the "blessed queen of heaven, whether Thou be the Dame Ceres ...; whether Thou be the celestial Venus ...; or whether Thou be the sister of the god Phoebus ...; or whether Thou be called terrible Proserpine...." After each name, he gives a lengthy recital of the deeds and qualities of the goddess.

The "heaping up of phrases" (6:7) and the "many words" in 6:8 are *not* a condemnation of long prayers. Jesus himself prays all night on a mountain (14:23–25). They refer instead to the array of divine names that were uttered in hopes of hitting the right combination that would win the supplicant an audience with the deity or deities. Catullus's poem to the goddess Diana is a typical example of pagan prayer that Jesus scorns. The poet recites all of the various names and qualities of the goddess and concludes with a catch-all formula in case he might have missed any crucial title: "Hallowed be thy name, whatever name you prefer" (*Poems* 34). Jesus teaches that one does not need to reel off a litany of divine aliases to conjure up a reluctant God in prayer; one need simply invoke God as Father and may then pray in a spirit of confidence that the Father will respond. Prayer is to be voiced in a spirit of intimacy, familiarity, and trust as one would direct requests to a loving father. One need not worry about omitting a key name for God any more than children worry about ceremoniously addressing their parents when they cry out for help or for joy. One also need not flatter God with a list of attributes. In the Talmud, one finds this story:

> A certain [reader] went down in the presence of R. Ḥanina and said, O God, the great, mighty, terrible, majestic, powerful, awful,

strong, fearless, sure and honored. He waited till he had finished, and when he had finished he said to him, Have you concluded all the praise of your Master? Why do we want all this? Even with these three that we do say [Great, mighty, and terrible in the first benediction], had not Moses our Master mentioned them in the Law [Deut 10:17] and had not the men of the Great Synagogue come and inserted them in the *Tefillah,* we should not have been able to mention them, and you say all these and still go on! It is as if an earthly king had a million *denarii* of gold, and someone praised him as possessing silver ones. Would it not be an insult to him? (*Babylonian Talmud Berakot* 33b)

Pagan prayers tended to be long on invocation and short on petition. The Lord's Prayer, by contrast, has a brief invocation and six petitions: three concerning God — let *thy* name be sanctified; let *thy* kingdom come; and let *thy* will be done — and three concerning ourselves — give *us* our bread; forgive *us* our debts; and deliver *us* from temptation and the evil one. The first three petitions ask the Father to act: to sanctify his name, to establish his sovereignty, to realize his redemptive purpose on earth. The reverential circumlocutions make it easier, however, to draw a connection between God's actions and human reaction. God's actions "demand a suitable human response" (B. Gerhardsson, "Matthew's Version of the Lord's Prayer [Matth 6:9b–13]: Some Observations," *The New Testament Age,* ed. W. C. Weinrich [Macon, Ga.: Mercer University Press, 1984], 213). It is this human response to God's mighty works that is of utmost interest to Matthew. The disciples have also already been instructed in the sermon to live in such a way that others may see their good works and glorify the Father in heaven (5:16; see *Testament of Naphtali* 8:4, "God shall be glorified among the Gentiles through you, but through him that does not that which is good, God shall be dishonored").

The model prayer contains no request for earthly favors, such as fortune, health, power, happiness, or peace. It makes no appeal to be anything or to do anything — to be more forgiving, to triumph over temptations, or to defeat evil. The "we" petitions focus simply on the minimal requirements that are needed for us to survive physically and spiritually.

(1) Daily bread. The word normally translated "daily" appears only here in Greek literature from the time of Jesus; and its meaning remains an enigma for translators. The content of the petition was probably intended to be self-evident, however; and it most likely refers to bread

for the existing day or for the morrow. The Lukan version refers unambiguously to bread given to us "each day." Those who see in this petition an appeal for the eschatological bread of the messianic banquet must go outside the Gospel of Matthew and appeal to Luke 14:15 to find a reference to breaking bread in the kingdom. The daily ration was a common motif in ancient literature, and an allusion to the daily supply of manna in the wilderness that was provided by God (Exod 16) is not unlikely. The petition in the Lord's Prayer has to do with a basic physical need, hunger.

(2) Forgiveness. The word "debts" assumes that sin is a failure to pay to God the obedience we owe. The petition also assumes that God is merciful and forgiving, but it requests forgiveness of our debts *as we have forgiven others*. This condition checks the natural tendency toward egoism in prayer where the "I" always seems to comes first. The axiom at the conclusion to the Lord's Prayer, "if you are not forgiving, you will not be forgiven" (6:14–15), underscores the point that persons should not expect to receive from God what they are not prepared to bestow on others; and the parable of the unmerciful servant (18:23–35) vividly illustrates it.

(3) Temptation. The lack of a definite article before "temptation" suggests that the petition has in view those occasions where our faith and obedience are put to the test, not the severe trial of the last days (Rev 3:10). According to some of the later Rabbis, it was proper to place oneself in temptation in order to overcome it (*Babylonian Talmud 'Aboda Zara* 17ab). Temptations were viewed as spiritual muscle builders for the faithful. For example, David prayed: "Prove me, O Lord, and try me; test my heart and my mind" (Ps 26:2). But other Rabbis tell the story of David this way: he asked God to test him so that he could be a proved man of God like Abraham, Isaac, and Jacob. Unfortunately for David, God sent him Bathsheba as a test (*Babylonian Talmud Sanhedrin* 107b). The petition in the Lord's Prayer takes precisely the opposite approach: "Do not test me, I am not able to hold up." Jesus does not teach us to pray for strength so that we might successfully hurdle all the various difficulties of life that might come our way but to pray that we might avoid them altogether. It is this confession of vulnerability that the spirit may be willing but the flesh is weak (26:41) that best arms a person against the onslaughts of the Evil One (see 13:19).

What to Do about Money
(6:19–34)

The next four sayings have to do with money and what disciples should do with it: (1) do not amass wealth on earth (6:19-21); (2) be generous (6:22-23); (3) do not try to serve God and money (6:24); (4) do not be anxious about material concerns but seek wholeheartedly the kingdom of heaven (6:25-34).

(1) The first saying (6:19-21) assumes that the final worth of one's treasure depends on where it is stored. Since the earth is temporal and heaven is eternal, it is only prudent to store treasures in heaven. The way to store wealth in heaven that will escape the ravages of earth is to give it away on earth. Jesus will later advise a rich man who inquires about how to inherit eternal life to sell his possessions and give to the poor, "and you will have treasure in heaven" (19:21; see also Sir 29:10-11; Tob 4:8-9; *Babylonian Talmud Baba Batra* 11a).

(2) The second saying (6:22-23) uses the image of the eye as the conduit that radiates the light that is within a person. Jesus concludes the first saying with, "Where your treasure is, there your heart shall be" (6:21). The next saying assumes that the eye reveals the condition of the heart. Literally, it reads, "if the eye is single," which means "simple" or "sincere." The noun form of the word "single" is used for "generosity" (Rom 12:8; 2 Cor 8:2; 9:11, 13; Jas 1:5). Someone who is single-eyed is generous and will do as Jesus commands in 5:42. The opposite of the "single eye" is the "evil eye," which has nothing to do with witchcraft but refers to stinginess or a begrudging spirit (see 20:15; Prov 23:6-8; Sir 14:10). A single eye shines forth the presence of inner light. An evil eye is the sign of a life engulfed in a darkness that is caused by the lack of generosity with one's possessions (see Prov 23:6-8; 28:22; Sir 14:10; Deut 15:9). It is bad enough to be in the dark but worse to have the darkness in you. Being generous with one's possessions is a sign that one has moved into the world of light.

(3) The third saying (6:24) uses the predicament of a slave who is the property of two different owners (see *Mishna Gittin* 4:5; *'Eduyyot* 1:13) to warn about money. The slave is placed in a terrible bind when one owner commands one thing; the other owner, something else. The result will be that the slave will be more faithful to one master than the other ("love" and "hate" again refer to preference; see on 5:43 above). God and Mammon are two totally different taskmasters, and one can no

more serve both than follow a road that forks. Jesus insists that loyalty to God must be undivided.

Most in Israel did not consider a life devoted to material gain to be in tension with a life devoted to God. Mammon, which in Jewish literature is a neutral term that refers simply to property or anything of value, becomes in the teaching of Jesus something tainted and dangerous. Jesus estimates that one inevitably will fall sway to mammon and become indifferent to the demands of God. Money will become the preoccupation of life. The saying assumes that humans will be enslaved to something; one can choose to be a slave to the things of this world or to God, but not both. The most prudent way to handle mammon, therefore, is to give it away to escape its snares.

(4) The last teaching concerning money issues (6:25–34) does not bid one to be indifferent toward life. It cautions against becoming so frantic about material concerns or an uncertain tomorrow that one is too distraught to function. The illustration from the world of flowers and birds to support Jesus' admonition not to worry is not forceful if one views them "as ordinary remarks about birds and flowers" (R. Tannehill, *The Sword of His Mouth*, 66). The portrait of birds and flowers only works if it engages our imagination so that it begins "to vibrate with deeper meaning."

The saying paints a rich landscape that illustrates the Father's care for his creatures. The picture of a heavenly Father feeding the birds without them having to sow or reap is an ideal world that contrasts with the hurry-scurry of our own. Jesus then asks, if the heavenly Father takes care of the birds, are we not of more value to him than they? Will the Father not also take care of us? Jesus awakens our imaginations with a picture of the Father's nurture of the birds. The second stage of the argument pictures the lilies of the field that neither toil nor spin and yet they increase. These wild flowers are not merely clothed; they are clad with a grandeur that cannot be matched even by Solomon, decked out in all his glory. Jesus then switches the direction of his argument by calling these breathtaking flowers "the grass of the field."

It is now clear that Jesus is not being sentimental about birds and flowers. The "grass of the field" was a standard image for something that was worthless. Jesus deliberately stresses the paradox between the glorious beauty of the flowers and their final insignificance. Today, the beauty of the flowers stun the observer; tomorrow, they are thrown into the oven as fuel. If the heavenly Father is so lavish in clothing field flowers that are destined to be consumed in an oven, how much more gracious will he be with humans? When we look at the canvas Jesus has painted for us, we see a God who makes clothes for the flowers and who prepares meals for the birds. We must then ask ourselves if our anxious concern to provide bread for ourselves is really necessary.

The argument is completed by the assertions that: (a) it is unnecessary to be anxious about food and clothing since the heavenly Father knows we need these things (6:32; 6:8; 7:7-11); (b) it is futile to be anxious since none can grow taller by worrying about his or her height (6:27); and (c) anxiously seeking all these things is a pagan activity (6:32; see the *Letter of Aristeas* 140: the title "men of God" is "ascribed exclusively to those who worship the true God, and not to those who are concerned with meat and drink and clothes, their whole attitude (to life) being concentrated on these concerns"). The pagans pursue all these things only because they do not know God as a loving Father and are deceived about what is crucial in life.

The future was something feared by one and all in the ancient world, since it was believed to be in the hands of Fate and Fortune, and who knew how the wheel of fortune would spin? The vulgar host Trimalchio in Petronius's *Satyricon* puts on a brave front by toasting the revelers at his dinner party:

> What comes next you never know.
> Lady Luck runs the show.
> So pass the Falernian [a wine], lad.
> (*Satyricon* 55.3)

But the account reveals a deep-seated anxiety that afflicts everyone at the table. The requests addressed to a legendary magician, Astrampsuchos, during the imperial period in Egypt, disclose that the cares and worries of ancient humans were little different from those of today: "Will I receive my wages? Will I be sold as a slave? Will I get money? Will I sign a contract? Will I be successful? Will I escape? Will I become a member of the council?" (H. S. Versnel, "Religious Mentality in Ancient Prayer," *Faith, Hope and Worship: Aspects of Religious Mentality in the Ancient World,* ed. H. S. Versnel [Leiden: Brill, 1981], 6; see Plutarch, *Moralia* 408C). According to Jesus, the awareness of God's love for us should cast out all anxiety and allow us to focus on what is important – the kingdom of heaven and its righteousness. Humans do not live on bread alone (4:4), and the most important clothing that they can possess is that which will keep them from being booted out of the wedding banquet and thrown into the outer darkness where there is weeping and gnashing of teeth (22:11–14). Anxiety that one will not have enough for oneself deters one from being generous to others, makes the eye, the lamp of the body, grow dark, and drains one's treasure in heaven.

Relating to Others
(7:1–12)

The next four sayings have to do with how disciples are to relate to others, that is, to be controlled by the love of the neighbor: (1) on judging (7:1–5); (2) on casting pearls (7:6); (3) on asking, seeking, knocking (7:7–11); (4) on the Golden Rule (7:12).

(1) The imperative "do not judge" hooks the attention of the listener because it challenges an everyday, taken-for-granted activity. Does it mean that a person is to suspend the faculty of judgment and never to find fault with others, or that one is always to overlook their sins and foibles in hopes that God will do likewise? Matthew 18:15–20 delineates a procedure for correcting a fellow member who is judged to have sinned, and therefore this saying is not encouraging a casual attitude toward the moral failings of others (see 1 Cor 5:12). Recognizing that the saying is in the form of a chiasm helps to target the key issue.

    a   Let me cast out the splinter from your eye

       b   and behold

          c   the beam is in your own eye.

             d   First cast out

          c′   the beam from your own eye

       b′   and then you will see clearly

    a′   to cast out the splinter from your brother's eye.

The crucial phrase is "first cast out." Jesus is not directing disciples never to judge others but stressing that their first responsibility is to purify themselves. They have not been called to be moral or theological watchdogs over others (see Rom 14:4). A cartoon typical of Semitic humor warns against trying to remove a sliver from a brother's eye without first doing the logging on oneself. The order is judge oneself first, *then* one can see clearly to *help,* not condemn, another. One is also to remember that the brother's sliver is just that, a sliver. The real danger of a judgmental spirit is not simply that one will get back what one dishes out to others (see 18:35), but that it strangles the love for the other (Gnilka, *Matthäusevangelium,* 1:262, cites *Testament of Gad* 4:2–3: "Hatred does not want to hear repeated his commands concerning love of neighbor, and thus sins against God. ³For if a brother makes a false step, immediately it wants to spread the tale to everyone, and is eager to have him condemned for it, punished and executed").

(2) It is helpful to recognize that the next saying (7:6) also forms a chiasm:

  a   Do not give what is holy to dogs

   b   Do not throw your pearls before swine

   b′ They will trample them under foot

  a′ And they turn to attack you

The point would seem to be that one should not give valued things to those who cannot appreciate them, but it also emphasizes the danger in doing so. Pigs trample the pearls when they discover that they are inedible, and packs of scavenging dogs viciously attack (see Ps 22:16). It is unclear, however, what it is that is holy and what are the pearls. The simile can have quite different meanings in different contexts. In a church context, it can be taken to refer to sacred rites (see Did 9:5; Exod 29:33; Lev 2:3; 22:6–7, 10–16; Num 18:8–19; *Mishna Temura* 6:5). In a missionary context, it can warn of the danger of sharing spiritual insights with those who are unable to value them. In the Matthean context, however, it would seem to be connected with judging members of the fellowship. "What is holy" and the "pearls" could refer to the character of the brother or sister that is to be held dear (see *'Abot de Rabbi Nathan* 15). One is not to expose them to humiliation and bring discredit to the community by making public one's judgments of a brother or sister. Since "pigs" was a term of abuse for the Romans (who trample their enemy; see Luke 21:24) and "dogs" a term of abuse for gentiles, the simile might also fit a context of persecution where love has grown cold (24:12) and brother is betraying a brother unto death (10:21; 24:10).

(3) The next saying is set off by an inclusio: "ask and it will be given to you" (7:7); "Your Father in heaven will give good things to those who ask him" (7:11). It pictures a situation of someone in want. "The one who asks, lacks something; the one who seeks, has lost something; the

one who knocks is shut out" (Gnilka, *Matthäusevangelium,* 1:262). The gracious response of the Father to his children is again emphasized with this argument: if you who are evil respond to the requests of your children, *"how much more"* will your heavenly Father respond with good things.

Jesus does not specify what it is that one is to ask for, to seek out, or where one is to knock. But elsewhere in the sermon, one is to ask in prayer for the kingdom to come (6:10) and to seek first the kingdom of God (6:33). The overwhelming demands made by Jesus in this sermon are tempered by this assurance that God is merciful and gives to those who ask, seek, and knock.

(4) The last saying in this section, the so-called Golden Rule (7:12), is said to be the gist of the law and the prophets. The phrase "the law and the prophets" forms an inclusio to the section that began in 5:17; and this saying again affirms that what Jesus teaches is not novel: it is the law and the prophets (see Rom 13:8–10; Gal 5:14). A famous parallel to Jesus' statement reveals that this ideal had been in circulation in Judaism for some time (see Talbert, *Reading Luke,* 73), but it also reveals Jesus' break with his tradition.

A certain heathen came before Rabbi Shammai and asked: "Make me a proselyte, on condition that you teach me the whole Torah while I stand on one foot." Rabbi Shammai responded by driving him off with the builder's cubit which was in his hand. When the heathen put the same question to Rabbi Hillel, he responded: "What is hateful to you, do not do to your neighbor: that is the whole Torah, while the rest is commentary thereon; go and learn it" (*Babylonian Talmud Šabbat* 31a). The proselyte asked for an explanation of the law in a nutshell. Shammai was apparently of the opinion that any philosophical system that could be put in a nutshell belonged there. Hillel, on the other hand, offered the proselyte a rule that summed up the entire law (see *Sipra Qedoshim* 4 on Lev 19:18: "Thou shalt love thy neighbor as thyself, R. Akiba said: 'That is the greatest principle in the Law' "). Hillel differs from Jesus in that the love of neighbor is the beginning of learning that everything in the law is valid. Jesus contends that the love of neighbor is the heart and soul of the law and the prophets and expresses God's will (see 19:19, where it caps off the list of commandments and 22:34–40). It is the canon for discerning what is God's will in the law and the prophets and for correctly interpreting them. The love for the neighbor that knows no bounds is the principle that governs Jesus' interpretation of the law.

The positive expression of the rule can lend itself to crass selfishness (*Tosepta Megilla* 4:16: "Do, that they will do to you, lend, that they will lend to you, mourn, that they will mourn for you, honor in burial, that they will honor you in burial"). But in the Matthean setting, it immediately follows 7:7–11, which emphasizes the Father's loving response to his children's needs. That benevolence is to be the norm for the disciples. Perhaps this explains why 7:7–11 is not affixed to the other sayings on prayer in 6:7–15, because it helps to clarify the golden rule. Disciples are to do unto others as they would ask, seek, and knock for God to do for them.

Warning: Obedience Is Not Optional (7:13–7:27)

The next three sayings about (1) the two ways (7:13–14), (2) false prophets (7:15–23), and (3) the two builders (7:24–27) serve as warnings that structurally balance the blessings that opened the Sermon on the Mount. They are strung together by linking words ("enter," 7:13, 21; "many," 7:13, 22; "false prophets," 7:15, 22; "all," 7:21, 24, 26; "do," 7:21, 26; "Lord," 7:21, 22).

(1) The concluding words to the sermon confront the crowds and disciples with a decision. They are told to enter the narrow gate. The saying assumes that the choice of gate will determine the state of the road. The imagery comes from the city and is surprising. If one is entering a city, a broad, constructed road leads to the king's palace or somewhere very useful and can be safely traversed. If one is exiting a city, a precipitous path would lead through robbers' territory (J. D. M. Derrett, "The Merits of the Narrow Gate," *JSNT* 15 [1982]: 20). The broad way offers a more pleasant excursion and avoids danger. The passage for the followers of Christ, if they choose the right gate, will be a tight squeeze and lined with suffering – one of many indications in the Gospel that discipleship in the kingdom will not be a festive field trip (5:10–12, 44; 10:16–33; 13:21; 23:34; 24:9–10). One must decide which gate to choose, and the decision will determine one's ultimate fate (see 4 Ezra 7:3–16).

(2) The second saying deals with the problem of false prophets (7:15–23), who were a recurrent problem for the early church (see 24:11, 24; Rom 16:17; 2 Pet 2:1; 1 John 4:1–3; Jude 4; Rev 2:20; Did 11:3–12; Hermas, *Mandates* xi.7–16; 3 Cor 1:2–5; 3:34–39). How is one to distinguish the true from the false since there is no such thing

as a spiritual Geiger counter to detect the presence of the Spirit? This passage asserts that true prophets are made known by their fruits and not their words.

But what is the nature of the fruits? These false prophets had all the credentials that are normally commended in the religious world, great deeds and orthodox confession; yet they still flunked the test. Bearing fruit has nothing to do with their confession of Lord, what signs and wonders they might pull off (see 24:24), or how successful they might appear. These kinds of fruits can be simulated and are the very garb that the wolves use to beguile the sheep. The metaphor of the good and evil tree makes it clear that bearing fruits is integrally related to one's inner existence. Only the truth that enters one's existence and transforms it is saving. Fruit is produced naturally and spontaneously because that is the very nature of a fruit tree. If there is a continuity between the being of the person and the external works, it is good fruit. If there is no such continuity, it is sham spirituality.

Jesus' sermon makes the point that zealous and scrupulous performance of the law is not sufficient for entering into the kingdom of heaven (5:20), nor the performance of mighty works, nor the protest of faith (7:21). One must bear fruit (3:8; 21:43), and fruits are related to "doing" (5:19, 47; 6:1; 12:50; 13:23; 21:31; 24:46; 25:40, 45). The Greek verb translated "bear" is the same verb used in 7:21 for doing the will of the Father. The verb reappears in 7:24 and 26: everyone who hears and *does* and everyone who hears and *does* not. Bearing fruit has to do with obedience, and obedience comes from a changed heart.

(3) A Rabbinic parallel makes the same point as Jesus' final saying: a house erected on the wrong foundation will collapse under stress. Rabbi Elijah ben Abuyah said:

> One in whom there are good works, who has studied much Torah, to what may he be likened? To a person who builds first with stones and afterward with bricks: even when much water comes and collects by their side, it does not dislodge them. But one in whom there are no good works, though he studied Torah, to what may he be likened? To a person who builds first with bricks and afterward with stones: even when a little water gathers, it overthrows them immediately. (*'Abot de Rabbi Nathan* 24)

But Jesus' parable is strikingly different in that it places the emphasis on obedience to *his* words and *his* interpretation of the law. With the emphasis on "my words," Jesus speaks with the authoritative voice of the living God. His words are synonymous with the will of the Father. Not surprisingly, the crowds respond with amazement to Jesus' authority (7:28–29), but the proper response to Jesus' teaching is not amazement but obedience. When Moses took the book of the covenant and read it to the people, they said, "All that the Lord has spoken we will do, and we will be obedient" (Exod 24:7).

The crowds are said to follow Jesus when he descends from the mountain, but what it really means to follow Jesus will be clarified in the next chapters.

RESTORING LIFE TO OTHERS

8:2–9:35

The compilation of Jesus' teaching in chap 5–7 is now complemented by episodes that profile Jesus' healing power (4:23–25). The marvel of the crowds over his mastery of demons at the end of this section (9:33) corresponds to their astonishment over the authority of his teaching at the end of the Sermon on the Mount (7:28–29). The narrative contains several motifs that intertwine throughout (see U. Luz, "Die Wundergeschichten von Mt 8–9," *Tradition and Interpretation in the New Testament,* ed. G. F. Hawthorne and O. Betz [Grand Rapids: Eerdmans/Tübingen: Mohr, 1987], 149–65).

(a) The first motif is the matchless power and authority of Jesus. E. E. Urbach observes that an outstanding feature of miracle stories in the Rabbinic literature "is the fact that the personality of the miracle worker is not emphasized. The sages were careful not to turn the person himself, who performed the miracle, into a wonder and marvel" (*The Sages* [Jerusalem: Magnes, 1975], 1:116–17). The opposite is true in the Gospels. Jesus' might and power is accentuated. When compared with the parallels in Mark and Luke, Matthew's account of Jesus' healing is so pruned of all auxiliary narrative details that the focus falls on the person's confidence in the power of Jesus and the words of Jesus in response. This economy of detail is not because the Evangelist eschewed vividness but because he has a "distaste for technical details of miracles as such" and does not want the reader to be distracted by the technique and miss the significance of the person of Jesus (Hull, *Hellenistic Magic,* 137, 168, n. 25). The miracles (ten mighty works, see *Mishna 'Abot* 5:1–6 for an emphasis on the number ten) demonstrate that Jesus is not simply a successful exorcist, the conclusion drawn by the Pharisees (9:34); his words and deeds are clothed with the authority of God (1:23; 10:40; 11:27).

(b) Jesus' power over disease, demons, and death establishes why one should want to follow Jesus, and the second motif that appears in this section has to do with discipleship. It surfaces in the opening

91

scenes in the use of the title "Lord" (see 7:21) by those who appeal to
Jesus for help (8:2, 6, 8). It is picked up again in 8:21, 25 in a section
that focuses on what it means to follow Jesus (8:18-27; "to follow" is
a key word appearing nine times in this section, 8:1, 10, 19, 22, 23;
9:9, 19, 27). The theme of following Jesus is then reviewed in 9:9, 27.
Faith is integrally related to discipleship, and it dominates 9:18-31 but
is previewed in 8:2, 8-10, 13, and 9:2. The faith that is exhibited and
commended is absolute confidence in the power of Jesus. The disciples
are specifically rebuked for their little faith when they panic during a
storm even though Jesus was with them in the boat (8:26).

(c) The third strand that is threaded through this section is the response to Jesus' power and authority. In 8:1, great crowds are present,
but they remain passive spectators and speak only in 9:8 and 9:33. It
is the reactions of the scribes and Pharisees that are featured. The rift
between them and Jesus appears in 9:2-17 and is taken up again in
the concluding episode in 9:32-34. Jesus is accepted by blind men as
Israel's messiah, the son of David; but his claims are rejected by these
Jewish teachers who bitterly allege that he blasphemes (9:3) and works
by the prince of demons (9:34).

It is difficult to provide an outline of this section that does justice
to the intertwining themes, but the number of parallels between 8:2-
17 and 9:18-34 suggest an ABA' structure. (a) The leper (8:2) and the
ruler (9:18) both come worshipfully to Jesus. (b) He touches the leper
to heal him (8:3) and is asked to lay hands on the ruler's dead daughter
(9:18; healing a leper was believed to be akin to raising the dead, see
Babylonian Talmud Sanhedrin 47a; Josephus, *Antiquities* 3.10.1-3
§258-64). He also touches the hand of Peter's mother-in-law (8:15),
seizes the hand of the girl (9:25), and touches the eyes of the blind men
(9:29). (c) The leper and the women with the flow of blood are both
cultically impure. (d) The centurion and the ruler both intercede for a
loved one, and both healings occur after an interruption (Jesus' word
to the crowd, and the woman's touch). (e) Jesus says to the centurion,
"Let it be done to you as you believed" (8:13), to the woman, "Your
faith has saved you" (9:22), and to the blind men (9:29), "Let it be
done to you according to your faith." (f) He commands the leper (8:4)
at the beginning of this section and the blind men at the end (9:30)
to tell no one about the miracles. (g) At the end of the first unit, the
demonized are brought to Jesus (8:16) and again at the close of the last
unit (9:32). (h) The conclusions of both units provide commentary on
Jesus' ministry. In 8:17, the Scripture affirms that Jesus is the suffering

servant. In 9:33–34, the crowds marvel at his mighty works, but the Pharisees counter that he works by Beelzebul.

The first and last units (8:1–17; 9:18–34) present Jesus as the incarnation of compassion and as a mighty healer. The emphasis falls on Jesus' will to heal with profiles of those who are willing to be healed by him. The middle unit (8:18–9:17) has to do with issues of discipleship, the forgiveness of sins, and the newness of Jesus' ministry.

(1) In the first unit (8:2–17), Jesus heals by touch, by word, and then again by touch. The first healing occurs when he descends from the mountain and is immediately confronted by a worshipful leper. The term "leprosy" was applied to a variety of skin maladies as well as conditions affecting clothes (Lev 13:47–48) and houses (Lev 14:34–53). Leprosy made the sufferer a prime transmitter of impurity (a "father of uncleanness"). The leper was identified as a living corpse, because, like a corpse, he could impart impurity to objects found within the same enclosure. The primary concern of the laws regarding leprosy (Lev 13) was the prevention of the spread of the impurity, not the disease.

To understand the miracles in this section one must set aside for the moment modern medical presuppositions about illnesses and their causes and remedies (see D. E. Garland, " 'I Am the Lord Your Healer': Mark 1:21–2:12," *RevExp* 85 [1985]: 327–43). The miracles should be interpreted against the background of the society in which they took place, a society that was governed principally by biblical presuppositions. The Bible does not treat illness as an organic malady but assumes that it is caused by God as a chastisement for sin or by some evil power. For example, it is implied in Scripture that leprosy is caused by God as a retribution for sin (Lev 14:34; Num 12:1, 9–10; Deut 24:9; 2 Kgs 15:5; 2 Chron 26:20). Later Rabbis, assuming that God operates according to the principle of measure for measure, tried to pinpoint the particular sin that brought on this "smiting," the name of the tractate (*Nega'im*) in the Mishna that deals with the laws of leprosy (see *Babylonian Talmud 'Arakin* 15b–16a; *Tosepta Nega'im* 6:7; *Sipra* on Lev 5:8). What is more important, however, is the implication in the Scripture that God alone can heal leprosy. When the king of Syria entreats the king of Israel to heal his army commander, Naaman, of leprosy, the king laments: "Am I God, to kill and make alive, that this man sends word to me to cure a man of leprosy?" (2 Kgs 5:7; see also Num 12:1, 9–13; 2 Kgs 15:5; Deut 32:39). When Naaman is eventually cured, he confesses: "I know there is no God in all the earth except in Israel" (2 Kgs 5:15). The point is clear: no one and no god can cure leprosy except the God of Israel.

The leper's petition, "If you want" (*not* "If you ask"!), assumes that Jesus is like God who can do as he wills (Wis 12:18) and who has the power to cleanse him from his leprosy. It was a common literary topos for a person enlisting a god's aid to remind the god that he has the power to do the thing asked (Horsley, *New Documents,* 3:115). What follows proves the leper right. Jesus does not call out to God to heal the leprosy as Naaman thought Elisha should have done (2 Kgs 5:10-11) and as Moses did on behalf of his sister, Miriam (Num 12:13). His touch and word alone effect the cure. As God worked by stretching forth his hand (Exod 4:4, 7:19, 8:1; 9:22; 14:16, 21, 26), so Jesus does to heal a disease that only God can heal.

While Jesus cleansed the leper of the disease, only a priest could inspect and pronounce him clean so that he could be reintegrated into society (*Mishna Nega'im* 3:1). Jesus' command that he go to the priest with the sacrificial gift (a guilt offering! Lev 14:10-32) shows that Jesus is one who complies, not competes, with the requirement of the Mosaic law (5:17-19).

Jesus next moves into Capernaum, where he is met by a centurion who entreats him on behalf of his severely ill servant. In Luke's account (7:1-10), the centurion sends elders of the Jews to Jesus to persuade him to come to heal his servant (7:3), and they plead his case by noting that he is a worthy recipient of attention because "he loves our nation and built our synagogue" (7:4-5). When Jesus goes with the elders, he is then met by more friends who bid him to come no further because the centurion considers himself unworthy to receive him in his home (7:6). He did not even deem himself worthy to come to give this message in person (7:7). In Luke's story, Jesus never deals with the centurion face to face. In Matthew's account, no Jewish middlemen make an appearance; the centurion approaches Jesus directly. The resulting dialogue between Jesus and the centurion mentions nothing of the centurion's good works, only his unworthiness. He is not presented as an exceptional gentile until he exhibits his exceptional faith in Jesus: "I have not found such faith in Israel" (8:10); "Let it be done to you as you believed" (8:13). The first point in this story is the display of exemplary faith by a complete outsider.

Like the leper, the centurion beseeches Jesus and addresses him as Lord. Supplication is not the normal posture of a member of the power establishment, but Jesus' response evokes even greater humility on the part of centurion. While 8:7 may be punctuated as an astonished and indignant question: "Am I to come and heal him?" the context, which emphasizes Jesus' mercy, suggests that Jesus responds as enthusiastically as he did with the leper, "I will come and heal him!" (8:7). The centurion modestly turns down this offer (8:8). He protests his unworthiness for Jesus to come under his roof, perhaps out of sensitivity to Jewish scruples (see John 18:28; Acts 10:28; *Mishna Oholot* 18:7). He expresses his confidence in Jesus' power to heal his loved one where he stands by drawing an analogy between his authority over troops and Jesus' authority. Even as a minor officer, the centurion can make things happen by just saying the word. The problem is that he has no clout when it comes to healing a sick loved one. As soldiers obey the authority of the centurion, however, so demons, who are assumed to be behind severe illness, will submit to the authority of Jesus' word.

At this statement of faith, Jesus' turns to his followers and marvels out loud. He says he has not found such faith as this in Israel and announces that many will come from east and west to eat with Abraham, Isaac, and Jacob in the kingdom of heaven while the sons of the kingdom are cast out (a saying that is recorded in Luke 13:38–39 in a quite different context). In Matthew's context, the gentile centurion must be an example of those who will come from east and west; and the figure of the banquet becomes a celebration where all social, racial, and national barriers have collapsed. Faith, like that exhibited by this centurion, will bridge the gap that currently exists between Jew and gentile. This context significantly modifies the image that appears in the prophets and the literature of second temple Judaism. Those who come from east and west referred to the scattered tribes of Israel, who were to be gathered up for a joyous reunion banquet. They were not associated with the eschatological incursion of gentiles (D. C. Allison, Jr., "Who will Come from East and West? Observations on Matt. 8.11–12 — Luke 13. 28–29," *IBS* 11 [1989]: 158–70).

5 Ezra indicates a significant shift in the tradition of a coming people. The coming people will replace God's former, sinful people and receive its patrimony and eschatological blessings (1:24, 35–37, 38–40; 2:10–11). 5 Ezra is either a Christian composition written to confirm that Christians would preempt the Jews or a Christianizing reinterpretation and reapplication of a Jewish theme of a coming people (T. A. Bergren, "The 'People Coming from the East' in 5 Ezra 1:38," *JBL* 108 [1989]: 675–83). The seeds for this reapplication of this biblical theme can be found in this text in Matthew. The reference to those coming from east and west and taking their places with Abraham, Isaac, and Ja-

cob at a banquet while the "sons of the kingdom," the legitimate heirs, are cast out is a hint of the reversal of all expectations that will occur at the last judgment – the second point of this story. It recalls the word of John the Baptist in 3:9 that God is able to raise up children to Abraham from these stones. One should be cautious, however, before pointing the finger at Israel as "the sons of the kingdom" who are destined to be cast out and consigned to the outer darkness. In 13:38, the "sons of the kingdom" refers to the good seed, presumably members of Matthew's community; and the great faith of this gentile primarily contrasts in the context with the little faith of the disciples in 8:26 (see also 6:30; 14:31; 16:8; 17:20). The messianic banquet that was supposed to bring joy and satisfaction may bring only despair and agony for so-called sons of the kingdom. There is no gloating in Matthew over the doom of those who have not responded to God's reign. The punishment that is assumed to have fallen on those in Israel who rejected their messiah is held up as a warning to the church lest they become complacent and their faith slacken. The Gospel of Matthew contains ample warnings that disciples may be the ones who are cast out (7:21–23; 13:36–43, 47–50; 22:11–14; 24:45–50; 25:1–13, 14–30).

The incident concludes with a report that the centurion's servant was healed "at that hour," which highlights the third point of this story, Jesus' ability to heal from afar. A tradition about Rabbi Ḥanina ben Dosa in the Babylonian Talmud provides an interesting comparison:

> Our Rabbis taught: Once the son of R. Gamaliel fell ill. He sent two scholars to R. Ḥanina b. Dosa to ask him to pray for him. When he saw them he went up to an upper chamber and prayed for him. When he came down he said to them: "Go, the fever has left him"; They said to him: "Are you a prophet?" He replied: "I am neither a prophet nor the son of a prophet, but I learnt this from experience. If my prayer is fluent in my mouth, I know that he is accepted: but if not, I know that he is rejected." They sat down and made a note of the exact moment. When they came to R. Gamaliel, he said to them: "By the temple service! You have not been a moment too soon or too late, but so it happened: at that very moment the fever left him and he asked for water to drink." (*Babylonian Talmud Berakot* 34b, see *Mishna Berakot* 5:5)

Ḥanina's statement about the fluency of his prayer meant that the words he uttered were not his own but were words placed in his mouth by God. When the words were placed in his mouth so that they flowed out, it was a sign to him that it was heaven's will for the sick person to recover; when that did not occur, it was a sign that heaven did not intend to provide the cure (G. Vermes, *Post-biblical Jewish Studies* [Leiden: Brill, 1975], 179). Whichever was the case, it is assumed that the cure was entirely dependent on heaven. The parallels between what Ḥanina is said to do and what Jesus does are only superficial; the differences, however, are significant. Jesus does not pray for healing but is portrayed as one who possesses divine power to effect the cure. What is also important is the inference that the reader can make from this incident. Distance does not affect Jesus' power to heal, and one may still solicit with confidence healing from the resurrected Christ.

Jesus next moves into Peter's house to find Peter's mother-in-law burning with fever. Fever was considered to be an illness in and of itself and was not viewed as a symptom of a disease (J. Preuss, *Biblical and Talmudic Medicine* [New York: Sanhedrin, 1978], 160). In Leviticus 26:16 and Deuteronomy 28:22, fever is cited as a punishment sent by God to those who violate the covenant; and it heads Philo's list of divine chastisements for impiety and disobedience (*On Rewards and Punishments* 143; see Josephus, *Jewish War* 1:654–58; *Babylonian Talmud Berakot* 34b). Fever could also be caused by the demonic (when one danced in the moonlight, for example, *Babylonian Talmud Nedarim* 41a, *Giṭṭin* 70a). Because of Deuteronomy 28:22, some considered fever to be curable only by the intervention of God. Rabbi Alexandri said in the name of Rabbi Ḥiyya bar Abba: "Greater is the miracle wrought for the sick than for Hananiah, Mishael and Azariah. [For] that of Hananiah, Mishael and Azariah [concerned] a fire kindled by man, which all can extinguish; whilst that of a sick person is [in connection with] a heavenly fire, and who can extinguish that?" (*Babylonian Talmud Nedarim* 41a). The answer is, none can extinguish it except God.

When Jesus sees Peter's mother-in-law and touches her hand, the fever forsook her (as if it were a demon). Jesus is shown to be one who can extinguish a heavenly fire — something that only God or God's agent could do. Her service, a characteristic of discipleship, is a sign that she has been restored to wholeness.

In Matthew, it is not the demons who first identify Jesus as the Holy One of God, as in Mark 1:24, or who recognize him as the Christ, as in Luke 4:41, but the authoritative Scripture. The narrator reports that many demonized persons were brought to Jesus, and he cast out the spirits with *a word* (see Ps 107:19–20) and healed *all* who were sick. This was done in fulfillment of Isaiah 53:4: "He took our infirmities and bore our diseases." Some commentators find it surprising that the citation follows the Hebrew text with "infirmities" and "diseases" in contrast to the LXX, which refers to "sins" (see 1:21). Sin and sickness, however, were integrally related in the mind of a Hebrew. This application of the Scripture is founded "on a deep theological truth: it is because Jesus, the 'Servant,' has come to take upon himself the expiation of sins that he could alleviate men's bodily ills, which are the consequence and penalty of sin" (Sabourin, *St. Matthew*, 2:468, citing P. Benoit).

(2) The middle unit (8:18–9:17) focuses on issues of discipleship and the unprecedented nature of Jesus' ministry. It contains two proposals about discipleship (8:18–22) followed by two demonstrations of Jesus' power over the demons of chaos (8:23–34). These are followed by three challenges, from the scribes (9:3), from the Pharisees (9:11), and from the disciples of John (9:14), that highlight the newness of Jesus' ministry and its relation to the forgiveness of sins.

The section begins with the narrator telling us that "when Jesus saw the crowd around him, he gave orders to go to the other side." The last time Jesus took notice of the crowd (5:1), he ascended a mountain to teach them. Now, he gives a command that forces the issue of discipleship. The reader is not told who, specifically, is addressed. The context suggests that it is the crowd that has followed Jesus (4:25; 8:1), witnessed his power, and brought the sick and possessed to him (8:16). When he embarks into the boat to go to the other side in 8:23, however, the narrator notes that *his disciples followed him*. The command to go to the other side will distinguish those who are simply tagging along from disciples who will obey and follow him. Disciples are those who both follow Jesus and his commands.

The disciples have been mentioned as a group previously only in 5:1; now they come to the forefront in the story (8:21, 28; 9:10, 11, 14, 19). The next three incidents have to do with discipleship. (a) A scribe will not be able to do what he thinks he can because discipleship entails sacrifice and the relinquishment of all earthly security (8:19–20). (b) A disciple will not be able to do what conventional mores dictate because discipleship requires uncompromising loyalty (8:21–22). (c) The disciples will not be able to do what Jesus commands without faith because discipleship requires absolute confidence in the power of Jesus (8:23–27).

The narrator provides no background information about the two anonymous persons who offer to follow Jesus. They function as straight men whose proposals give Jesus an opportunity to make a point about discipleship. The first, identified as a scribe, proposes a joint venture. J. R. Butts explains why the scribe's offer is rebuffed:

> there is no such thing as successfully *volunteering* to follow Jesus or any other master teacher in the Greek biographical tradition. A prior call, an immediate, unconditional response, and the willingness to sever all ties to convention are the necessary ingredients for a successful teacher-student concoction. ("The Voyage of Discipleship: Narrative, Chreia, and Call Story," *Early Jewish and Christian Exegesis,* ed. C. A. Evans and W. F. Stinespring [Atlanta: Scholars, 1987] 205, paraphrasing A. Droge, "Call Stories in Greek Biographies and the Gospels," *SBLSP* [1983]: 257).

This conclusion accords with the evidence in the Gospels; but this scribe's pledge implies that he thinks Jesus is a teacher who is going to go places, and he is offering to go with him. Jesus' comeback, that the son of man has no place to lay his head, discloses that discipleship is not a road that leads to success, tranquility, or security. Eagerness that cloaks ambition is no virtue in disciples. Neither is hesitancy, as the next saying makes clear.

One who is identified as "another of the disciples" asks, "Lord, permit me first to go and bury my father." Jesus callously, it seems, does not even offer a word of condolence but demands, "Follow me, and leave the dead to bury the dead." One can hardly think of a more reasonable excuse for delaying discipleship than the need to bury one's father. To disallow it runs counter to the law, which commanded one to honor parents (see Tob 4:3; 6:15; Josephus, *Jewish War* 5:545), to piety, which had so exalted burying the dead that it was one of the highest of all good works (see 26:10), and to custom, which in both the Greek and Hebrew world considered the refusal to bury anyone, let alone parents, the greatest irreverence. Scholars have duly noted that this saying was uniquely offensive, something "completely unthinkable to Jewish sensitivities, a purely sacrilegious act of impiety" that cannot be excused on the grounds of "interests in humanitarian freedom or higher morality" that might justify Jesus' other challenges to piety and custom (Hengel, *Charismatic Leader,* 14). The request also has a biblical precedent. When Elijah passed on his prophetic mantle to Elisha, Elisha asked, "Let me kiss my mother and my father and then I will follow you" (1 Kgs 19:19-21). Elijah consented; and Elisha went to his home, bade farewell to his parents, and even threw a going-away banquet for his friends. Jesus' response to this son who wants to bury his father is scandalous.

The only parallel for this kind of absolute demand is when God forbade the prophet Ezekiel to lament his dead wife or to carry out a mourning ritual for her (Ezek 24:15–24). The purpose of this unsocial, unthinkable behavior was to convey God's judgment against the people. God also forbade Jeremiah from lamenting the dead or comforting the mourner, again to show God's displeasure with the people (Jer 16:5–7). When Jesus insists that this disciple disregard the fourth commandment and common decency, he requires what only God had commanded of the prophets. Jesus is therefore depicted as calling disciples with the authority of God. Hengel interpreted the saying to mean: " ... there was no more time to be lost and so he had to be followed without procrastination and to the abandonment of all human considerations and ties" (Hengel, *Charismatic Leader,* 15). Disciples learn from this that there are no excused absences from the kingdom of God whether they be business commitments, social obligations, or sacred family duties. Disciples cannot shuttle back and forth between the old life and the new. Jesus labels those who do not follow him the spiritually dead; and there will be plenty of them around to take care of the task of burying the physically dead. This incredible statement makes it quite clear that discipleship for Jesus " ... is not merely another commitment which we add to the long list of our other commitments, but it is *the* commitment – demanding a reordering of our lives from the bottom up" (Tannehill, *The Sword of His Mouth,* 159). The kingdom of heaven is to come first in the lives of disciples, even before love of father and mother (10:37; 19:29).

As the disciples cross over to the other side with Jesus, the lake undergoes a "great shaking" (24:7; 27:54, 28:2), which represents the upheaval of the powers of chaos that dwell in that realm (Ps 74:12–14; Dan 7:2–3; 1QH 3:13–18). The boat is "hidden" by the waves, and the disciples rouse a sleeping Jesus with mournful pleas to save them from perishing. While it may be true, as some have suggested, that Jesus slept because he was exhausted by the demands of itinerant preaching and that he could sleep peacefully through storms because of his complete trust in God's protective power, the description of the disciples having to rouse a sleeping Jesus points in another direction. Rest is a divine prerogative (see 11:28), and sleeping is a symbol of divine rule in Ancient Near Eastern literature (B. F. Batto, "The Sleeping God: An Ancient Near Eastern Motif of Divine Sovereignty," *Bib* 68 [1987]: 153–77). Isaiah 51:9–10 provides an important backdrop to this story:

> [9]Awake, awake, put on strength, O arm of the Lord! Awake, as in
> the days of old, the generations of long ago! Was it not you who
> cut Rahab in pieces, who pierced the dragon? [10]Was it not you who
> dried up the sea, the waters of the great deep; who made the depths
> of the sea a way for the redeemed to cross over? (NRSV)

The disciples do not ask Jesus to call on God to save them as the frightened sailors had implored Jonah (Jon 1:6). They ask him directly to
save them as if he had the power of God (8:25). Jesus' rest is a sign of
his divine sovereignty, and the terrifying power of chaos is promptly
overcome when he arises.

In Matthew's account, Jesus scolds the disciples for their little faith
before calming the sea. Following Jesus as a disciple promises to lead
one into storms (see 7:24–27), and those who lack confidence in Jesus'
mastery of the demonic powers will only shrink back in cowardice.
When Jesus rises, he rebukes the winds and the sea as if they were
demons (8:26); and the immediate calming of the sea is punctuated by
the astonished question of the men: "What sort of man is this that even
the winds and the sea obey him?" In the Hebrew Scriptures, the sea
obeys only the God who created it (Job 38:8–11; Pss 29:3–4; 65:5–7;
89:8–10; 93:4; 106:9; 107:23–32; 2 Macc 9:8). By now, readers are able
to answer the disciples' question. This is God with us. The real question
is, however, Will the answer govern their faith?

In Psalm 89:9–10, God is praised for ruling "the ragings of the sea,"
"stilling the waves," and "crushing Rahab like a carcass" (see Job 26:11–
12). With this psalm and Isaiah 51:9–10 as a backdrop, the story about
Jesus' exorcism of demons in Gadara (8:28–34) clearly belongs together
with the story of the storm. In contrast to Mark's much longer account
of the exorcism (5:1–20), we learn nothing from Matthew about the
previous attempts to tame the demoniac(s) or their self-destructive ten-
dencies. In Matthew's edition, the demons also do not attempt to ward
off an exorcism when they confront Jesus but simply ask why he has
come to torment them before the time (8:29). There is no description
of the recovery of the demoniac, his desire to be with Jesus, the sub-
sequent command to go to his house to announce what the Lord has
done, or the report of the reaction to his preaching (Mark 5:15, 18–20;
Luke 8:35, 38–39). The focus of the Matthean account is entirely on
the demons' recognition of Jesus and their destruction. "All element of
struggle, of menace, of tension is gone. The spirits have not been exorcised by a wonder worker; they have perished for ever before the face

of the messiah" (Hull, *Hellenistic Magic*, 132). In the narrative, they provide the answer to the question of the men in the boat (8:27): Jesus is the son of God (8:29). They also immediately recognize his mission. He has come to punish them.

Matthew's version alone, abbreviated as it is, has the demons ask, "Why have you come to torment us before the time?" Jewish traditions assumed that demons were free to operate as they wished until the day of consummation (*1 Enoch* 16:1; *Jubilees* 5:6–10; 10:7–9; *Babylonian Talmud Pesaḥim* 112b). The Gadarene demons may have assumed the same, but their timetable is wrong. Jesus' presence means that the time of reckoning has arrived (see 12:24–30). The demons get no answer to their question, so they beg Jesus, "If you cast us out, send us into the swine." They are clearly at the mercy of Jesus' power and are felled by one little word, "Go!" (8:32). They are destroyed in the waters that Jesus has just demonstrated he rules. The disciples can learn from this effortless destruction of the demons and from the calming of the sea that those who follow Jesus have nothing to fear from the demonic. It has been neutralized.

As the demons came to "meet" Jesus in 8:28, "the whole city" comes out to "meet" him in 8:34. They do not invite him to stay nor do they bring their sick and demonized to him (8:16; 9:32) but instead plead with him to leave. If the inhabitants are assumed to be gentiles, their reaction reveals that not all gentiles are going to recognize the help that Jesus offers or to outshine Israel in faith. Jesus has liberated the area from the noted danger of the demons (8:28), but they are more at home with the demons they know than with a power they cannot comprehend. It is easier for Jesus to deal with ungovernable demons than with unwilling humans.

Jesus' tour of Israel takes him back to his own city where a paralytic is brought to him (9:1–8). The paralytic and the ones who carry him serve as another example of those who have confidence in his power to bring about healing. The dramatic efforts to get the paralytic to Jesus, recorded in Mark 2:4 and Luke 5:19, deflect attention away from Jesus, however, and are absent from Matthew. The spotlight is only on Jesus; and when he sees "their faith," he announces to the paralytic, "Take heart [be of good courage], child, your sins are forgiven." "Take heart" is associated with God's deliverance in the Scriptures (Exod 14:13; see Isa 35:4), which also affirm that it is God who forgives sins (Exod 34:7; Ps 103:2–3; Isa 6:7; 43:25; 44:22).

E. Haenchen (*Der Weg Jesu* [Berlin: Alfred Töpelmann, 1966], 101) commented on this announcement that the men did not bring their friend to have his sins forgiven him but to be healed. It is inappropriate, however, to read modern expectations of what should happen when one goes to a physician with a malady into the thoughts of these friends who bring the paralytic to Jesus. Moderns tend to see no connection between sickness and sin; the Hebrews did (see 2 Chron 7:14; 21:13-15, 18-19; Pss 41:3-4; 103:3; Isa 38:16-17; 4QPrNab; *Babylonian Talmud Nedarim* 41a; *Megilla* 17b). The story presupposes a direct linkage between sin and sickness (see John 5:14). The paralysis was viewed as a consequence of sin (see 1 Macc 9:55; 3 Macc 2:21-23), and the man cannot be healed without its forgiveness. When Jesus asks the scribes, "Which is easier, to say, 'Your sins are forgiven,' or to say, 'Rise, and walk' " (9:5), he is not only asking them which is easier to do. He is asking, "What is less important?" The question implies that the forgiveness of sins is absolutely essential before healing can take place. This incident now makes explicit what was implicit in all of Jesus' healing. In healing infirmities, he also takes away sins (1:21; 8:17; 26:28). Jesus' ability to forgive sins and his bypassing the proper channels of temple sacrifice will take on greater significance in light of the whole story and his atoning death and vindicating resurrection.

At Jesus' pronouncement of the forgiveness of the man's sins, the scribes make a pronouncement of their own: "This one is blaspheming!" The dispute between Jesus and other Jewish teachers would have revolved around such issues as: On what terms does God forgive? What is to be required of those who are forgiven? Who makes it official that a person is forgiven or not? But this debate is muffled in Matthew. No theological rationale is given for the scribes' assertion that Jesus blasphemes (compare Mark 2:7 and Luke 5:21, "Who is able to forgive sins except God alone?"). In Matthew, the only reason that the scribes consider Jesus to be guilty of blasphemy is because they think evil in their hearts (9:4), which can only mean that they are evil (12:34-35; 15:19).

Matthew concludes the incident with the crowds in awe and glorifying God who gave such authority to humans (9:8). The plural noun alludes to the fact that the community will also have this power to pronounce forgiveness of sins (16:19; 18:18; see John 20:23).

The call and the instant response of Matthew (9:9) continues the theme of forgiveness and again elicits suspicion when Jesus hosts toll collectors and sinners (9:10-11). Jesus embodies God's mercy and purpose to take away the diseases, infirmities, and sins of all the people; and the meal was a concrete expression of the acceptance of sinners.

The Pharisees would have had no objection to sinners repenting. What would have been reprehensible to them was the tacit approval and forgiveness of a coven of sinners who had done nothing that would pass for traditional repentance (confession and restitution) except to follow Jesus (9:9).

The scribes and Pharisees are consistently portrayed in Matthew as misreading Scripture and God's will. Jesus' directive to "go and learn what this means, 'I desire mercy and not sacrifice' " (Hos 6:6) implies that they have failed to understand the basic tenor of the Scripture. M. J. Borg argues that Jesus challenged the dominant holiness paradigm for the life of Israel (represented by the Pharisees) with an alternative one based on inclusive mercy that redefines holiness (*Conflict, Holiness and Politics,* 124-43). The Pharisees' holiness paradigm concentrates on separation and insulation from those things that have the power to defile. Borg writes, "in the teaching of Jesus, holiness, not uncleanness was understood to be contagious," and it could "overpower uncleanness rather than the converse" (*Conflict, Holiness and Politics,* 135). Jesus has already touched a leper (8:3), healed a gentile (8:13), and ventured into a land infested with pigs and demons (8:28-34). He will be touched by a menstruant (9:20) and will touch a dead girl (9:25) almost as if to illustrate what he means in 9:13 about mercy, not sacrifice.

The statement "I came not to call the righteous but sinners" spells out the issue that was so offensive to both Hebrews and Greeks (see Talbert, *Reading Luke,* 63-67). The popular and successful god of healing, Asclepius, was considered just because he granted to suppliants that which was their due and rejected those who were impure: "O Asclepius, the philosophy you teach is secret and congenial to yourself, in that you suffer not the wicked to come hither, not even if they pour into your lap all the wealth of India and Sardis" (Philostratus, *Life of Apollonius of Tyana* 1.11). Jesus and his church embraced indiscriminately those whom many regarded as unworthy sinners, sick in body and soul, and pronounced God's forgiveness and acceptance. The message is that true holiness is related to one's being as indiscriminate in one's love and acceptance as God is (5:43-48).

The disciples of John the Baptist next bring up the issue of fasting: Why is it that Jesus' disciples do not fast? In the ancient world fasting was sometimes associated with the fear of demons, who could gain power over someone through eating, and one could therefore ward off demons by fasting. Fasting was considered to be one of the distinguishing marks of Jews (Tacitus, *Histories* 5.4; Suetonius, *Augustus*

76.3). For Jews, it could be linked to mourning or an act of penance intended to stave off disaster (1 Kgs 21:27-29), to prompt mercy (2 Sam 12:22-23), or to attain forgiveness for sin. According to the *Psalms of Solomon,* the righteous one on the day of Atonement "atones for (sins of) ignorance by fasting and humbling his soul" (3:6-8; see Sir 34:31). In the *Apocalypse of Elijah* 1:21, true fasting releases sin, heals diseases, and casts out demons.

One can now see why fasting is unnecessary in the presence of the bridegroom, Jesus (see 22:2; 25:1-14; 2 Cor 11:12; Eph 5:23-33; Rev 19:7-9; 21:2), who casts out demons, heals diseases, and releases sin without requiring any preparatory works of devotion. There is no need to fast for forgiveness of sins; it is freely offered in Jesus. The only reason the disciples might fast is to mourn when the bridegroom is taken from them, but that is only temporary because Jesus will not remain absent (28:20). The only fast that is required by God is to loose the bonds of injustice, to undo the thongs of the yoke, to let the oppressed go free, to share your bread with the hungry, to bring the homeless poor into your house, and to cover the naked (Isa 58:6-7; see Matt 25:31-46).

The implication of the inquiries of the Pharisees and the disciples of John the Baptist is that what Jesus is doing is novel. Jesus uses two images to convey that the new is incompatible with the old. No sensible person patches an old garment with a piece of unshrunk cloth; its "fullness" ("that which completes or restores," E. Lohmeyer, *Das Evangelium des Markus* [Göttingen: Vandenhoeck & Ruprecht, 1959], 61) will ruin both the garment and the patch (9:16). Putting new wine in old wineskins also only spells disaster. New wine must be put in new wineskins if the wine and the wineskin are to be preserved (9:17).

"Wedding," "garment," and "wine" were symbols of eschatological salvation (J. Jeremias, *The Parables of Jesus* [London: SCM, 1962], 117-18). Jesus is not just another exorcist; he brings a "fullness" and "new wine" connected with God's salvation. In the context, what is new is the emphasis on mercy and the authority to forgive sins. The old is represented by the complaint about Jesus' lax attitude toward traditional religious standards and such things as fasting to attain release from sins. The old is not to be allowed to ruin the new.

(3) The third unit (9:18-34) returns to the theme of faith in Jesus' miraculous powers that is so prominent in 8:1-17. The incidents that follow reveal that Jesus, the son of David, is able to raise the dead, give sight to the blind, and give the speechless their voice and that faith in Jesus heals.

The first story about the ruler's daughter and the woman with the flow of blood (9:18-26) is characteristically pruned of all novelistic details when compared with Mark's account (5:21-43). We do not have a ruler of a synagogue making a last minute appeal to save his daughter but a ruler (of what, we are not told) who beseeches Jesus *after* his daughter is already dead (9:18). As Jesus returns with the desperate father, an equally desperate woman seeks to be healed from her twelve years of flux and consequent impurity (see Lev 15:19-33; the *Mishna* tractate on the menstruant is entitled *Niddah*, "banished"). She believes that she will be healed merely by touching the fringes of Jesus' garment (Num 15:38-39; Deut 22:12). Matthew's version makes no mention of any power leaving Jesus, and he does not need to ask who touched him (Mark 5:30; Luke 8:45-46). He has direct knowledge of the woman's secret thoughts (9:22), and he tells her that her faith (not the touch) has saved her. Jesus speaks to her, and she is "saved from that hour."

When Jesus finally arrives at the home of the ruler, he directs the flute players and mourners to depart, saying the child is not dead. Their laughing disbelief starkly contrasts with the faith of the ruler who sought out Jesus out after she had died and that of the woman who daringly touched the hem of his garment. Jesus takes the girl by the hand and raises her, which is precisely what the ruler requested Jesus to do: "Come lay your hand upon her and she will live" (8:18).

As Jesus leaves, two blind men cry out for mercy (9:27-31). They are the first persons to identify Jesus as the son of David in the Gospel, and this may be connected to the tradition that the son of David was to be a healer. Jesus' question, "Do you believe that I am able to do this?" (9:28), explicitly equates faith with confidence in the power of Jesus. On the one hand, the faith of the blind men becomes a model. They follow Jesus (9:27). They come inside the house (9:28; see 13:36; 17:25); and they respond without hesitation to Jesus' question, "Do you believe?" with "Yes, Lord!" They are healed according to their faith (8:13; 9:22), and their eyes are opened. On the other hand, their faith exposes how benighted the Pharisees are – even the blind (and a pagan gentile) could see who Jesus was.

For the second time, Jesus commands someone he has healed to tell no one (9:30; 8:4). This attempt to hush his healing power is somewhat unusual in the ancient word. As partial repayment for their beneficence the gods in the ancient world frequently demanded that their miracles be recorded, preferring to be honored and admired rather than simply thanked (H. S. Versnel, "Religious Mentality in Ancient Prayer,"

Faith, Hope and Worship: Aspects of Religious Mentality in the Ancient World, ed. H. S. Versnel [Leiden: Brill, 1981], 60). By trying to stifle the publication of his feats, Jesus is shown to be meek and humble (11:29; 12:16-21) and unlike other popular gods of healing that were prevalent in the Hellenistic world.

The last miracle (9:32-34) brings the total number of miracles in this section to ten. Jesus again operates with the authority of God by healing a mute demoniac ("Who gives speech to mortals? Who makes them mute or deaf, seeing or blind? Is it not I, the Lord?" [Exod 4:11]). The crowds score the point: "Never was anything like this seen in Israel." But it was promised. Isaiah 35:4-6 would have been an appropriate fulfillment passage at this point, "Here is your God.... He will come and save you. Then the eyes of the blind shall be opened, the tongue of the speechless shall sing for joy." But it is left for the reader to make that connection when this passage is alluded to in 11:5. The focus falls instead on the reaction of the crowds and Pharisees. The Pharisees do not deny that Jesus has worked miracles but accuse him of using magic. This allegation is a prelude for ever more intense encounters with the Pharisees, who are seeking to drive a wedge between Jesus and the crowds.

The summary in 9:35 brackets the cycle of teaching and miracles, examples of Jesus' "wisdom and power" (13:54), with 4:23-25. Jesus teaches in "their synagogues," preaches the gospel of the kingdom, and heals every sickness and disease. To summarize, chapters 8-9 display Jesus' power to heal by touch, to heal at a distance, to cast out spirits with a word, to still a storm with a word, to destroy demons, to forgive sins, and to raise the dead. He also calls disciples with the authority of God. Jesus is equal to every occasion, and those who recognize that fact are healed. The narrative reveals that one does not fully learn who Jesus is from the various titles that occur in the Gospel — son of God, son of David, son of man, Lord — but only from the whole story of his preaching and deeds. The one who has power over demons and storms is God with us, who has come to restore humans to wholeness.

The miracles also show that Jesus discounts the demarcation of society along purity lines. He does not shun the impure and unholy. He touches a leper, a menstruant, and a corpse. He obliges a gentile, enters the space of demons, eats with toll collectors and reputed sinners, and has contact with the blind and lame. The kingdom of heaven does not respect the boundaries of purity that the Pharisees and others use to categorize persons and places and to isolate them.

The rumblings from the scribes and Pharisees indicate that not all will accept who Jesus is or his beneficence. His rejection of the Pharisees' holiness paradigm will lead to bitter conflict. The consistent reference in Matthew to "their synagogues" (9:35; 10:17; 12:9; 13:54; see also 6:2, 5; 23:6, 34) and once to "their cities" (11:1) hints of his own community's alienation from those who have disowned Jesus. Matthew's perspective is decidedly defensive: it is them versus us. The next cycle of teaching and narrative will reveal the breach between Jesus and Israel growing ever wider in spite of Jesus' compassion for the lost sheep of the house of Israel. One gets the impression from Matthew that the crowds would have accepted Jesus as their messiah were it not for the perverse opposition and slander of the Pharisees who thwart their belief.

GREAT HARVEST
AND GREAT DANGERS

9:36–10:42

A fter the recap of Jesus' teaching, preaching, and healing in 9:35, the next verses, 9:36–38, form a transition to the mission discourse in chapter 10. When Jesus sees the crowd, he has compassion on them and uses two images to describe their dire situation: (a) sheep, harassed and helpless, and without a shepherd, and (b) a great harvest with few ready field hands.

Sheep without a shepherd is a biblical figure of speech that describes the desperate situation of a nation without proper leadership (Num 27:16–17; 1 Kgs 22:17; 2 Chron 18:16; Jer 50:6; Ezek 34:1–16; Zech 11:15; see 2 Sam 24:17). It is an implicit indictment of Israel's current leaders. The image of abandoned sheep exposes the guilt of the faithless shepherds who have failed to give the people either spiritual nurture or direction. Their incompetence is evident from the fact that they see only the demonic in Jesus' works of mercy (9:34). If Israel, who was supposed to be a light to the nations, is lost, as Jesus divulges in 10:6 (see 15:24), how great must be the darkness for the nations? When things are at their worst, however, God has sent the compassionate messianic shepherd (Ezek 34:23; Mic 5:4; Matt 2:6), who has come to teach and heal the people and to renew their vocation in the world (5:13–16; 28:19–20).

The change in metaphors from sheep to harvest indicates that the situation is even more critical; the harvest is ripe and the workers are few. The harvest is an image that holds out both threat and hope. It is a figure for coming judgment and for restoring the fortunes of the people (Isa 27:12–13; Jer 51:33; Hos 6:11; Joel 3:1, 13; Amos 9:13–15; 4 Ezra 4:26–40; *2 [Syriac] Apocalypse of Baruch* 70:2; Rev 14:15; compare the image of fishing for humans in 4:19 and Jer 16:14–16; Amos 4:2; 1 QH 5:8). In the explanation of the parable of the wheat and the tares, the harvest represents the end of the age, and the harvesters are angels sent

109

out to execute final judgment by gathering up all those who are causes of sin and casting them into the fire (13:39–42; see 3:12). Jesus is not appealing for workers to help execute this final judgment. The parable makes clear that disciples have no business trying to separate tares from wheat (13:24–30). Sending workers into the harvest therefore must have the positive goal of alerting Israel to the coming kingdom (10:7). They will also warn that refusal to heed their summons (11:4–5) will result in judgment at the harvest (10:15; 11:20–24). The mission will get only a mixed response; and, in the end, the good fish will be separated from the bad (13:47–48) and the wheat from the tares (13:41–43).

The reference to "his twelve disciples" in 10:1 and 11:1 forms an inclusio around the discourse that reintroduces the basic task of the disciples: mission (see 4:18–22). The discourse begins with (1) the commissioning of twelve with the authority to expand Jesus' ministry of healing (10:1–4). It is followed by (2) specific mission instructions (10:5–23) that are bracketed by the reference to "Israel" in 10:6 and 23. This unit divides into two subunits, 10:5–15 and 10:16–23. Both begin with the verb "send" (10:5, 16) and end with a saying introduced by "Truly, I say to you" (10:15; 10:23). The first has to do with the nature and manner of their mission; the second warns of its perils. (3) The next unit, 10:24–33, ties the calling of discipleship to fearless confession. Two general statements about disciples frame an argument about whom to fear (10:26–31): the disciple is not greater than the teacher and can expect no better treatment (10:24–25), and everyone who confesses Jesus before others he will vouch for before his Father in heaven, and everyone who denies him before others he will renounce before his Father in heaven (10:32–33). The phrase "therefore, do not fear" brackets this unit (10:26, 31). (4) The last unit of the discourse, 10:34–42, warns that confession will bring division, requires sacrifice, and promises reward for those who welcome the missionaries even if it is only with a cup of cold water.

Throughout this discourse, one can hear Jesus speaking beyond the disciples to the church who knows itself as sent out and has faced persecution and the temptation to wilt under pressure. Four prominent themes in the discourse are particularly relevant to the church's life.

(a) The mission of the disciples is related to God's eschatological work (10:7–8, 15, 40).

(b) What the disciples do conforms to and extends the work of Christ. They are not simply a gallery of onlookers and eavesdroppers. To follow Jesus as disciples means to join in his mission as Lord of the harvest. He gives to them authority to do the very same things that he has been doing (10:1, 7–8). They are to preach what he has preached, the kingdom of heaven is at hand (4:17; 9:35), and to do the same works that he has done: to heal the sick (see 8:16; 9:35), to raise the dead (see 9:18–26), to cleanse lepers (8:2–4), and to cast out demons (8:28–34). Those who receive them therefore receive him as well and the one who sent him (10:40).

(c) Persecution is certain. They are sent as sheep in the midst of wolves (10:16), a less than rosy prospect that promises anything but tranquility (Sir 13:17–18). They will be handed over (10:17, 19, 21), hated (10:22), and vilified (10:25). The disciples not only will face the same ill treatment endured by the prophets before them (5:10–12); they will share the same travail that their Lord endures. He has had to flee to Egypt (2:13–15; 10:23) and has nowhere to lay his head (8:20). His mission will sever him from his family (12:46–50; 10:37). He will be betrayed by an intimate (10:4, 21), handed over to the Sanhedrin and the governor, scourged (10:17–18), and crucified (10:38). If the disciples are to accept the benefits of his power and share in that (10:1, 7–8), they must accept his suffering and share in it as well (10:38; see Rom 8:16–17; 2 Cor 4:10–11; Phil 1:29; 3:10; Acts 5:41).

(d) The disciples' mission forces a decision. Some will accept the message and demonstrate themselves to be worthy; others will refuse to be shepherded by Jesus (2:6; 10:11–14). Everything that Jesus says implies, however, that rejection will be the norm and that acceptance will be unusual. The message will cause strife even among the closest of kin (10:21, 34–35). But those who do not receive them do not receive him and the one who sent him and are left to the judgment of God (10:14–15; see 1 Thess 2:14–16).

(1) The discourse opens with the commissioning of the disciples (10:1–4). The disciples presumably obeyed Jesus' command to pray for laborers for the harvest (9:38), and the next scene shows them being mobilized in answer to their prayer (10:1). They are commissioned for a particular task, not promoted to an exalted status. Peter heads the list as "the first," the leader of the disciples, as Judas, the betrayer, comes last as the most dishonored. The number twelve is stressed, and it is obviously related to the twelve tribes of Israel (see 19:28; Acts 26:7). Jesus sends out twelve to ready the entire people of God for the coming harvest.

(2) Jesus gives the disciples their marching orders in 10:5–23. The first half of this unit (10:5–15) clarifies the character of the disciples' mission. (a) They are to engage only Israel, where Jesus' fame has al-

ready spread (9:31; 10:5-6, 23; although a reference to testimony to the gentiles slips in, 10:18). A gentile mission is anticipated elsewhere in the Gospel (24:14; 26:13; 28:19), but the command in 10:5b to go nowhere among the gentiles or Samaritans (who are mentioned only here in the Gospel) may sound harsh. How does one explain it?

Matthew is not a sloppy editor who retains conflicting traditions on mission (10:5b-6; 28:19-20), as some have charged. This passage highlights the priority of the mission to Israel during the lifetime of Jesus (4:23, 9:35; see Tertullian, *On Flight during Persecution* 6). As the son of David, the messiah of Israel, Jesus naturally must first go to Israel; and while gentiles are not denied help, all contact with them is considered to be exceptional during Jesus' earthly ministry. The Jewish mission and the gentile mission are not two unrelated issues: the one precedes the other (Gnilka, *Matthäusevangelium*, 1:363). The priority of mission to Israel makes sense if Israel is to fulfill its vocation as the light to the nations (Isa 42:6; 49:6). Israel must be renewed and gathered before it can carry out its task for the nations. The restriction to Israel therefore accords with Paul's perspective, "to the Jew first and also to the Greek" (Rom 1:16; 2:9, 10). In Romans 15:8, Paul states: "Christ became a servant to the circumcised to show God's truthfulness, in order to confirm the promises of the fathers." He then adds that God did this so that the gentiles might glorify God for his mercy (15:9-13). Matthew would concur with this view.

The command to go only to the lost sheep of the house of Israel makes it clear that God did not abandon Israel for the gentiles, who, in Matthew's day, were responding positively to the Christian message (an issue Paul addresses in Rom 9-11). Later developments in the story will reveal, however, that many in Israel, under the sway of false leaders, abandoned God instead by rejecting the messiah and his messengers. Nevertheless, the gentile mission is inaugurated only after the death and resurrection of Jesus as a consequence of that event and not because of any presumed failure of the mission to the Jews. That mission is carried out by those in Israel who responded faithfully to the call of their messiah.

Matthew never reports the return of the disciples from their mission, and one can only conclude that the mission to Israel does not come to an end (Gnilka, *Matthäusevangelium*, 1:379). It is not that Israel gets the first shot but only one shot. The mission to Israel is to continue until the son of man comes (10:23).

(b) The disciples are also instructed to carry out their mission without seeking pay. They cannot expect to cash in on blessings and authority that they received free of charge (10:8b; see 1 Cor 9:18; 2 Cor 11:7; *Mishna 'Abot* 1:3, 13; 4:5; *Mishna Bekorot* 4:6; *Babylonian Talmud Nedarim* 37a). They are to take (acquire) no money and no belt where they would carry their money (10:9). They are to take no bag for food and other necessities; nor are they to take a change of tunics, sandals, or a staff for walking or to fend off the wolves. Why this austerity? The urgency of the mission is not the point, since they will not be able to move faster without sandals. These instructions pertain to the character of their mission. Possessing only one garment, being dependent on the table of another for food, and being without shoes is a token of extreme poverty (see *Mishna Beṣa* 32b; *Babylonian Talmud Šabbat* 152a; Luke 15:22). Traveling in this way means that they are totally reliant on God to provide for them (6:11, 25-34). They are to go out as the poor to those who are also poor and hungry. It may also be a prophetic sign of the coming judgment, akin to God's instructions to Isaiah to walk naked and barefoot, as if he were a captive of war, to signal the judgment coming upon Egypt and Ethiopia (Isa 20:2-4; Luz, *Matthäus (Mt 8–17)*, 2:97).

Comparison with the parallels in Mark and Luke suggests that Matthew may want to make a further point that is particularly applicable to his church's setting (see Did 11:3-12). They are not to discredit the message by seeking financial gain. Mark 6:8 has "do not take bronze." Luke 9:3 has "do not take silver." Matthew 10:9 has "do not *acquire* gold, silver, or bronze." The use of the verb "acquire" suggests a concern beyond the insistence that the disciples rely only on God to supply all their needs. If they are to proclaim the kingdom of heaven that is not of this world, they must loose "their ties to this present age" (Davies and Allison, *Saint Matthew*, 2:171). Religion is not to be used for profit, but avarice has always plagued the church. Lucian mocked the Christians for how easily they were duped by rascals in their midst. They "despise all things indiscriminately and consider them common property, . . . so if any charlatan and trickster, able to profit by occasions, comes upon them, he quickly acquires sudden wealth by imposing upon simple folk" (*The Passing of Peregrinus* 13). Jesus' words assure the disciples that they may count on sustenance, and, if obeyed, insure that they will not become affluent at the expense of others.

(c) In whichever town or village the disciples find themselves, they are instructed to seek out a worthy host (10:11). A host is judged to be worthy by whether he or she accepts the message and the messenger (in

22:8, the invited guests who snub the invitation to the marriage feast are declared not worthy). Jesus tells them to let "your peace" come upon the household. Since the message has to do with the coming kingdom of heaven, the peace must be associated with the blessings of the messianic age (Isa 11:1-9; see Ezek 34:25; 37:26). The blessing is not irrevocable, however. If the message is rejected, the peace can be caused to return to the disciples. Withdrawing that peace from those who spurn the message is a sign that they will be cut off from those blessings. Shaking the dust from their feet is an even more graphic gesture for those who had shared assumptions about sin and its consequences. In Mark 6:11, this gesture is a witness "to them," a warning that they are cutting themselves off from the kingdom. In Luke 9:5, it is a witness "against them," a threat, or, in Luke 10:11, a grievance: "Even the dust of the town that clings to our feet, we wipe off in protest against you. Yet know this: the kingdom of God has come near" (NRSV). Matthew makes no mention of the witness value of the gesture. Instead, Jesus solemnly affirms that this place will be worse off in the judgment than the proverbially sinful cities of Sodom and Gomorrah (10:15). This saying makes shaking the dust from their feet a dramatic prophetic action that symbolically dissociates the disciples from those who do not respond (Acts 13:51; 18:6). Without guilt, they can leave them to their fate for refusing the message.

The implication is that the community of Israel will be split by the mission. Everyone will be harvested (see 10:21-22; 34-46), but some will be like chaff or tares that will be burned. The command requires that the disciples be free from any worldly entanglements. The more one is entrenched in the power structures of society and at home with its values, the harder it is to shake the dust from one's feet.

The second half of this second unit (10:16-23) contains three warnings that the mission is fraught with dangers. (a) Jesus' commission of the disciples was prompted by the fact that the crowds were like unprotected sheep, harassed and helpless (9:36). Now, Jesus tells them that they are sheep sent out in the midst of wolves (10:16). As sheep, they are as powerless and as vulnerable as the ones they are sent to help. A frequently cited parallel helps to put the following instructions in perspective. The Roman emperor Hadrian purportedly said to Rabbi Jehoshua: "There is something great about the sheep (Israel) that can persist among the seventy wolves (the nations)." He replied: "Great is the Shepherd who delivers it and watches over it and destroys the wolves before them" (Tanḥuma 32b; cited by H. L. Strack and P. Billerbeck *Kommentar zum Neuen Testament aus Talmud und Midrasch* [Munich: C. H. Beck, 1926], 1:574). Jesus does not promise to protect the sheep so that they will not be harmed or to destroy the wolves before them. The disciples are given authority to cast out demons and to heal every disease but not to fend off persecution. There are no safe-conduct passes for their mission, and the situation calls for wariness as well as purity.

(b) The disciples are also given fair warning that they can expect to be handed over to various authorities for disciplinary action (10:17–18; see 24:9–14, and Paul's list of travails in 2 Cor 11:25–27). This note of warning is followed by a word of assurance in 10:19–20. It begins with the phrase "and whenever," followed by a command, "do not be anxious," and the assurance. Jesus assumes that their only anxiety in this moment of duress will be over what to proclaim, not how to save themselves. He comforts them with the pledge that the Spirit of the Father will speak in them. They are not to resist the evil except by their speech.

(c) Jesus then gives a third warning: they will be handed over to death by family members and hated by all (10:21–22a). In 24:9b, there is the warning that they will be hated "by all nations." What happens to them within Israel will therefore happen everywhere: they will be caught in a no man's land between a hostile community and a resentful family. This forewarning is followed by a second word of assurance, "the one who endures to the end will be saved" (10:22b). This assurance is amplified in 10:23, a verse that is notoriously problematic. It should be interpreted in its context as a word of consolation to disciples caught in the web of danger. Like 10:19–20, it begins with the phrase "and whenever," followed by a command, "flee," and the assurance "you will not have completed all the cities of Israel until which time the son of man comes." It affirms that the coming of the son of man, the time of vindication (13:41–43; 16:27; 24:27–44; 25:31), is not far off.

Jesus does not call for heroics on the part of disciples. He himself prudently withdraws in the face of opposition (4:12; 14:13; see 2 Cor 11:32–33), and he advises threatened disciples to flee to the next town when persecuted. He only assures them that they will not run out of places of refuge before their vindication.

(3) The next instructions deal with courage under fire (10:24–33). It may be small comfort to be promised only that there will be plenty of hiding-places before the end comes, but the disciples must know that they have committed themselves to one who is a byword of contempt.

As members of the same household they can only expect to be maligned as well (10:24–25). Intimidation may spark fear, and the question of whom and what to fear is probed in 10:26–31, where the verb "fear" appears four times.

The command not to fear in 10:26 may seem paradoxical. Jesus has forewarned them that they will be handed over, scourged, hated, pursued, and put to death; "therefore, do not fear!" What Jesus calls for is a cool appraisal of the situation. If the foe is able to kill only bodies, but God is able to destroy both bodies and souls in Gehenna, who should rate the most awe? Jesus seems to be saying about those who menace the community, "Don't worry! The only thing they can do is kill you. After they kill you, they are through and can do no more. But God is not through."

Similar sentiments about courage before death can be found elsewhere. Seneca, for example, argued that there was nothing to fear in death:

> Death is the ultimate threat, and injustice and the most cruel tyrants have nothing beyond death with which to threaten us. Death is Fortune's final expenditure of energy. And so if we accept death with a calm and steadfast mind, and we realize that death is not an evil and therefore not even an injury, we will much more easily endure other things — losses and insults, humiliations, exiles, bereavements, and separations. These things cannot overwhelm the wise man even if they all beset him at one time, and still less does he complain when they attack him singly. (*An Essay about Constancy* 8.3)

But Jesus contends that indeed there is something to fear in death — God. Each one will be confronted by the judgment of God. This Jewish perception of things is reflected in the story about Rabbi Johanan ben Zakkai on his death bed. He wept when his disciples came to visit him, and when they asked him why he was weeping, he answered as follows:

> If I were being taken today before a human king who is here today and gone tomorrow in the grave, whose anger if he is angry with me does not last forever, who if he imprisons me does not imprison me for ever, and who if he puts me to death does not put me to everlasting death, and whom I can persuade with words and bribe with money, even so I would weep. Now that I am being taken before the supreme King of Kings, the Holy One, blessed be He, who lives and endures for ever and ever, whose anger, if He be angry with me, is an everlasting anger, who if He imprisons imprisons me for ever, who if he puts me to death puts me to death for ever, and

whom I cannot persuade with words or bribe with money – nay more, when there are two ways before me, one leading to Paradise and the other to Gehinnom, and I do not know by which I shall be taken, shall I not weep?" They said to him, "Master, bless us." He said to them: "May it be [God's] will that the fear of heaven shall be upon you like the fear of flesh and blood." (*Babylonian Talmud Berakot* 28b; see also *Berakot* 61b; 4 Macc 13:14-15)

Jesus' admonition to fear the one who can destroy both body and soul in Gehenna warns disciples against the danger of renouncing their faith under pressure, and the concluding statement in 10:32-33 assumes that Jesus is the final arbiter of one's ultimate fate and that it will hinge on whether one acknowledges or denies him before others. Paul exemplified this courage in the face of death, and his greatest anxiety when imprisoned was that he might be put to shame by breaking under the stress (Phil 1:13-26). By the time of Lucian, Christians have apparently become renowned for their fearlessness: "The poor wretches have convinced themselves, first and foremost, that they are going to be immortal and live for all time, in consequence of which they despise death and even willingly give themselves into custody, *most of them*" (*The Passing of Peregrinus* 13, my italics). Jesus' words are recorded by Matthew to fortify the courage of those Christians in his community who are fainthearted.

The image of the sparrows in 10:30 deserves special attention because it offers an answer to those who might question why God allows evil to be inflicted on disciples. It brings to mind the image of the birds of the air who neither sow nor reap nor gather into barns and yet are fed by the heavenly Father (6:26). The sparrows are not worth two cents to humans, yet Jesus insists that not one falls to the earth "without [the knowledge or consent] of your Father" (see *Jerusalem Talmud Šebiʿit* 9:1, 38d, "Without [the intervention of] heaven, [even] a bird does not perish; all the more so a human being"; see also *Genesis Rabba* 79:6). The punch line asserts that the hairs of your head are numbered and asks, "Are you not worth more than many sparrows?" (the cheapest living things).

The image of numbering hairs refers to something that human beings cannot count or know (Ps 40:12; 69:4; D. C. Allison, Jr., "The Hairs of Your Head Are All Numbered," *ExpT* 101 [1990]: 334-36). The passive verb "are numbered" is a divine passive; God has counted them (as God has the clouds, the drops of rain, the sand, and the stars). This saying about the hairs contrasts with a number of biblical passages that promise persons that not a hair of their heads will be harmed (1 Sam 14:45; 2 Sam 14:11; 1 Kgs 1:52; Luke 21:18; Acts 27:34). Jesus does not say that the disciples' hairs will not be harmed, only that they are numbered. He does not promise that his disciples will be able to duck danger, only that God knows about it. The implication is that when disciples fall to the earth it is not without the knowledge and consent of the Father. How can humans who cannot give even an approximate number for the hairs on their heads expect to understand why evil or suffering occurs or how it fits into God's plans? They can only trust that somehow it does and that the reign of God will soon put all things right. They are therefore not to allow their message to be muted by external pressures or by internal fears.

(4) The last unit (10:34-42) brings together the threads of the discourse. Some Jewish traditions (Isa 9:5-7; Zech 9:9-10; 1 Chron 22:9; *Testament of Levi* 18:2-4; *Mishna 'Eduyyot* 8:7; see Luke 2:14) might lead one to expect that the messiah would bring only peace. But the wolf and the lamb are not yet going to lie down in peace or to feed together (Isa 11:6; 66:25). In the first saying (10:34-36), Jesus cautions against any false expectations; he does not bring peace but a sword. The sword is not the sword of judgment that will mow down the oppressors (*1 Enoch* 91:12). It is the sword of decision, and the call to decision will bring division (Bruner, *Christbook,* 1:392-93). It will sunder even the closest relations (Mic 7:6; see *1 Enoch* 100:2; 4 Ezra 6:24; *Mishna Soṭa* 9:15; *Babylonian Talmud Sanhedrin* 97ab), particularly if they are sure that the disciple has been enticed by a false prophet (see Deut 13:6-11). Jesus does not intend to split families (see D. E. Garland, "A Biblical Foundation for Family Ministry," *The Church's Ministry with Families,* ed. D. S. R. Garland [Dallas: Word, 1990], 20-34), but he concedes that ruptures will result from the choices that individuals make for or against the kingdom of heaven as priorities are reordered (see 8:21-22). This disruption of families cannot be avoided as long as there are some who prefer darkness to the light (John 3:17-21).

The disruption of family life is graphically illustrated in some of the acts of the Christian martyrs. For example, in *The Martyrdom of St. Perpetua and Felicitas,* Perpetua is described as a newly married woman of good family and upbringing who has an infant son at her breast. When she is arrested for her faith during the African persecution, her father pleaded with her to recant. She responds that she could be nothing other than what she is, a Christian. Her father "was so angered by the word 'Christian' that he moved towards me as though he would pluck my eyes out" (3.3). Later, he begs:

> "Daughter have pity on my grey head – have pity on me your father, if I deserve to be called your father, if I have favoured you above all your brothers, if I have raised you to reach this prime of your life. Do not abandon me to the reproach of men, think of your brothers, think of your mother and your aunt, think of your child, who will not be able to live while you are gone. Give up your pride! You will destroy all of us! None of us will ever be able to speak freely again if anything happens to you." (5.2-4, H. Musurillo, *The Acts of the Christian Martyrs* [Oxford: Clarendon, 1972], 113)

Life was believed to be tied up in one's family, but Jesus contends that true life can be found only in giving oneself completely to the reign of God.

The final saying of the discourse (10:40-42) recalls the opening scene when Jesus tells the disciples to pray to the Lord of the harvest to send workers (9:38). The disciples are sent by God and are therefore not only envoys of Jesus but of God as well, like the prophets and righteous before them. That fact only underscores the gravity of rejecting them. Even a minimal act of acceptance (see Horsley, *New Documents*, 3:153) receives much beyond what it would seem to merit (Josephus, *Antiquities* 18.6.6 §193-94, reports that Agrippa richly rewarded a slave who had given him a drink when he was under arrest). If such a small token of hospitality will not go unrewarded; those who go out may take comfort that they certainly will be rewarded as well.

The conclusion to the discourse in 11:1 turns the spotlight back on Jesus. The narrator reports that he, not the disciples, moved on from there teaching and preaching in their cities (11:1). The ominous predictions of rejection and peril for the disciples prepares the reader for the repudiation of Jesus that will be recorded in the narrative that follows.

Part 2

Rejection and Confession
11:1-16:20

he resumption of the narrative launches the second half of the large division, 4:17-16:20. It opens with a question about who Jesus is, raised by John the Baptist, and a beatitude for a positive response to Jesus (11:2-6) and concludes with a question about who Jesus is, raised by Jesus himself, and a beatitude for Peter's response (16:13-20). The preceding discourse warns the disciples to be prepared for hostility when they go out on mission to Israel, and the narrative now offers some clues as to why they will be ostracized: Jesus himself is rejected. The narrative begins with doubts about Jesus raised by none other than John the Baptist. This is followed by reports of indifference to Jesus' salvific ministry in Galilean cities (11:16-24) even though his fame has spread throughout the whole land (9:26). An open confrontation with the Pharisees ensues (12:1-14) with the result that they map out plans to destroy Jesus (12:14) and to defame his reputation (12:24). Reasons for this turn of events are interspersed throughout the narrative (11:25-27), but a fuller explanation is provided by the discourse of parables in 13:1-52. The parables also make it clear that rejection of Jesus will result in condemnation at the end of the age. The disciples, however, are affirmed as those who understand; and Jesus turns increasingly to them as the fertile ground who will produce the desired fruit. The narrative that follows in 13:53-16:20 shows Jesus continuing to minister to the needs of Israel but concentrating on giving the disciples further instruction.

Like the first half of this large block (4:17-11:1), this second half can be outlined as a chiasm:

   a   11:2 Question about Jesus

      b   11:3–5 Jesus' answer

         c   11:6 Beatitude for those who respond to Jesus

           d   11:7–15 John's role explained

              e   11:16–12:45 Unbelief and rejection from the Jewish leaders

                 f   2:46–50 Jesus' mothers, brothers, and sisters

                    g   13:1–52 Parables of the kingdom that explain the reaction to Jesus

                 f′   13:53–58 Jesus' mothers, brothers, and sisters

              e′   14:1–16:12 Belief and acceptance by the disciples and warnings about the Jewish leaders

a′   16:13–20 Question about Jesus

      b′   16:14–16 Answers from various ones and from Peter

         c′   16:17 Beatitude for Peter's response

           d′   16:18–20 Peter's role explained

DOUBT, INDIFFERENCE, AND DISSENT

11:2–12:45

The new section of narrative recapitulates something of what has happened in the story. John the Baptist reappears. The miracles of chapters 8–9 are reprised in 11:5. The climax of the chapter, 11:25–30, harks back to the voice from heaven at Jesus' baptism that identified him as the son of the Father (3:17), and the invitation to "learn of me" renews the theme of Jesus as the teacher. The image of violent ones assaulting the kingdom of heaven (11:12), the parable of the bickering children (11:16–19), and the bitter reproach of the cities that fail to respond to Jesus' mighty works (11:20–24) recall Jesus' warnings to the disciples that they would be rejected in their mission to the lost sheep of the house of Israel (10:14–25). They also foreshadow the bitter clashes with the Pharisees that are to come.

By informing the reader from the beginning that Jesus' messianic works are at issue (11:2), the narrator brings into the foreground the question whether or not Jesus is the fulfillment of Israel's hopes. Various responses to these works will be depicted in what follows. The cautious approach of John the Baptist who, upon hearing the works of the Christ, asks, "Are you he who is to come, or shall we look for another?" is the first in a string of questions about Jesus' identity that will climax at the end of this large section when Jesus asks his disciples: "Who do you say that I am?" (16:15). In between, the crowds will inquire uncertainly, "This is not the son of David, is it?" (12:23). The synagogue in Nazareth will ask skeptically, "Where did this man get this wisdom and these mighty works?" (13:54). Herod Antipas will persuade himself that Jesus must be John the Baptist raised from the dead (14:2). The correct answer, however, will be given by the disciples and a Canaanite woman – he is "the son of God" (14:33), "the son of David" (15:22) – and most memorably by Peter: "the Christ, the son of the living God" (16:16).

123

This section divides into three parts. (1) The first part (11:2-19) is composed of three units each beginning with a question: (a) 11:2-6 (Are you he who is to come?), (b) 11:7-15 (What did you go out into the wilderness to see?), (c) 11:16-19 (How shall I compare this generation?). Each paragraph contains a reference to "coming:" "Are you the coming one?" (11:3), "he is Elijah who is to come" (11:14), "John came" (11:18), "the son of man came" (11:19). The reference to the works of the Christ in 11:2 and Wisdom's works in 11:19 form an inclusio. (2) The second part of the section (11:20-24) contains a condemnation of three Galilean cities for their failure to repent. (3) The third part (11:25-30) contains an explanation for the indifference, a declaration about Jesus and his mission, and an invitation to discipleship.

(1) John has been imprisoned during the entire course of Jesus' public ministry (4:12). When he hears about "the works of the Christ," he appears to have misgivings about whether Jesus is the one who is to come. He sends his disciples to sound Jesus out about whether they should wait for another. In Matthew's narrative, John's uncertainty could only have been prompted by the disparity between what he had forecast would soon happen and what he was hearing about Jesus. He had predicted a cataclysmic judgment and a severe judge who would come with an ax in one hand and a winnowing shovel in the other (3:10-12). But the ax that John said was laid at the root of the trees was not falling, and the winnowing shovel was still. Nothing eschatologically momentous seemed to be happening. John hears only about acts of divine mercy. Where was the final separation and the fierce baptism with Spirit and fire that he had forecast? The gap between what John had preached (3:10-12) and what Jesus has been doing forces the reader to come to grips with the question, What are the works of the messiah? John's doubt also raises the issue of how those works will cause some to stumble.

In Luke's account of this incident, Jesus cured many "in that hour" in preparation for the response to the question of John (7:21). Jesus then tells John's disciples to relay to him what they have seen and heard. The disciples are themselves witnesses of Jesus' miracles. In Matthew, no miracles are performed for them. If one cannot see the truth from hearing it, it is futile to do anything more. They are to report back to John only what Jesus tells them has happened, which might not seem to provide any new information. The works cited in 11:5 recall Jesus' deeds in chapters 8-9 and match various passages from Isaiah (Isa 29:18, "the deaf shall hear, the blind shall see"; 35:5-6, "the eyes of the blind shall be opened; the ears of the deaf will be unstopped; the lame shall leap"; 42:18, "listen, dead; look up, blind"; 26:19; "the dead shall live"; and 61:1, "to bring good news to the oppressed"). It might also seem that the last item on the list, preaching good news to the poor, is anticlimactic after the raising of the dead. But "the poor" denotes those who are completely dependent upon God for help (see above on 5:3) and therefore sums up the condition of all those in the list.

A recently released fragment from Dead Sea Scrolls, 4Q521, reveals that similar expectations about the signs of the messiah (or the messianic time) were shared by others during the time of Jesus and that they were derived from the study of a common nucleus of texts from the Prophets and the Psalms.

> 1 [The heav]ens and the earth will obey His Messiah,
> 2 [The sea and all th]at is in them. He will not turn aside from the commandment of the Holy Ones.
> 3 Take strength in His mighty work, all ye who seek the Lord.
> 4 Will you not find the Lord in this, all ye who wait [for Him] with hope in your hearts?
> 5 Surely the Lord will seek out the pious, and will call the righteous by name.
> 6 His spirit will hover over the poor, by His might will He restore the faithful.
> 7 He will glorify the pious on the throne of the eternal kingdom.
> 8 He will release the captives, make the blind see, raise up the do[wntrodden.]
> 9 For[ev]er I will cleave [to Him aga]inst the [po]werful, and [I will trust] in his lovingkindness.
> 10 a[nd in His] go[odness forever. His] holy [Messiah] will not be slow [in coming.]
> 11 And as for the wonders that are not the work of the Lord, when he [i.e. the Messiah] will not be slow [in coming.]
> 12 then he will heal the sick, resurrect the dead, and to the poor announce glad tidings.
> 13 . . . he will lead the [Hol]y Ones, he will shepherd [th]em. he will do
> 14 . . . and all of it. . . . (text and translation from M. O. Wise and J. D. Tabor, "The Messiah at Qumran," *Biblical Archaeology Review* 18 [1992]: 62)

These allusions to Isaiah echo a prominent Matthean theme: what is happening in Jesus' ministry is a fulfillment of the prophets. They also affirm that it is not yet the time for judgment (or for mourning, 9:14–15). The word about proclaiming the day of vengeance in Isaiah

29:20; 35:5; and 61:2 is omitted (as well as any reference to setting prisoners free, Isa 42:7; 61:1). What is emphasized is the presence of good news and the offer of mercy.

The concluding beatitude in 11:6, "Blessed is the one who takes no offense at me," does three things. First, it implies that Jesus' works are not unequivocal. Those who are not let in on the proofs from Scripture and the authoritative pronouncements from heaven are at some disadvantage. Second, it implies that there is something scandalous about Jesus, something that will always jolt preconceived notions of what a messiah should be and do. The temptation will be to remove the cause of offense by making Jesus over in our image so that he fulfills our agenda. Or, the temptation will be to remove him altogether. Third, unlike other beatitudes in the Gospel, this one issues a challenge and underlines the alternatives of faith or offense.

The disciples of John had come to ask Jesus who he was; in the second unit, Jesus now clarifies for the crowds who John is (11:7-15). He asks them if they ventured out into the wilderness to see a shaking reed or a prophet. Many readers take the shaking reed to refer to something quite ordinary. The plentiful cane grass would hardly be worth a special outing to the wilderness to behold. The unspoken answer to the question is that they did not go out to the desert, the traditional place of God's revelation (Isa 40:3; 1 QS 8:12-14; Josephus, *Jewish War* 2.13.4 §259; 7.10.1 §438), to see something commonplace, but to encounter a prophet. The reed, however, was an emblem for Herod Antipas that appeared on his coins celebrating the foundation of Tiberias with its plenteous reeds. The shaking reed parallels the image of the man (singular!) clothed in soft raiment and found in the houses of kings (11:8). It is likely that these two images, a shaking reed and an elegantly clothed dandy (contrast John's apparel in 3:4), are pointed barbs aimed at Herod Antipas, whom Jesus elsewhere brands a fox (Luke 13:32; G. Theissen, *Lokalkolorit und Zeitgeschichte in den Evangelien*, Novum Testamentum et Orbis antiquus 8 Göttingen: Vandenhoeck & Ruprecht, 1989], 25-44). The shaking reed may refer to Antipas's bending with the wind to survive politically, or to his cowardice. Whatever the image may insinuate about Antipas, the saying harks back to the biblical motif of the conflict between prince and prophet. The crowds did not go out to see Herod Antipas, but his prophetic nemesis; and they were not mistaken in their impression that John was someone worth going out to see in the wilderness. He was indeed a prophet (21:26). But he was far more than they realized; he was the greatest of the prophets (11:9). Jesus declares him to be the eschatological prophet of whom Scripture speaks, "Behold I send my messenger before your face, who will prepare *your* way before *you*" (a conflation of Mal 3:1 and Exod 23:20; see Matt 3:2).

The evaluation of John becomes more ambivalent in 11:11. On the one hand, no one born of woman is greater than John; on the other hand, the least in the kingdom of heaven is greater than he. Why? The answer must be related to John's query in 11:2–3. He has not been privileged to perceive the full significance of the arrival of the Christ. The implication is that John had set the stage for God's great drama of salvation and did not realize the significance of his role or how the drama would unfold. He is a perfect example of human finitude; he was profoundly right and profoundly wrong at the same time. Even being the greatest of the prophets does not insure full recognition of what God is doing. Nor does it spare one from having a crisis of faith. In many ways, John is like Moses, who brought the people of Israel to the outskirts of the promised land but who did not enter the land of rest himself (Manson, *Sayings,* 70). John and his disciples still belong to the old (9:14–17), primarily because they are not disciples of Jesus. That the least in the kingdom are greater than John also implies that status in the kingdom of heaven is conferred by grace. The concluding unit of this section (11:25–30) makes it clear that those who understand who the son is are nobodies, dismissed by the "wise and understanding" as "simpletons." They understand simply because it has been given to them (11:27; 13:11, 51; 16:17).

The modern reader might want to know how John reacted to Jesus' answer, but the Evangelist offers no clues. What is important to Matthew is only the eschatological status accorded John by Jesus and what that implies about Jesus. The next verse, 11:12, is obscure and has puzzled interpreters from the beginning (see P. S. Cameron, *Violence and the Kingdom: The Interpretation of Matthew 11:12,* ANTJ 5 (Frankfurt/Bern/New York: Peter Lang, 1988). The issues are these: Does the kingdom suffer violence (passive voice)? Or, does the kingdom come with violence (middle voice)? Are the men of violence to be condemned or commended? An analysis of the words and the context suggests that this saying denounces those who do violence to the kingdom (see E. Moore, "*BIAZŌ, HARPAZŌ* and Cognates in Josephus," *NTS* 21 [1974–75]: 519–43; and Jewish traditions about violent ones, 1QpHab 2:6; 4QpPs37 2:14; 1QH 2:11, 21–22; *Mishna Soṭa* 9:15). The kingdom of God suffers violent attack by violent ones who attempt to plunder it. In this case, the kingdom ("it") is personified by its heralds.

The saying offers an explanation for imprisonment of the greatest of the prophets and why Jesus had to warn the disciples about the enmity they will face (10:17-18; 21-22). It also prepares the reader for John's execution by Herod Antipas (14:1-12) and the fate of Jesus (16:21; 17:10-13; see 21:33-41). The violence directed against John, Jesus, and the disciples is a manifestation of the clash taking place between God and the powers of evil in their various guises.

The statements "from the days of John the Baptist until now" (11:12a) and "for all the prophets and the law prophesied until John" (11:13) divide salvation history into different stages. They imply that the dispensation of the law and the prophets has reached an end with the appearance of John. With John a new era begins, which explains why John is identified as more than a prophet. Jesus says that John is Elijah, the one who is to come – if you can accept it (11:14). First-century Jewish listeners must completely rethink whatever expectations they may have had about Elijah. For example, in Malachi 3:1-3; 4:5, Elijah is not said to come before the messiah but to come before the great and terrible day. According to Sirach 48:10, Elijah was to have an almost messianic function. He is "destined to calm the wrath of God before it breaks out in fury, to turn the heart of the father to the son, and to restore the tribes of Israel." Jesus himself affirms that Elijah comes to restore all things (17:11). Fabulous expectations about what Elijah would do may have been rife and were probably as varied as modern Christians' expectations about the end of time. Some thought that Elijah would bring back Moses and the generation of the wilderness, revive the messiah, reveal lost sacred temple vessels (the ark, the vessel of manna, and the vessel of sacred oil), show the scepter received from God, crush mountains like straw, and reveal great mysteries. The later Rabbis, riveted by more mundane matters, maintained that Elijah would settle property disputes (*Mishna Baba Meṣi'a* 1:8; 2:8; 3:4-5; *Šeqalim* 2:5). If the audience shared any of these expectations about Elijah (see 27:47), Jesus' declaration that the imprisoned John was Elijah would have been hard to swallow. Since Jesus identifies John as Elijah, who is to come, and implicitly links his ministry to John's, the reader is left to ponder: Who then is Jesus if John is the greatest of the prophets, and what will happen to him?

The sudden castigation of "this generation" in 11:16-19 in the third unit ties into the overarching theme of the response to the advent of the kingdom and the works of the Christ. The illustration comes from the world of children's play. It pictures children playing the wedding game, piping and dancing, and the funeral game, wailing and mourning. One group sits, piping and wailing; and they complain that their playmates do not respond by dancing or mourning. To which group of children is "this generation" compared? It may be the aloof children who sulk on the sidelines, the active children who expect everyone to dance to their tune, even prophets from God, or both groups who are too busy squabbling to recognize that a grave crisis has burst in upon them. The most likely interpretation in the context of Matthew is that the parable likens "this generation" to the children who do not respond. They would not be aroused by the piping of Jesus' joyous announcement of a wedding celebration (see 9:14–15) as they were not moved by the wailing of John's call to radical repentance. The pattern forms a chiasm:

A   piping the wedding

  B   wailing the funeral

  B′   John came

A′   the son of man came

"This generation," a phrase that calls to mind the infamous wilderness generation (Pss 78; 95; 106; Acts 7:35–53; 1 Cor 10:1–12; Heb 3:7–4:13), did not repent at John's preaching (see 21:32) nor at Jesus' preaching. Instead, they grumbled that John had a demon because he came neither eating nor drinking (only supernatural beings can exist without food or water), and that Jesus was a glutton and a drunkard (see Deut 21:20) because he came eating and drinking as a friend of toll collectors and sinners (see 9:10–13). Nevertheless, Wisdom, which refers to God's wise design or purpose for humankind, will be proved right from her works. This last line declares that if it were to go to trial to determine who was at fault for the failure of this generation to respond, Wisdom would be exonerated. The works are clear for those who have ears to hear (11:15).

(2) The second part of this section (11:20–24) opens with Jesus uttering woes on the unrepentant cities of Capernaum, Jesus' home base, Chorazin, and Bethsaida. This outburst comes as a surprise for a couple of reasons. The response of the Galilean towns, to this point, has not been portrayed as negative (9:31). To contend that they will suffer a fate worse than the infamous Sodom in the judgment is surely a terrible fate, and for what sins? Capernaum is not accused, as Sodom was, of adultery and walking in lies (Jer 23:14; Jude 7; see *Testament*

of Levi 14:6; *Testament of Benjamin* 9:1) or of pride and the neglect of the poor (Ezek 16:49); it has only given Jesus the cold shoulder. This startling judgment does two things. (a) It impresses on the reader that indifference toward Jesus or rejection of him is the deadliest of sins (see the warning in *Testament of Asher* 7:1: "Do not become like Sodom, which did not recognize the Lord's angels and perished forever"). (b) It prepares the reader for what will follow. Judgment is first announced, and then the developing story shows how it is justified (Luz, *Matthäus (Mt 8–17)*, 2:194). The failure of these towns to respond marks a new stage in the relationship between Jesus and Galilee. The gap between Jesus and the people will only continue to widen. In chapter 12, the rejection of Jesus becomes more evident in the heated disputes between Jesus and the Pharisees.

Jesus' miracles have attracted large crowds who marvel, but the call to repentance has fallen on deaf ears. This failure underscores the fact that miracles do not produce faith (see John 2:23–25), and Jesus will refuse all requests for signs (12:38; 16:1–4; 27:42). The woe stresses the danger of smugly presuming that one has an exclusive relationship with God that will guarantee preferential treatment (11:23). It also makes clear that privilege brings with it both greater responsibility and judgment. John the Baptist was right: failure to repent will lead to catastrophe; and these cities can expect only doom on the day of judgment and will fare worse than notorious pagan sinners.

(3) The third part of this section (11:25–30) divides into three pieces: (a) thanksgiving (11:25–26); (b) pronouncement (11:27); and (c) invitation (11:28–30). Each saying contains a significant theological affirmation.

(a) The introductory phrase "at that time" places the thanksgiving saying (11:25–26) in the setting of Jesus' grievance about the carping generation of spoiled children and the impenitence of the Galilean cities. The thanksgiving is an indirect way of asserting a truth about something (F. W. Danker, *Jesus and the New Age: A Commentary of Luke's Gospel* [Philadelphia: Fortress, 1988], 218; see Ps 118:19–21; Luke 18:11; 1QH 5:20–21; 25–26), and it offers the explanation for why this generation did not repent. God in God's mysterious wisdom (cf. Rom 11:25–36) has hidden these things from the wise and understanding and revealed them to babes. But there is also something about the mentality of those who regard themselves as "wise and understanding" that makes them unreceptive to God's revelation and something about the spirit of the "babes," the simple-minded, that makes them well-disposed to it.

Wisdom and learning are not to be despised; the problem arises when one considers oneself to be wise and learned (cf. 1 Cor 1:18–30). The wise and understanding regard themselves as the theological elite. They have their own wisdom and are convinced that they have nothing to learn from one so meek and lowly as Jesus. Their years of learning serve only to blind and deafen them to the presence of God's saving activity in Jesus. They are sure of themselves, but they do not have ears to hear and are not able to accept such preposterous declarations that John the Baptist is Elijah (11:14–15). Their preoccupation with their own exaltation to heaven (11:23; 23:6–7) also makes them unresponsive to one who comes as a suffering servant and who seems to offer only inglorious affliction. The "babes," on the other hand, are those who possess no wisdom of their own (Rabbi Johanan is said to have complained: "Since the temple was destroyed, prophecy has been taken from prophets and given to fools and children," *Babylonian Talmud Baba Batra* 12b; see *Mishna 'Abot* 3:11). They are beginners in wisdom, the meek and humble who count for nothing, the childlike, as opposed to the childish. They are more disposed to being helped and to being taught.

Here lies a paradox. In Jewish apocalyptic literature revelation is not concealed from the wise and prudent but disclosed to them so that they might possess knowledge (U. Wilckens, *"sophia,"* *TDNT* 7:517). Daniel exults after the mystery of the king's dream was revealed to him (Dan 2:18–23):

> [18]Blessed be the name of God from age to age, for wisdom and power are his.... [21]He changes times and seasons, deposes kings and sets up kings; he gives wisdom to the wise and knowledge to those who have understanding. [22]He reveals deep and hidden things; he knows what is in the darkness, and light dwells with him. [23]To you, O God of my ancestors, I give thanks and praise for you have given me wisdom and power, and have now revealed to me what we asked of you, for you have revealed to us what the kings ordered. (NRSV)

An explanation for the principle that wisdom is given only to the wise (see 4 Ezra 12:35–38) is found in a late midrash:

> A matron asked R. Jose b. Ḥalafta, "What means that which is said, 'He giveth wisdom unto the wise'? The text should have stated, 'He

giveth wisdom unto them that are not wise and knowledge to them that know not understanding!' " He answered her, "I will explain with a parable. If two persons came to borrow money from you, one rich and the other poor, to whom would you lend, the rich man or the poor?" She replied, "To the rich man." "Why?" he asked; to which she answered, "Because if the rich man loses my money he has wherewith to repay me; but if the poor man loses my money, from where can he repay me?" He said to her, "Does your ear hear what you have uttered with your mouth? If the Holy One, blessed be He, gave wisdom to fools, they would sit and meditate upon it in privies, theatres, and bath-houses; but the Holy One, blessed be He, gave wisdom to the wise who sit and meditate upon it in the Synagogues and Houses of Study. Hence 'He giveth wisdom unto the wise, and knowledge to them that know understanding' " (*Qoheleth Rabba* 1:7).

Jesus' announcement that "these things" are hidden from the "wise and understanding" and given to the "simple" hints that something is awry. If revelation is accessible to "babes" then it is accessible to all (A. M. Hunter, "Crux Criticorum — Matt xi. 25–30 — A Reappraisal," *NTS* 8 [1962]: 244) — which is something for which to be thankful. It is even accessible to the wise and understanding if they would only humble themselves and become as little children (18:3), if not "babes."

(b) The pronouncement in 11:27 characterizes Jesus' vocation as revealing God. Jesus declares that all things have been delivered to him (a word used in Rabbinic literature for passing on tradition; see also 1 Cor 11:23; 15:3) by his Father. As teacher, Jesus has exclusive knowledge of God. But why mention first that the son is known by the Father? The entire section shows the problem of comprehending Jesus. Not even John, the greatest of the prophets, is sure who he is (11:3). The statement affirms that only God knows the son (see 3:17), and therefore recognition of the son can come to humans only as a gift from the Father (13:11; 16:17). The assertion raises an important question for the reader: How does one becomes a recipient of this privileged knowledge?

The pronouncement also boldly affirms that the Father can only be known through the son. The reason for this is to be found in their mutual knowledge, which far surpasses the relationship between Moses and God (Exod 33:12–14). This reciprocal knowledge is unique and testifies to a mystical relationship between them. It takes like to know like (see Luz, *Matthäus (Mt 8–17)*, 2:213). The declaration embraces a high christology and an exclusive theological claim that decisively divides Christian Judaism from its counterpart, nascent Rabbinic Judaism.

(c) In spite of rejection, the invitation remains open (11:28). It is an invitation to discipleship, which for the first time in the Gospel is now extended to all. For the reader, the appeal comes appropriately after the presentation of Jesus' teaching (5-7), the demonstration of what Jesus is able to do for others (8-9), and the not so subtle warnings about what will happen to those who reject him (11:20-24).

Jesus invites people to come to him and to take his yoke. The yoke, used on draft animals and on prisoners of war, was a common metaphor for toil, submission, discipline, duty, and obedience. The image, in Jewish literature, expresses a paradox: "it represents burden, labor and obligation, and yet it symbolizes freedom and life" (C. Deutsch, *Hidden Wisdom and the Easy Yoke: Wisdom, Torah and Discipleship in Matthew 11.25-30*, JSNTsup 18 [Sheffield: JSOT Press, 1987], 128). One can find references to the yoke of serving God (Jer 2:20; 5:5), the yoke of Wisdom (Sir 6:30; 51:26), the yoke of the law (Acts 15:10; *2 [Syriac] Apocalypse of Baruch* 41:3; *Mishna 'Abot*. 3:5), the yoke of the commandments (*Mishna Berakot* 2:2), the yoke of repentance (*Babylonian Talmud 'Aboda Zara* 5a), and the yoke of the kingdom of heaven (*Mishna Berakot* 2:2). Nowhere does anyone refer to the yoke of Moses nor does any teacher have the temerity to invite others to put their necks under "my yoke" and to "learn from me." Jesus, however, does and invites persons to enroll in his school of Wisdom where he is both the teacher and the core curriculum. If one does not recognize the union between the Father and the son, this offer borders on blasphemy. If one does recognize this union, then one also knows that the only way to rest is through Jesus. In the Hebrew Scriptures, it is God who offers rest (Exod 33:14; Jer 6:16; 31:25); here it is Jesus, God with us.

The invitation to take "my yoke" may also assume that persons will be under one kind of dominion or another. One only has a choice of which kind of yoke. For the weary, the burdened, the harassed, and helpless (9:36), Jesus' yoke is easy. Again, there is a paradox. The easier yoke does not mean that Jesus makes fewer demands. He does not alleviate the requirements of the law (5:21-48). He describes his way as hard and narrow (7:13-14), as a cross that needs to be borne (10:38), and as something that will split families (10:34-37). How can it be said that his yoke is easy? The answer from the text is that he is meek and gentle. Jesus treats his disciples as yokefellows rather than as camels and donkeys to be loaded down (23:4). One might also conclude that his yoke is easy because it "fits." His demands grow out of our need. Hate is a greater burden to bear than love. Forgiveness lightens the load; anger only makes it heavier.

The next section (12:1-45) portrays overt controversy and falls into two parts. (1) The first part (12:1-21) contains two sabbath controversies (in a field, 12:1-8; in their synagogue, 12:9-14) and concludes with a long fulfillment quotation from Isaiah 42 (12:15-21). The opening phrase, "at that time" (12:1), ties these disputes to Jesus' offer of rest in 11:28-30, which is closely related to the sabbath (Gen 2:1-4a; Heb 4:4, 8-10). It is a one-sided debate that bears out Jesus' claim that his yoke is kind by showing that he interprets the law according to the needs of individuals. (2) The second part (12:22-45) contains the churlish reactions of the Pharisees to Jesus (12:24, 38) and corroborates Jesus' observation that the significance of his works is hidden from the "wise and understanding." It begins with Jesus healing the demon-possessed, blind, and lame (12:22). It concludes with a parable about a house swept clean of a demon, but because nothing has filled the void (=belief in Jesus), the demon returns with a vengeance (12:43-45).

(1) The disputes over the sabbath (12:1-8, 9-14) raise the basic issue of Jesus' fidelity to God's covenant with Israel. Was Jesus a scofflaw?

God commanded that the sabbath be kept holy by refraining from work (Exod 20:8-11). That command elicited the question: What precisely is to be classified as work? Pietist groups tried meticulously to clarify things with an increasing number of finely spun arguments and rules (see CD 10:14-11:18). The *Mishna* contains three tractates that specifically address sabbath issues, *Šabbat* (sabbath), *'Erubin* (sabbath limits), and *Beṣa* (festival days). The Rabbi who said, "The rules about the sabbath, festal offerings and sacrilege are as mountains hanging by a hair, for Scripture is scanty and the rules many" (*Mishna Ḥagiga* 1:8; *Tosepta 'Erubin* 8:23), concedes that the guidelines for conduct on the sabbath had multiplied exponentially while the scriptural basis for them was slim.

Some commentators have so belabored the complexity of Rabbinic casuistry that they overlook the fact that faithful Jews did not consider sabbath observance to be something irksome. They welcomed the sabbath as a joyful entry into the sacred time of the beginning before human work (see Philo, *Moses* 2.209-11). Fasting was banned, and eating and drinking encouraged. Sabbath observance was both a way to honor the holiness of God and a bulwark against assimilation to creeping paganism (Borg, *Conflict, Holiness and Politics,* 147–48). The significance of the sabbath for Israel went beyond the fact that it was one of the two positive commands in the decalogue. It was a sign of the exclusive relationship between Israel and God throughout the generations, "that you may know that I, the Lord, sanctify you" (Exod 31:13). Many reveled in the fact that the Creator sanctified only Israel of all the nations to keep the sabbath (*Jubilees* 2:31). The sabbath was therefore considered to be a symbol of what made Israel distinct and special to God, and by observing it Israel celebrated the act of creation and imitated God, who rested on the seventh day (Gen 2:1–3; Exod 31:12–17). As a kind of national banner, the breach of the sabbath would have been similar to desecration of the flag in modern times; and it triggered similar reactions. Dishonoring the sabbath was viewed as part of Israel's apostasy that resulted in the exile, according to Jeremiah (Jer 17:27; see Neh 13:15–18: "you bring more wrath upon Israel by profaning the sabbath"). This background should make suspect any interpretation that argues that Jesus abolishes the sabbath or endorses wanton violations of it in these controversies; in fact, he does not. He proclaims the disciples to be "guiltless" of any infraction (12:7) and that it is "lawful" to do good on the sabbath (12:12).

The first incident (12:1–8) answers the suspicion that Jesus condoned transgression of one of the ten commandments and set aside what made Israel distinct in all the world. The disciples pluck grain and eat it as they travel with Jesus through a field on the sabbath. Exactly why they were traveling on the sabbath (were they fleeing?) and possibly exceeding the limits of a sabbath's day journey is not revealed. In Mark 2:24, the Pharisees ask why the disciples do what is unlawful on the sabbath; in Matthew, they bring a direct accusation to their master (12:2). This charge, or perhaps warning, since later Rabbis stipulated that a warning was to be given prior to prosecution (*Mishna Sanhedrin* 7:8), cannot be ignored. Unintentional violations of the sabbath required a sin offering (Lev 4:27–35). Intentional violations of the sabbath were punishable by death and cutting off (not having progeny in Israel; see Exod 31:14; 35:2; Num 15:32–36; *Jubilees* 2:25–26; 50:8).

According to Deuteronomy 23:25, it was permissible to go into a neighbor's field to pluck grain to satisfy one's hunger as long as one did not use a sickle – which would be tantamount to stealing. Whether it was permissible to do this even on the sabbath probably depended on whom one asked. The later Rabbis, intent on putting a fence around

the law to forestall breaking an ordinance, classified plucking as a form
of reaping that is forbidden on the sabbath; and this seems to be the
basis of the Pharisees' protest (Exod 34:21; see *Mishna Šabbat* 7:2;
Philo, *Moses* 2.22, also maintains that it is not lawful to pluck any fruit
whatsoever on the sabbath or even to touch them).

Matthew's account alone mentions the hunger of the disciples
(12:1), so that the story begins with a defensible explanation for their
actions. It also makes the parallel with David and his men closer since
they were also hungry (12:3). Jesus defends and justifies their behavior with three arguments and a declaration: (a) the precedent from
David and those with him (12:3–4); (b) an analogy from the law and
the priests' temple service on the sabbath with an argument from the
lesser to the greater (12:5–6); and (c) a critical judgment about the
Pharisees' knowledge of Scripture (12:7). (d) The incident culminates
with the declaration that the son of man is the Lord of the sabbath
(12:8).

One searches in vain in this account for a clear policy of what disciples may or may not do on the sabbath, which reveals a major difference
between the concerns of the Evangelist and those of a Rabbinic scholar.
The Rabbinic scholars were interested in compiling and scrutinizing legal decisions (*halakah*) and would want to know what Jesus' teaching
on sabbath issues was. The Evangelist wants to show Christians who it
is that teaches this. His primary interest is christology, and the incident
affirms both the authority of the son of man and the primacy of the
love command and does not clarify what is or is not permissible to do
on the sabbath.

(a) Jesus' first justification of his disciples' action refers to David
and his fleeing troops eating the shewbread (1 Sam 21:1–6) that was
permitted only to the priests (Lev 24:8–9; Num 28:9–10). They did
what was unlawful. The question is, What does this incident have to
do with the breaking of the sabbath? How does the conduct of David
help explain the conduct of Jesus' disciples? The point in Matthew
has nothing to do with the priority of human need over regulations.
Matthew does not have the saying in Mark 2:27, "The sabbath was made
for humankind and not humankind for the sabbath." Matthew's point
is christological. The argument turns on the relationship between the
great David and his retinue and the greater Jesus and his disciples. David
is a type of the messiah who took liberty with the law in a situation of
urgency and is not condemned by Scripture. "If David, because of who
he was, was entitled to do what no other layman might dare, so too

Jesus, because of who he is, has no less authority" (France, *Evangelist and Teacher*, 170).

(b) The second argument is also christological. The temple duties of the priests compel them to violate the strict letter of the sabbath, and yet they remain guiltless (see *Babylonian Talmud Yebamot* 32b). If sabbath law can be overridden by the requirements of the temple cult, it also would hold true for something even weightier than the temple cult. Jesus does not explicitly say that he is greater than the temple, but the implication is that the disciples of Jesus are able to break the sabbath as the priests do because they are with him and are carrying on a greater work than the priests serving in the temple. The temple was the place of God's presence (23:21). This statement implies that in Jesus God's presence is more immediate than in the temple (A. Schlatter, *Der Evangelist Matthäus,* 6th ed. [Stuttgart: Calwer, 1963], 396).

(c) The third argument recalls the earlier citation of Hosea 6:6 in Matthew 9:13. The phrase "if you had known" insinuates that the Pharisees do not know the Scripture and what it requires (see 12:3; 19:4; 21:16, 42; 22:31). They are guilty of insisting on punctilious obedience to their interpretation of sabbath rules while condemning the hungry. God's demand for mercy always overrides the command to observe rules or ritual. Jesus does not stand over against the law but over against the Pharisees' interpretation of the law that discounts the principle of mercy.

(d) Jesus' arguments imply that he is greater than David and greater than the temple, but the concluding statement declares that the son of man is Lord of the sabbath, who alone determines what does and what does not conform to God's merciful will for the sabbath. One can infer from this incident that the sabbath was not made to occupy the casuists but for human well-being.

The next incident (12:9–14) shows Jesus entering into enemy territory – "their synagogue." When he faces a man with a withered hand, those in the synagogue do not watch him to see what he would do (as in Mark 3:2 and Luke 6:7); they directly challenge him by questioning whether it is lawful (see 12:2) to heal on the sabbath. It is almost as if they "egg him on" (Gundry, *Matthew,* 225) so that they might accuse him (see 27:12). These tactics serve to heighten their guilt.

Jesus again argues from the lesser to the greater: they will not hesitate on the sabbath to pull a sheep out of a pit (perhaps dug and camouflaged to snare predators, see Longus, *Daphnis and Chloe* 1.11.1–2; 1.12.2–5). Some specifically forbade this: "Let no beast be helped to give birth on the sabbath day; and if it fall into a cistern or into a pit, let it not be lifted out on the sabbath" (CD 11:13–14); "if an animal falls into a stream of water [on the sabbath], provisions are made for it where it lies so that it should not perish" (*Babylonian Talmud Šabbat* 128b). One doubts, however, that a poor Galilean shepherd would have been so conscientious: saving a sheep takes precedence over sabbath because it might mean saving the farm. The "wise" Jerusalem lawyer might disdain this argument, but the "simple" peasant grasps the point immediately. Jesus then proclaims (rather than inquires, as in Mark 3:4 and Luke 6:9): "It is lawful to do good on the sabbath!" (12:12b).

All later Rabbis agreed that saving a life could take precedence over the sabbath (*Mishna Yoma* 8:6). They only disagreed about the scriptural basis for that conclusion (see *Mekilta Shabbata* 1 to Exod 31:12). The problem is that the man with the withered hand is not in a life-or-death situation. Jesus could ask him to come back tomorrow. It would not hurt the man unduly to go one more day with a withered hand, and controversy could be avoided. But it must be made clear that demands of love always override. The Pharisees were intent on setting up boundary stones that marked out clearly what could and could not be done on the sabbath. Jesus shows that love and mercy can know no boundaries.

The command to stretch out a hand whereby it is healed is hardly an infringement of any sabbath law. Nevertheless, the Pharisees took council on how to destroy Jesus (see 22:15; 27:1, 7; 28:12). They condemned Jesus for "doing good" on the sabbath but have no qualms about forming a caucus on the same sabbath to conspire how to destroy him.

Jesus does not counter the Pharisees' plot by huddling with his disciples on how to destroy the Pharisees. Instead, he withdraws (see 10:23) and heals all those who follow him. He forbids them from making him known, however. The crowds are unreliable witnesses to Jesus. It is better to hear the divine perspective from Scripture than the mercurial opinions of the crowds (16:13–14). The Scripture citation in 12:17–21, the longest in the Gospel, is a free rendering of Isaiah 42:1–4 that clarifies six things about Jesus. (a) It names Jesus as the chosen of God, "my beloved in whom my soul is well pleased" (12:18ab; see 3:17; 17:5), which attests to Jesus' authority over the sabbath (12:8) and provides in advance the answer to the crowds' question about Jesus' identity in 12:23. (b) It affirms that Jesus works by the Spirit of God (12:18c), which negates in advance the Pharisees' charge that he is in league with Beelzebul (12:24). It also confirms that since Jesus works by the Spirit of God, the kingdom of God has come upon them (12:28) and that they are indeed guilty of blasphemy against the Spirit (12:31–32). (c) It connects Jesus' withdrawal with the humility and lowliness of the servant of God (12:19a). The unassuming servant does not shout on the streets (like Wisdom, Prov 1:20; 8:1; Sir 24:1) or force response. He is not a messiah who comes to take power and thrash his enemies but one who prevails through his humble and compassionate care for others. (d) It affirms that the servant announces justice (12:18d) but makes it clear that he will not be heard (12:19b). The active translation "nor will anyone hear" underscores the deliberate rejection of his voice. (e) It confirms the healing role of the servant. Jesus comes to save the weak and broken and those with little or no life left in them (12:20ab). (f) It affirms that his ministry will open up the door of hope to gentiles (12:21). The heirs of the inhabitants of Tyre and Sidon, of Sodom and Gomorrah, and of Nineveh and the queen from the South will come to know God's justice (12:18d).

Lucian's description of Demonax communicates in a Greco-Roman setting what Matthew ascribes to Jesus using the Scripture:

> He was never known to make an uproar or excite himself or get angry, even if he had to rebuke someone; though he assailed sins he forgave sinners, thinking that one should pattern after doctors, who heal sicknesses but feel no anger at the sick. He considered that it is human to err, divine or all but divine to set right what has gone amiss. (*Demonax* 7)

(2) The second part of this section (12:22–45) presents allegations and demands from the Pharisees and includes comments by Jesus that help the reader evaluate these opponents and their blindness. (a) In 12:22–30 Jesus heals a blind and mute demoniac. The crowds ask if Jesus is the son of David, and the Pharisees accuse him of black magic. (b) This is followed by a unit that helps the reader assess those who lead the smear campaign against Jesus. It is bracketed by two "I say to you" pronouncements: on blasphemy against the Spirit (12:31–32) and on accountability for every idle word (12:36–37). In between is a statement about good and evil trees and good and evil treasure (12:33–35). (c) The scribes and Pharisees come back on stage to demand a sign from Jesus, and he warns them that they will receive only the sign of Jonah and that the Ninevites and queen of the South will arise to condemn them (12:38–42). (d) He concludes with a further warning about an unclean spirit that returns with a vengeance to an empty house (12:43–45).

In 9:32–34, Jesus healed a mute demoniac and the crowds marveled, "Never was anything like this seen in Israel." Now, Jesus heals a blind and mute demoniac, and again all of the crowds are amazed and begin to ask whether or not he might be the Son of David (see 9:27). David had success in driving out the evil spirit from Saul (1 Sam 16:14–23), and Solomon's wisdom was associated with his power over demons (Josephus, *Antiquities* 8.2.5 §45–49; see *Pseudo Philo, Biblical Antiquities* 60:3: "one from David's loins" would rule over evil spirits). The crowds are still groping in the dark because the Greek phrasing expects a negative answer: "This is not the son of David, is it?" This negative answer is exactly what they get from the Pharisees. They claim that Jesus is a secret agent for Beelzebul, an accusation anticipated by Jesus in 10:25. According to later Jewish tradition, Jesus was condemned to death for practicing sorcery and misleading the people (*Babylonian Talmud Sanhedrin* 43a; 107b; *Soṭa* 47a; *Tosepta Šabbat* 11:15; see John 7:20; 8:48, 52; 10:20; and Justin, *Dialogue* 69:7). It is a charge that Matthew cannot ignore.

The first time that the Pharisees alleged that Jesus worked by the "prince of demons" (9:34) he did not respond. Theirs is not the last word, however. Jesus now counterattacks to expose the absurdity of their accusation, unless they regard Satan as a bungler. Would the powers of evil vanquish themselves and collaborate in widespread acts of mercy? How can the Pharisees attribute the same activity of exorcism to two different sources: God works in their sons, but Beelzebul in Jesus? It takes one with greater strength to plunder the possessions of a strong man. The allegory of the strong man who is bound evokes the apocalyptic hope of the binding of the powers of evil (*Jubilees* 5:6; 10:7, 11; *1 Enoch* 10:4; 13:2; 14:5; 18:16; 21:6; *2 Enoch* 7:1; *2 [Syriac] Apocalypse of Baruch* 56:13; *Testament of Levi* 18:12; Rev 20:2). If the Pharisees were to come at this from another perspective and suppose that Jesus casts out demons by the Spirit of God, as the reader already knows (3:16, 12:18), then they would realize that the reign of God that sets all things right has come upon them.

The next unit condemns the Pharisees as blasphemers, bad trees, and a brood of vipers (12:31–37). It is unfortunate that the statements regarding blasphemy against the Spirit have caused so many to worry about whether they may have committed the unpardonable sin when the text emphasizes God's mercy in forgiving all sin (12:31–32). Jesus employs biblical hyperbole to stress how urgent it is to respond to the Spirit's working through him. Serious or defiant sin was often spoken of as "unpardonable" (Num 15:30-31; 1 Sam 3:14; Isa 22:14; *Mishna 'Abot* 3:11). It is one thing to reject Jesus when it is done in ignorance (Acts 3:17); it is something else to do so with careful premeditation. If one is ignorant, one can be informed. If one is willfully blind and deaf, nothing can be done. It is not that God is unwilling to forgive, but that one cuts oneself off from what might lead to repentance. The Pharisees have spoken against the Spirit of God and fall into the category of enemies who will not be forgiven. Ironically, they have accused Jesus of blasphemy in 9:3; but it is they who, in Matthew's opinion, are guilty of far greater blasphemy that severs them from God's people.

The only explanation for how the Pharisees reached their blasphemous conclusion about Jesus is that they are evil, and it is impossible for anything evil to produce anything good (12:33-37; see 3:7, 10; 15:13, 19). They have only an evil treasure from which to draw (see 6:21; 13:52). They will be liable for every word that they speak against the Spirit that directs the people away from faith in their messiah (12:36-37).

The next unit has the Pharisees demand some irrefutable sign from Jesus (12:38-45). In Mark 8:29, Jesus asks, "Why does this generation seek a sign?" In Matthew 12:39, he declares that "an evil and adulterous generation seeks a sign." Those who seek signs are evil, and only false prophets will provide them (24:23-26; Deut 13:1-3). Since Satan demanded signs from Jesus in the wilderness (4:3, 5-6; see 16:1), the Pharisees show themselves to be allied with him.

For Matthew, there will be only one unambiguous sign, Jesus' death and resurrection. Just as Jonah was miraculously delivered from death after spending three days and nights in the belly of a great fish (Jonah 1:17), so the son of man shall be delivered from death after being in the heart of the earth three days and nights (see 27:63). The resurrection will be God's answer to the intrigue of the Pharisees (12:14). The Pharisees, however, will conspire with the Jewish leaders to cover up this one incontrovertible sign! Only Matthew reports their push to secure the tomb, the stationing of guards, and the suppression of what had happened at the tomb through a campaign of lies (27:62-66 and 28:11-15).

The last sin is unforgivable; and this evil generation will be the ones on trial when gentiles – the Ninevites and the queen of the South – will be raised up as witnesses against them. The Ninevites responded on the basis of a prophet who performed no signs and preached only reluctantly. This generation does not respond to something far greater than Jonah, the son of God who performs mighty deeds by God's Spirit. The queen of the South (the queen of Sheba, 1 Kgs 10:1) came from a far corner of the earth "to test Solomon with hard questions" and submitted to Solomon's wisdom when he answered all of them (1 Kgs 10:6–10). As Wisdom incarnate, Jesus is far greater than Solomon; but this generation will not acknowledge his wisdom.

The final warning turns the parable of the unclean spirit into an allegory about "this generation" (12:45). Even the Pharisees must reluctantly admit that Jesus has exorcised demons. But liberation from demonic powers does not make repentance superfluous; it points to the coming kingdom of God that demands repentance (12:28; 3:2; 4:17). The parable assumes that as nature abhors a vacuum so does the spiritual world. It will be filled either by the Spirit of God or by Satan. The house may have been momentarily swept clean; but if it remains empty, it is vulnerable to another invasion from Satan. Because this generation snubs Jesus and his call to repentance (4:17; 11:20–24), the demon will return with ample reinforcements to guard against the possibility of ever being driven out again. The last state will be worse than the first.

This last saying is echoed in 27:64. When the Pharisees and high priests agitate for guards to be posted at Jesus' tomb to prevent his disciples from stealing the body and fudging a resurrection, they claim that if that were allowed to happen "the last fraud will be worst than the first." We can sense the bitter crossfire between two opposing groups who have traded charges and countercharges. The allegory expresses Matthew's evaluation of "this generation" of Israel that has rejected Jesus and the mission of his disciples. It lays under the spell of a demon possession from which it may never escape. The entire section serves to provide further legitimation of Jesus' new community, his household (10:25), over against its parent which has now become a rival. Those not with Jesus (12:30) have been corrupted by the malicious slander of the Pharisees, who have been shown to be evil to the core. When it comes time for the judgment, Matthew bitterly claims they would have been better off in ignorance (compare Rabbi Trypho's remark that it would have been better for Justin to have remained a heathen than to become a Christian, which he considered to be intentional opposition to Judaism, *Dialogue* 8.3).

THE MYSTERIES
OF THE KINGDOM REVEALED

12:46–13:58

The previous narrative sections disclose that Jesus' salvific ministry in Israel has met with confusion, indifference, and hostility. As Jesus predicted (10:34–35), division is occurring within Israel. Two scenes that mention Jesus' own immediate family dramatize this polarization (12:46–50; 13:53–58), and they also bracket the parable discourse in 13:1–52.

In the first scene (12:46–50), Jesus stretches his hand over his disciples and says: "my mother and brothers and sisters are those who do the will of God." It seems to be an ungracious remark, but the point is clear: participating in the kingdom has nothing to do with kinship. While biological family relationships are not based on choice, becoming a member of the family of the kingdom of heaven is. It is therefore open to all who have ears to hear and the daring to follow up with commitment to Jesus.

The second scene is set in Nazareth (13:53–58) and records Jesus' last teaching in "their synagogue." His hometown is mystified by his wisdom and deeds of power. Their astonishment compares to the astonishment of the crowds after the Sermon on the Mount (7:28). The difference is that following the Sermon on the Mount Jesus performs a variety of miracles. Because the synagogue in Nazareth is scandalized by him (13:57; see 11:6) and is unbelieving, he does not do "many miracles." Jesus' humble, local origin makes him seem implausible as some great figure of wisdom: "Where did this one get this wisdom and the miracles?" (13:54); "Where then did this one get all these things?" (13:56). Their inability to answer these questions springs from their ignorance of who Jesus truly is. They assume that he is simply a carpenter's son. The story has shown, however, that he is, in truth, the son of God (1:18–25). They ask, "Are not his mother, brothers, and sisters in our midst? Jesus has made it clear that his true family comprises those

143

who do the will of his Father. Matthew and Mark have Jesus respond: "A prophet is without honor in his own country and in his own house"; but Matthew does not include the statement "and among his kinsmen" (Mark 6:4). In Matthew's view, Jesus' disciples are his kinsmen; and he will turn increasingly to them as the only ones who understand his revelation and commit themselves to it. To the rest, it is nothing but riddles and unanswered questions.

The works of the Christ have been done in Israel; why does Israel not embrace its messiah? Why are so many, including Jesus' own family and hometown, scandalized? The collection of parables in chapter 13 explains this tide of events. Part of the blame can be pinned on slander from such as the Pharisees who malign the work of the Spirit (12:24); but this discourse traces the failure to respond to three other sources: (a) human hardness of heart (13:3-23), (b) the wiles of Satan (13:24-30; 36-43), and (c) the deceptively humble presence of the kingdom prior to its final apocalyptic manifestation (13:31-34).

New themes emerge in this discourse that address the following issues: (a) the different kinds of response among persons (13:3-9, 18-23); (b) the parables and their purpose (13:10-17, 34-35); (c) the requirement of understanding (13:11, 19, 51); and (d) the nature of the kingdom of God (13:31-33, 44-46). (e) A theme found in every discourse reappears: the threat of judgment (13:40-42, 48-50).

Among the many structures of this discourse that have been proposed, two are worthy of consideration. One suggests that the discourse falls into two halves, each containing four parables (D. Wenham, "The Structure of Matthew 13," *NTS* 25 [1979]: 516-22, detects a striking chiasm). The first half is directed to the crowds by the sea (13:1-35); the second is directed privately to the disciples in the house (13:36-52). The main weakness of this proposal is that the interpretation of the parable of the tares is not structurally related to the parable itself.

Davies and Allison propose a three-part structure that has much to commend it (*Saint Matthew,* 2:371). (1) The first part (13:1-23) contains the parable of the sower (13:1-9), the discussion of the parables with a scriptural citation (13:10-17), and the interpretation of the parable of the sower (13:18-23). (2) The second part (13:24-43) contains the parable of the tares (13:24-30), the complementary parables of the mustard seed (13:31-32) and leaven (13:33), a discussion of the parables with a scriptural citation (13:34-35), and a concluding interpretation of the parable of the tares (13:36-43). (3) The third part (13:44-52) contains the parable of treasure (13:44), the complementary parables of the pearl (13:45–46) and the net (13:47–48), the interpretation of the parable of the net (13:49–50), and a final discussion of the parables with a mention of treasure (13:51–52). In this structure, each part begins and ends on the same note (inclusio). No parable is separated structurally from its interpretation. A question or request for clarification follows the parabolic part of each section: "Why do you speak in parables?" (13:10); "Explain the parable of the tares" (13:36); "Do you understand all these things?" (13:51).

(1) The first part of this discourse (13:1–23) offers an explanation for the mixed response with the parable of the sower. When one first reads this parable, one might be tempted to ask, what kind of careless farmer is this who casts good seed on the pathway and rocky ledges and among thorn bushes? Concern to make the parable realistic by claiming that sowing preceded plowing, however, is misguided. It is unnecessary to require realism of the parables in all their details, particularly since the Matthean parables often contain an element of the fantastic. The evidence for the claim that sowing preceded plowing is much debated; and the parable never mentions plowing, only sowing. The parable describes a sower who sows with abandon, hoping for the best.

The hope is not in vain, but the sowing does not result in a spectacular harvest. The hundred, sixty, and thirty fold yield refers to the yield of individual plants, not that of a single field. It is, in fact, an average harvest (Pliny, *Natural History* 18.21.94–95, mentions that wheat with branching ears yielded a hundred grains; see Columella, *On Agriculture* II.9.5–6; Varro, *On Agriculture* I.44.1–3; Strabo, *Geography* XV.3.11, mentions a yield of three hundred and sixty fold). If one cannot talk about an abundant harvest, what is the point?

A parallel in 4 Ezra 8:41 sheds some light on the matter.

> For just as the farmer sows many seeds upon the ground and plants a multitude of seedlings, and yet not all that have been sown will come up in due season, and not all that were planted will take root; so also those who have been sown in the world will not all be saved (NRSV).

This analogy concisely draws attention to the fact that not all seed that is sown prospers. Jesus' parable would seem to make the same point but devotes considerable attention to the failure of the seed. The emphasis falls on the utter waste of seed in poor soil conditions with three different types of failures and the reasons for them. Some seed is lost immediately and does not even get into the ground. Some is lost eventually when it withers at the root. Some is ultimately choked out by the thorns. There are also three different types of success for the seed in good soil, but no reasons are given to explain why they vary. The parable makes it clear that the yield from the seed is directly affected by the condition of the soil.

Everyone can understand the story about the sower, but only the disciples will recognize its implications for the successes and failures of Jesus' sowing. The parable compares the kind of reception Jesus' mission to Israel has received to what happens to the average farmer when he sows seed. But the sower in this parable is not an average farmer. In Jewish literature, sowing is a metaphor for God's work (Jer 31:27-28; Ezek 36:9; Hos 2:21-23; 4 Ezra 8:6; 9:31; *2 [Syriac] Apocalypse of Baruch* 70:2). God promises to sow Israel to begin the renewal of Israel. The image of sowing implies that a new Israel, an end time Israel, is being planted by God (*1 Enoch* 62:8; Ignatius, *To the Ephesians* 9.1). The sower is the Lord of the harvest (9:38).

Given the nature of some of the soil, the rate of failure is not surprising. The reasons for the failures are not a lack of intellectual insight and understanding that one finds in the sowing imagery from Hellenistic literature (see Plato, *Phaido* 276E-77A; Plutarch, *The E at Delphi* 1 [394 E]; Seneca, *Epistles* 38:2; Antiphon, *Fragments* 60; Quintilian, *Institutio Oratoria* V.xi.24). According to the parable's interpretation, the failures are caused by (a) a lack of spiritual insight compounded by Satan snatching the seed; (b) withering under persecution because of the word (see 5:10-12; 10:22-23; 23:34; 24:9, 21, 29; 26:31-33); and (c) temporal anxieties and the lure of prosperity (see 6:19-34; 19:16-26). In other words, the reason for the failure of the seed is the lamentable spiritual state of the hearer's heart. All of the soils are said to have heard the word (13:19, 20, 22, 23)! Some are fruitful, and some are not. Bearing fruit depends on hearing rightly, and that depends on the nature of the soil (=the individual's heart). The parable identifies what makes bad soil bad (path, rocks, thorns), but what makes good soil good so that it produces a good yield? The next paragraph on the purpose of the parables (13:10-17) offers some explanation.

The disciples do not ask Jesus about the meaning of the parables but why he uses them when speaking to the crowds. Their question implies that they understand (contrast Mark 4:10, 13) but want to know, "Why do you speak to them in this way? Why don't you come right out and say what you mean?" Jesus' answer to this question is given in 13:11: "Because knowing the mysteries of the kingdom of heaven has been given to you [the disciples] and not to them [the crowds]." The plural "mysteries" may refer to Jesus' teaching as a whole, the variety of lessons in the parables of this chapter, and/or the relationship of Jesus to the advent of the kingdom. This answer is then amplified by an appeal to a basic principle: "To the one who has, more will be given and he will have in abundance; to the one who has not, what he has will be taken away" (13:12). Just as in the economic world where the rich get richer because they have capital to invest and the poor get poorer because they have no capital, so it goes in the spiritual world (Gundry, *Matthew*, 256; see Prov 1:5; 9:9). This principle is then applied to the crowds (them) in 13:13–15 and to the disciples (you) in 13:16–18.

In Matthew's presentation, Jesus' parables are not brain teasers intended to stump people. There is nothing hard to understand about the parables unless one's mind is already hardened to the truth. Jesus begins to "speak" (not teach) in parables to the crowds (13:3), not to prevent them from understanding, but *because* they do not understand (13:13). The separation between those who do and do not understand has therefore occurred before Jesus speaks in parables. C. A. Evans (*To See and Not Perceive: Isaiah 6.9–10 in Early Jewish and Christian Interpretation*, JSOTsup 64 [Sheffield: JSOT, 1989], 110) writes, "obdurate people deserve only parabolic teaching. The parables do not promote obduracy, they only make it easier to remain obdurate, and to 'lose what one already has.'" Obduracy is therefore assumed to be a prior condition in the people, and they are culpable for it (13:13–15). They have closed their eyes, shut their ears, and refused to repent (11:20–24; 12:41); as a consequence, they get only parables, which reinforce their blindness and deafness. If one fails to understand, one will become mired further in ignorance. In the interpretation of the parable of the sower it is because the person *does not understand the word of the kingdom* (13:19) that the evil one comes and snatches what has been sown and not the reverse, that the evil one snatches it before they get a chance to understand.

The disciples are blessed because they not only see what prophets and the righteous of old longed to see (5:11–12; 10:41), they see with understanding. If one has the right instinct for understanding, it opens the door to further illumination. The explanation of the parables for the disciples (13:18–23, 36–43) comes as a gift in order that they may have more.

This first unit presents one explanation why Israel did not embrace its messiah. While there may be a variety of individual causes, the primary reason falls under the general category: hardness of heart, something that was not a new circumstance in Israel's history.

(2) The second reason for the lack of response to Jesus is charged to the malicious ploys of Satan in the parable of the sower of weeds (13:24-30, 36-43). The evil one not only snatches away the good seed (13:19); he has sown the field with weeds. The appearance of weeds in a field would hardly be cause for surprise; it must have been the large amount of the tares that dumbfounded the servants. The householder explains that it was a deliberate sowing by an enemy that produced so many weeds (13:28) and that he is not to blame. The interpretation of the parable in 13:37-43 provides a glossary that deciphers the details of the parable. The sower of good seed is the son of man (presumably also the sower in the first parable, 13:3). The field, identified as "his field" in 13:24, refers to the world. The good seed is the sons of the kingdom (13:38; see 8:12; also 5:9, 45); the tares, the sons of the evil one. The enemy is the devil (4:8, 13:39; see 13:19), who works under the cover of darkness while people sleep.

In the Matthean context, the parable explains why so many do not respond: those who are sons of the evil one naturally will not respond to the son of man. It also explains the continuing existence of opposition to the sons of the kingdom. The householder, in his wisdom, allows the sons of the evil one, who cause others to stumble and who work lawlessness (13:41), to persist side by side with the sons of the kingdom until the end. The parable does not so much encourage tolerance as assure that the sons of the evil one will be dealt with in due course by God in the judgment (13:30; see 3:12; 1QS 4:25). Angelic reapers will cut down the weeds, and they will be gathered into bundles to be burned in a fiery furnace where there will be "weeping and gnashing of teeth" (13:41-42; see 8:12, 13:50, 22:13, 24:51, 25:30). It also affirms that the vindication of the righteous must await the end (13:30, 43). In the meantime, it is not the servants' responsibility or task to purge the world of evil.

The parable of the drag net (13:47-50) is another grim assurance that all of the wicked who reject the kingdom will be separated out and destroyed. When one uses a drag net, one knows that the catch will be a mixed one. But one must wait until reaching the shore before the final separation. The separation of the righteous from the evil that is already occurring in Jesus' proclamation of the kingdom will become final at "the end of the age."

(3) A third reason for the lack of response is attributable to the

inglorious nature of the advent of the kingdom before the consummation. For the first time in the Gospel, Jesus reflects upon the nature of the kingdom. There have been hints that it is something "hidden" (11:25), and the hidden nature of God's eschatological intervention becomes more explicit in the parables of the mustard seed (13:31–32) and leaven (13:33).

Most readers can recognize that the point of the parable of the mustard seed has to do with contrast: small beginnings, surprising end results. As God transforms a tiny speck of mustard seed into an eight-to-ten-foot-high shrub, so God will transform the ministry of Jesus. As one cannot judge the future outcome of the mustard seed by its present microscopic dimensions and may be fooled by first impressions, so one cannot judge the future outcome of the kingdom from its present manifestation in Jesus.

While this point is obvious, the reader also should not overlook the emotive nature of language and symbols. The statement that the mustard seed becomes a "tree" so that "the birds of heaven come to make nests in its branches" is an exaggeration that causes one to ponder further the meaning of the parable. Mustard is a fast-growing, annual plant that is large but does not grow to tree size. It is hardly a suitable nesting place for birds of (hence many would render the verb "make nests" as "roost" or "light upon"). While its seeds are considered by Pliny to be beneficial for health, he also cautions that it grows like a weed and will quickly get out of control (*Natural History* 19.14.170–71). Mustard is therefore an odd image. When one is talking about the kingdom of God and the birds of heaven lodging under the protection of trees with great branches, the Jewish auditor would have been conditioned by Scripture and tradition to think in terms of pagans finding refuge with a triumphant Israel. The mighty cedar would seem to be a more appropriate image of the kingdom. The great and strong tree is used in the Old Testament as a symbol of the dominion of mighty kingdoms in the world, Egypt (Ezek 31), Babylon (Dan 4:9–12, 22–22), and then the proud hope of Israel, which is promised a future kingdom to rival that of all others (Ezek 17:22–24; see Ps 104:12, 16–17; Sir 24:13; 1QH 6:14–17; 8:4–8). The Lord, Israel hoped and believed, would one day bring the high tree low and make the low tree high (Ezek 17:24).

The lowly mustard plant hardly competes against the majestic cedar of Lebanon; it is almost a caricature of it (R. W. Funk, "The Looking-Glass Tree Is for the Birds," *Int* 27 [1973]: 3–9). When read against this imagery of a mighty kingdom, Jesus' parable hints that the kingdom is breaking into the world in a disarming and, for many, disenchanting form. We do not sing, "A mighty mustard bush is our God." The parable implies that the kingdom "is not a towering empire, but an unpretentious venture of faith" (Funk, 8). It will not come "as a mighty cedar astride the lofty mountain height" reaching to the topmost part of the sky but as a lowly mustard bush. The incongruity between glorious expectations about what the kingdom should be like and its unassuming manifestation before the end is a cause of stumbling for many in Israel.

The parable of the leaven (13:33) confirms the view that Jesus chose startling images to convey the humble and mysterious nature of the kingdom. Leaven was a symbol of corruption in the Hebrew Scriptures (Exod 12:17–20; 23:18; 34:18; Lev 2:11, 6:17; Hos 7:4), in Matthew (16:6, 11), and elsewhere in the New Testament (1 Cor 5:6–13; Gal 5:9; see also *Mishna 'Orla* 2:8–12; *Menahot* 5:1–2; *Genesis Rabba* 34:10; *Babylonian Talmud Berakot* 17a; Plutarch, *Roman Questions* 289F: "Yeast [leaven] is itself also the product of corruption, and produces corruption in the dough with which it is mixed; ... and altogether the process of leavening seems to be one of putrefaction"). What leaven meant to the first-century Jew has been obscured by its translation as "yeast," as if yeast and leaven were one and the same thing. Leaven was produced by keeping back a piece of the previous week's dough, storing it in suitable conditions, and adding juices to promote the process of fermentation. After several days the old dough was sufficiently fermented to be used in a large mass of dough to give it lightness. This homemade rising agent, however, was fraught with health hazards. If it became tainted, it would spread poison to the rest of the dough in baking, and that batch of dough could infect the next batch and so on (see Pliny, *Natural History* 18:26). For this reason, leaven became a symbol for the infectious power of evil.

The parable is not simply a meditation on insignificant beginnings. No reference is made to the small amount of the leaven as in 1 Corinthians 5:6 and Galatians 5:9. To compare the kingdom of heaven to leaven is to invert the common images of sacred and profane (R. W. Funk, "Beyond Criticism in Quest of Literacy: The Parable of the Leaven," *Int* [1971]: 149–70). It would be like saying that the kingdom of heaven is like "rust" or a "virus." It is a rather iconoclastic image, but it accords with Jesus' assertion that the tax collectors and the harlots enter into the kingdom of heaven before the chief priests and elders (21:32) and Matthew's conviction that one must believe that the kingdom has come in Jesus, the son of God who was crucified. The question is not:

"Can something *so contemptibly small* be representative of the work of God?" but "Can something *so contemptible* be representative of the work of God?"

Does the kingdom work like corruption? Does it undermine and pervert? From the perspective of Jesus' opponents, the kingdom he proclaimed, which accepted sinners and toll collectors and ignored issues of purity, was indeed a corrupting force. But the kingdom does not pervert; rather, it inverts. Jesus in his preaching and teaching and ministry to the outcast set in motion a disturbing process that would change Israel and the world. In this sense, the kingdom is like leaven in that it has an inward vitality of its own that gives it the power to affect with its own quality whatever it touches. It has the power to transform the dough into something new, while at the same time maintaining continuity with the old.

Two details in the parable deserve comment. The amount of meal is about thirty-nine liters, enough for a large banquet. It seems to have in view "party baking," which may allude to the festive flavor of the kingdom of heaven (see 9:10–11; 11:19). The leaven is also said to be "hidden" (instead of "kneaded" or "placed"). Like leaven, the presence of the kingdom may be invisible to unbelieving eyes, but its effect soon becomes obvious (see 13:35).

The parables of the finder of hidden treasure and the pearl merchant illustrate how one should respond to the presence of the kingdom (13:44–46). One must be decisive, resourceful, and willing to risk everything. The first parable suggests that encountering the kingdom comes as an unexpected surprise. The treasure trove was not discovered by a cunning treasure hunter. The advice "Seek and ye shall find" (see Prov 2:4) does not apply here. It was discovered by a field hand who was seeking nothing more than a day's wage. The second parable suggests that the kingdom is encountered as an expected surprise. The pearl merchant did not discover the magnificent pearl simply by chance; he had a skilled eye and was looking deliberately for pearls to buy. Both parables make the point that the kingdom comes as a chance of a lifetime. Its presence elicits joy, but decisiveness is required if one is to capitalize on the opportunity. One cannot possess the treasure or the pearl without making a major commitment. The price is high because both finders must sell everything to acquire it. Neither gets something for nothing. They get something for everything. But what formerly had value pales beside the supreme worth of the kingdom (see Phil 3:7–10). The behavior of the finders in selling all contrasts with the thorn-infested soil where the seed is choked by the snares of wealth (13:22) and matches the reaction of the disciples who have left everything to follow Jesus (19:27).

The discourse of parables concludes in 13:51–52 with Jesus' question to the disciples, "Do you understand all these things?" "All these things" refers to the mysteries of the kingdom conveyed in the parables (13:34). The disciples answer in the affirmative because understanding is a key component of discipleship in Matthew (13:23; 15:10; 16:12; 17:13). It involves more than intellectual comprehension, however; it requires submitting to the word in one's heart and producing fruit.

The reference to the discipled scribe recalls the image of the ideal teacher of the law (see Sir 38:24–39:11). But the scribes Jesus refers to are not simply trained in the law, they have heaven-granted understanding and are "instructed in the truths of the kingdom." The disciple-scribes are able to become teachers for the community and, like a householder with an amply stocked storeroom, provide for the needs of the household from both the new and the old.

Two things can be gleaned from this confirmation of the disciples. First, the order, new and old, is the reverse of what is expected. "The new is not added to old; the old has as its central focus the new, which has thereby become new" (D. A. Carson, "The Jewish Leaders in Matthew's Gospel: A Reappraisal," *JETS* 25 [1982]: 171; see 9:34). The tradition of Israel and its Scripture are not rejected, but they must be reread in light of the new, eschatological situation brought to pass by Christ's death and resurrection. Second, Jesus has said that the Pharisees can draw only from an evil storeroom (12:35). They may sit on the seat of Moses (23:2), but they are plantings that will be uprooted by God (15:13, see 13:29) who offer only an infectious leaven of lies (16:6). The disciples-scribes are being groomed to take their place as the true teachers (28:19), and the next section shows Jesus preparing his disciples for their role as leaders of his church.

POWER AND MERCY
FOR GOD'S PEOPLE

14:1-36

Why does Jesus continue his ministry to Israel in the face of blindness and rejection? The context of the quotations from the Old Testament cited in chapter 13, Isaiah 6:9-10 (13:14-15) and Psalm 78:2 (13:35), may offer some explanation. In Isaiah 6, the prophet agrees to be God's spokesman to the people, but God warns him that Judah is rebellious and that they will not obey the word. When the prophet asks, "How long?" the answer comes, until the land is utterly desolate, until the Lord sends everyone far away. But amid the desolation a holy seed will persist (Isa 6:13). The covenant remains in force. The promise of Immanuel (Isa 7:14) and of a light for those walking in darkness will follow. Psalm 78 summarizes the history of Israel from the Exodus to David and emphasizes the importance of hearing and obeying (Ps 78:1, 7); but it also refers to God's judgment on the stubborn and rebellious generation whose heart was not steadfast (Ps 78:8, 37), who did not keep the covenant (Ps 78:10, 37), who forgot the miracles (Ps 78:11-16), and who did not believe in God's wonders (Ps 78:32). They did not have faith in God or trust God's saving power (Ps 78:22). Yet God rained down manna to eat so that they ate and were filled (Ps 78:23-30). God led them to safety so that they were not afraid, while the sea overwhelmed their enemies (Ps 78:53). God chose his servant David to tend and guide them (Ps 78:70-72). These Scriptures affirm the basic principle that even when Israel disobeys, God does not discard it. God is ever faithful and compassionate, and Jesus follows the same pattern in his ministry to Israel. Despite obduracy among the people, little faith among the disciples, and peril from the Jewish leaders, Jesus has come to save. This next section demonstrates that he is their provider and divine deliverer who has power to overcome sickness, hunger, and the storms of the waters (the demonic).

It is composed of two parts: (1) The report of the death of the great-

153

est of the prophets (14:1–12) and (2) further demonstration of Jesus as both divine provider and savior (14:13–36). The summaries of Jesus' healing the crowds in 14:13–15 and 14:34–36 enclose the report of the miracles of the feeding of five thousand and the walking on the sea, which demonstrate Jesus to be both divine provider and savior.

(1) In the first part (14:1–12) Antipas, tetrarch of Galilee (4 B.C.E. to 39 C.E.), is the third Herod to make a threatening appearance in the story. Like his father and brother before him (2:1–12, 16–18, 22), he is intent on murder (14:5). Again, Jesus must retreat beyond the long arm of an unnerved Herod. This account shows the continuing confusion about Jesus' true identity. Herod is just as perplexed as the hometown folk in Nazareth about the source of Jesus' mighty works (13:54, 56; 14:2). He also draws the wrong conclusions. His best guess is that Jesus is John the Baptist raised from the dead (14:2). This surmise may have elevated his lingering fear of political unrest that, according to Josephus (*Antiquities* 18:2 §117–19), he believed John had fomented against him. The flashback relating Herod's execution of John explains the risk for Jesus to remain in the tetrarch's domain (14:3–12).

The story recalls the traditional run-in between king and prophet alluded to in 11:7–10 (see Ahab, Jezebel, and Elijah) and Jesus' saying about the "violent ones" who "do violence" to the kingdom (11:12). As Nazareth provides an example of how a prophet is not received by his own people (13:57), Herod provides an example of how Israel's leaders treat its prophets (14:5; see 23:29–31). What happens to John also foreshadows what will happen to Jesus. His handing over (4:12) portends that Jesus will be handed over as well (27:2, 18, 26). John was "seized" and "bound" (14:3), and Jesus will be "seized" (26:4, 48, 50, 55, 57; see 21:46) and "bound" (27:2). Herod's fear of the people who regarded John as a prophet (14:5; see 21:26) frustrated his desire to kill John but did not ultimately prevent him from doing so. The Jewish leaders' fear of the people who also regarded Jesus as a prophet restrained them from seizing Jesus (21:46) but will not ultimately keep them from succeeding in doing away with him (26:3–5). Herod's reluctance to execute John (14:9) will be paralleled by Pilate's reluctance to execute Jesus (27:1–26). Both, however, accede to external pressure: Herod, to honor his hasty oath before guests (14:7, 9); Pilate, to honor his ill-considered proposal to release Jesus or Barabbas (27:15–17). The wives of both men figure behind the scenes: Herodias as the successful instigator of the death of John (14:3, 8, 11); Pilate's wife as the unsuccessful advocate for Jesus (27:19). The violent and shameful death of

John foreshadows the violent and shameful death of Jesus (see 17:12). John was buried by his disciples (14:12), and Jesus will be buried by a disciple (27:57-61). The slaying of John, the greatest of the prophets (11:11), therefore prepares the reader for Jesus' death.

(2) The second part (14:13-36) shows Jesus, who did not do many miracles in Nazareth because of lack of faith (13:58), performing miracles for the crowds because of their faith. For Matthew, faith is confidence in Jesus' power. The crowds' faith in Jesus is implied by the fact that they do the same things that others, inspired by faith, have done earlier in the narrative. They bring to him all those who were sick like the men who brought the paralytic to Jesus (9:2). They believe that they can be healed by touching the fringe of Jesus' garment, like the women with the hemorrhage who touched Jesus' garment (9:20-21). Their faith in Jesus' power contrasts with the little faith of the disciples, who appear to lack that same confidence (14:17, 31).

The fast-approaching evening prompts the disciples to implore Jesus to send the crowds off into the villages to secure something to eat for themselves. Jesus' command, "You give to them something to eat" (14:16), is met with a helpless response that they have only limited resources, five loaves and two fishes (14:17). They doubt Jesus' divine power in their midst to supply whatever is needed to feed the crowd as Moses doubted God's power in the wilderness (Num 11:21-22). They will slowly begin to learn of Jesus' capacity to supply in abundance and of their task to feed the people (24:45, to give the household their food at the proper time).

The miracle of the loaves and fishes also lends itself to several other impressions. (a) It recalls the exodus theme (as the first redeemer, so the last; *Qoheleth Rabba* 1:9), where Israel is fed in the wilderness (Exod 16; Pss 78:18-30; 81:17; 105:40). (b) The abundance may signify the presence of the messianic age and salvation: "And it shall come to pass at the self-same time that the treasury of manna shall again descend from on high, and they will eat of it in those years, because these are they who have come to the consummation of time" (*2 [Syriac] Apocalypse of Baruch* 29:8). (c) The parallels with the narrative of the Lord's supper (26:20, 26) may suggest that Jesus is the source of spiritual nourishment. The feeding of five thousand with the excess collected in twelve baskets (distinctively Jewish baskets? see Juvenal *Satires* 3.14; 6.542) indicates the abundant supply for all Israel. The Eucharist, however, will offer bread for all humankind. (d) The story also bears witness once again to Jesus' compassion for the needy: they do not have to be sent away hungry. Jesus has compassion for their needs as God does (Ps 22:26, "the afflicted shall eat and be satisfied"; Ezek 34:23, "And I will set up my servant David, and he shall feed them: he shall feed them and be their shepherd"; see also 1 Kgs 17:8–16; 2 Kgs 4:1–7, 4:42–44).

After the miracle of the feeding, Jesus compels his disciples to get into the boat and go before him to the other side while he dismisses the crowd (14:22). The narrator offers no clue as to why Jesus does this, but their departure in the boat means that they will experience a divine manifestation apart from the crowds. When Jesus disperses the crowds, he ascends a mountain to pray privately (14:23).

The disciples have been able to get only several stadia (185 meters) from the shore because the boat is "being tormented by the waves" (14:24). They are in the middle of the lake in the deep waters, which have always represented for Israel the threatening powers (Pss 18:7; 32:6; 69:2; 1QH 3:6, 13–18), with the wind against them. It is the darkest hour of the night during the fourth and last watch (3:00–6:00 A.M.), but it is also the time of God's help (see Exod 14:24, Ps 46:5, cited by Luz, *Matthäus (Mt 8–17),* 2:406, n. 22). Jesus has already calmed a storm from the boat (8:22–27); now he comes to his disciples in the midst of a storm, walking upon the wind-driven sea. The disciples' vision is dim, however; and they cry out in fear, thinking it to be a phantom.

One might conclude that they are more frightened by Jesus' presence than his absence, but fear is the normal reaction to a theophany (17:6, 7; 27:54; 28:4, 5, 8, 10). Trampling the waves and walking in the recesses of the deep is something that God and God alone does in the Old Testament (see Job 9:8; 38:16; Ps 77:19; Isa 43:16; Hab 3:15; Sir 24:5–6). He does not come to them "on a calm, sunny day"; his striding across the heaving sea at the peak of its strength is a token of his conquest over the powers of chaos (Heil, *Jesus Walking on the Sea,* 43). Jesus' reassuring words, "Take heart, I am; have no fear," suggest the divine name in Exodus 3:14 (see Deut 32:39; Isa 41:4; 43:1–13 particularly verse 2a, "When you pass through the waters, I will be with you, and though the rivers, they shall not overwhelm you," and verses 10–11 "so that you may know and believe me and understand that I am he . . . I, I am the Lord, and besides me there is no savior"; 45:18; 51:12). Matthew presents Jesus coming to the boat as the divine savior, God with us (Matt 1:23; on the assimilation of Jesus to God in the Gospel traditions, see B. Blackburn, *Theios Anēr and the Markan Miracle Traditions,* WUNT 2/40 [Tübingen: J. C. B. Mohr (Paul Siebeck), 1991], 133–82).

Only Matthew records Peter's venture on the waters (14:28-32). It begins with his request, "Lord, if it is you, command me to come to you on the waters" (14:28). Jesus says, "Come." Peter takes a few steps, takes a look at the wind, and begins to sink (the same word for "drown" in 18:6) like a rock. Peter then cries out, "Lord save me" (not "if it is you, save me"); and Jesus immediately stretches out his hand and catches him. The one who asks to be able to go out on the waters must now be saved from them and is berated as of "little faith:" "Why did you doubt?"

This incident is the first of several where Peter takes center stage as the foremost disciple. How is the reader to evaluate his attempt to walk on water, positively or negatively? On the positive side one can argue that (a) Peter wants to go to Jesus and will not go until Jesus issues a command and obeys when Jesus says, "Come." H. J. Held claims that the whole scene "presents a disciple on the way of discipleship" ("Matthew as Interpreter of the Miracle Stories," 206). Many understand Peter's request to be a believing response to the appearance of his Lord:

> Peter's response shows that he recognizes the significance of Jesus walking on the sea as an act of dominance over the wind and the waves. Jesus has crossed the sea through wind and waves and now Peter wants to do the same. He manifests the faith that Jesus can save him by allowing him to likewise cross the sea on foot even before the wind has ceased. (Heil, *Jesus Walking on the Sea,* 60)

(b) Peter had enough faith to venture out of the boat and try the impossible. His insufficient faith is true of all the disciples during Jesus' ministry. They seem caught between faith and doubt (28:17). (c) With what faith he has, he cries to Jesus, his Lord, to save him when he starts to drown (see Pss 18:5, 7, 13; 69:1-3; 107:28-29; 144:7). This incident reveals Jesus' readiness to help the faltering disciple.

On the negative side, Peter's desire to leave the boat in distress and share in the unique divine power of Jesus may be understandable, but is it praiseworthy? (a) Peter's desire to walk on water may be due to the same impulsive bravado that will lead him to even greater failure later in the story when he denies his Lord (26:35). (b) To want to walk on water is to want to do what only God can do and is presumptuous. The disciples share Jesus' divine power to extend God's merciful healing to others (10:8), not to do the spectacular. No disciple is to be honored as a semi-divine figure (see Acts 28:1-6). (c) Jesus is coming to save the boat; Peter wants to make a spectacular exit from the boat. If one can walk on water one can abandon the boat and the people in it. Jesus comes to get in the boat with them. If they stay in the boat through the storms, Jesus will not fail to save them and help them reach the other side. (d) Jesus rebukes Peter for doubt. Readers may too quickly assume that Peter doubted when he became frightened by the gale-force wind; but the text does not say that he doubted, rather, that "he became afraid" (14:30). He first expressed his doubt when he asked the question, "Lord, if it is you . . . " (compare other "if you are" questions in Matthew, 4:3, 6; 26:63; 27:40). He leaves the boat in a context of hesitation about whether it is really Jesus. (e) If this is a story about discipleship, what is the lesson? Are disciples supposed to learn to walk on water in the midst of howling storms without doubt? If one considers the boat to be a symbol of the church, as interpreters have done from the beginning, it seems that disciples belong in the boat rather than trying to walk on water to prove to themselves and to others who Jesus is.

Matthew's interest in christology, discipleship, Peter, and ecclesiology are all blended together in this story. Jesus, however, is the primary focus of the story. He comes to the distressed disciples as God and calms their fears. He saves Peter from drowning. When he enters the boat, the wind that was tossing it about stops, and those in the boat confess that Jesus is the son of God. That confession answers the question raised in 8:27 when Jesus calmed an earlier storm: "Who is this that even the winds and the sea obey him?" It also provides an answer to the doubts raised by others, the questions of John the Baptist (11:2-6), the crowds (12:23), and the synagogue of Nazareth (13:55).

The story also places emphasis on the boat (compare *Testament of Naphtali* 6:1-10). It is the *boat*, not the rowers, that is tormented by the waves (14:24) – a fitting description of the persecution of the church. When Jesus and Peter entered the *boat*, the wind ceased (14:32). *Those in the boat* worshiped him saying, "Truly you are the son of God" (14:33). Jesus does not promise to deliver it from the storm but through the storm. The disciple's task is therefore to stay in the boat worshiping and confessing, not attempting the sensational.

BREAD FOR ALL

15:1–16:12

The structure of this section centers on the theme of food and bread, which ties the units together. It begins with (1) a controversy with the Pharisees over eating bread with unwashed hands and the purity of food (15:1–20), bracketed by the phrase "to eat with unwashed hands" (15:2, 20). This unit contains three segments: (a) 15:1–9, the condemnation of the tradition of the Pharisees; (b) 15:10–11, the calling of the crowds to hear and understand; and (c) 15:12–20, the explanation of true purity to the disciples. (2) The following incident with the Canaanite woman (15:21–28) raises the question of the possibility of healing (bread crumbs) for gentiles. (3) The feeding of the four thousand (15:29–39) reveals the abundance still available for Israel. (4) The warning about the leaven of the Sadducees and Pharisees (16:1–12) returns to the condemnation of the Pharisees' tradition.

(1) Pharisees and scribes return to the story in 15:1–20. As if on religious patrol from Jerusalem they question why Jesus' disciples transgress the traditions of the elders by eating bread with unwashed hands (15:2). Their challenge assumes that the disciples should obey the tradition of the elders and that unclean hands defile food. The tradition about washing hands stems from Leviticus 15:11 (uncleanness is not transmitted by one with a discharge if he has rinsed his hands with water) and Exodus 30:17–21 (the priests are instructed to wash their hands and feet before entering the tent of meeting), but handwashing before eating was not biblically mandated. Jesus' rebuttal is three pronged. He first attacks them for transgressing the commandment of God "for the sake of your tradition," then gives an extreme instance of how they negate the word of God, and concludes with the accusation that they are hypocrites and a quotation from Isaiah that condemns them as those who perform lip service but not heart service and who teach human precepts as doctrine.

The validity of the law is not at issue but only the Pharisees' interpretation of the law. The extreme example of a son who spitefully or

159

selfishly vows that his property is an offering dedicated to the temple while his parents have no benefit from it is used to reveal how the tradition of the elders subverts God's will. Two divine commands, the command to honor parents, which included providing them with material necessities (Exod 20:12; Deut 5:16; Prov 28:24; see *Babylonian Talmud Qiddušin* 31b), and the command to honor vows (Deut 24:21–23), clash head on. Later Rabbis discussed and developed grounds for the release of vows, but Matthew's narrative assumes that the Pharisees who encountered Jesus required that the vow be kept regardless of the consequences for the parents.

One example from the *Mishna* shows how intricate casuistry and legal fictions developed around vows:

> If a man was forbidden by a vow to have any benefit from his fellow, and he had naught to eat, his fellow may give [the food] to another as a gift, and the first is permitted to use it. It once happened that a man at Beth Horon, whose father was forbidden by a vow to have any benefit from him, was giving his son in marriage, and he said to his fellow, "The courtyard and the banquet are given to thee as a gift, but they are thine only that my father may come and eat with us at the banquet." His fellow said, "If they are mine, they are dedicated to Heaven." The other answered, "I did not give thee what is mine that thou shouldst dedicate it to Heaven." His fellow said, "Thou didst give me what is thine only that thou and thy father might eat and drink and be reconciled one with the other, and that the sin should rest on his head!" When the case came before the Sages, they said: Any gift which, if a man would dedicate it, is not accounted dedicated, is not a [valid] gift. (*Mishna Nedarim* 5:6)

God's purpose expressed in the love command makes any vow that wrongs parents automatically invalid. The Pharisees are consistently portrayed as those who are concerned more with legal niceties than with love, and their confirmation of such a merciless vow depicts their tradition as routinely contravening the very law of God. Matthew's "God said, Honor your father and mother" in 15:4 (instead of "Moses said . . . ," Mark 7:10) underscores this opposition.

The crowds are distinct from the Pharisees, and Jesus calls them away from them. He continues to speak to the crowds in enigmatic language, however. He gives them a general principle about what defiles a person: "It is not what enters a person's mouth that defiles one, but what comes out of the mouth that defiles one" (see 12:34, "for out of the abundance of the heart, the mouth speaks"). The crowds are left to themselves to figure out the implications of this statement. As in chapter 13, the disciples get a special explanation both about the Pharisees and the meaning of purity.

They inform Jesus that the Pharisees (not the Jews) took umbrage over this saying directed to the crowds. Jesus responds with two negative verdicts about the Pharisees. (a) They are plants not planted by the heavenly Father that will be rooted up (15:13). This statement looks back to the parable of the tares. The tares sown by the evil one will also be rooted up (13:29). Just as the master tells his servants to "leave" the tares for the harvest (13:30), Jesus tells his disciples to "leave" the Pharisees (15:14). This connection to the imagery of the parable essentially writes the Pharisees off as sons of the evil one as well as repudiating them as a part of the true Israel. Israel is God's planting:

> All Israelites have a share in the world to come for it is written [Isa 60:21], *Thy people also shall be all righteous, they shall inherit the land forever, the branch of my planting, the work of my hands, that I may be glorified. (Mishna Sanhedrin* 10:1)

> ³The Lord's devout shall live by it [the law] forever; the Lord's paradise, the tree of life, are his devout ones. ⁴Their planting is firmly rooted forever, they shall not be uprooted as long as the heavens shall last. ⁵For Israel is the portion and inheritance of God. (*Psalm of Solomon* 14:3-5)

Jesus' saying implies that nothing can be done about the alien plantings, the Pharisees, except to leave them to the judgment of God.

(b) They are blind guides who cannot interpret the law correctly (see 23:16, 17, 19, 24, 26), which underscores the urgency of "leaving them." They will lead those who follow them into a pit, which may refer simply to misfortune (Ps 7:15; Prov 22:14; 26:27; Qoh 10:8; Isa 24:18; Jer 48:44; Sir 27:26; *Testament of Reuben* 2:9) or worse, to the Pit of Sheol (Job 33:18; Pss 16:10; 30:9; Isa 38:18).

Peter is emerging as the spokesman for the disciples (as the later interpreter of church tradition), and his request for clarification of the parable to the crowds (see 13:36) allows Jesus to make a statement about the purity that matters to God. Food impurity is implicitly dismissed (see Rom 14:14) in the first argument that all food entering the mouth passes through the digestive system and ends up in the latrine, the most obvious form of impurity. Even without the statement in Mark 7:19b ("cleansing all foods"), the argument in Matthew is just as radical in dismissing the external causes of impurity. It is the logical consequence of Jesus' indifference to contact with a leper, a menstruant, and a corpse (see Lev 5:3). Jesus goes far beyond the incompetent student who is condemned by later Rabbis for breaking down the fences erected by the Sages by pronouncing the clean unclean and unclean clean (*Sipre Deuteronomy* §48) and strikes at the heart of Pharisaism and Judaism (Meier, *Matthew,* 169-70). Food that enters the mouth is part of a purely transitory process that hardly compares with what really matters: the sins that come from a person's innermost being.

The second argument asserts that the locus of purity should be the person's heart (see 5:8). Holiness does not dwell in the stomach (contrast *Babylonian Talmud Ta'anit* 11a-b). What does not reach the heart cannot defile a person; what is in the heart and what comes from it does. "Evil thoughts" heads the list followed by six actions that stem from evil thoughts (see 5:21-22, 27-28): murders, adulteries, sexual sins, thefts, false witnesses, slanders (see Exod 20:13-17; Deut 5:17-21). The opponents of Jesus are guilty of nearly all these things in Matthew's story: evil thoughts (9:4); murder (12:7; 21:35-39; 22:6; 23:29-36; 26:27); adultery (12:38; 16:4, "an evil and adulterous generation"); false witness (26:60-61); and slander (9:34; 11:18-19; 12:24; 26:60-61, 64-65; 28:13).

The conclusion that eating with unwashed hands does not defile (15:20) would seem to leave the impression that Jesus has only offered a legal decision on clean/unclean hands, but his statements about something so crucial to Pharisaic Judaism are more far reaching. The Pharisees are accused of annulling God's will in their tradition, so Jesus declares their tradition null and void. What matters to God is not ritual observance and ethical behavior, but ethical behavior alone. God desires mercy, not food laws (see Isa 1:16-17). Like the command to honor the sabbath, the dietary laws were also thought to be a result of God's consecration of Israel (Deut 14:1-21). As God separated Israel from the nations, so Israel, as a holy nation, imitates God by separating clean from unclean foods (Lev 20:35-36; see J. D. Levenson, "The Jerusalem Temple in Devotional and Visionary Experience," *Jewish Spirituality: From the Bible through the Middle Ages,* ed. A. Green (New York: Crossroad: 1986], 36-37). But the gospel of the kingdom will reveal that God intends for God's people to make disciples of the nations as a light to the world and not to segregate themselves from others. The dismissal of Pharisaic dietary laws is the prelude to the disciples' mission to all the nations.

(2) Jesus again withdraws in the face of controversy (15:21-28),

this time to the regions of Tyre and Sidon, previously mentioned in 11:21–22 as notoriously godless cities that would have responded to his mighty works with repentance in sackcloth and ashes. But when a woman comes to him from that region, Jesus only reluctantly responds to her cries for help.

The description of the woman as a Canaanite conjures up the image of the pagan enemies of God's people who were to be exterminated by Israel (Gen 9:24–27; Josh 7:9; Judg 1:1, 31–33). Her cry, "Have mercy on me, Lord, son of David!" is the same as that of the blind men in Galilee (9:27; see 20:31–32) and is aroused by the plight of her daughter who is described as "terribly demonized." Jesus' record of compassion and power (4:24; 8:16, 28–32; 9:32–33; 12:22) leads one to expect him to cast out the demon post haste. His gruff reaction is therefore surprising and, to the modern gentile reader, disturbing.

The account contains four verbal appeals to Jesus. The mother's first appeal is met only with stony silence (15:22–23a). The second is made by the disciples who are annoyed by the woman who cries after them. It is possible that they want Jesus to dismiss her without granting her request (see 14:15). But his response, "I have been sent only to the lost sheep of the house of Israel" (15:24; see 10:6), only makes sense if it is a negative reply to their wish to get rid of her by granting her request. In the third appeal, the mother's fervor intensifies: she comes to him, worships him (see 8:2; 9:18; 14:33; 20:20; 28:9, 17), and cries, "Lord, help me" (compare Peter's cry, "Lord, save me" in 14:30). Jesus spurns this plea with a sharp insult: "It is not good to take the children's bread and toss it to the dogs" (15:26). Mark's palliative statement, "Let the children be satisfied [fed] first" (7:27), holds out some ray of hope for gentiles if they are but patient and wait their turn. It is absent from Matthew. Matthew's version does not hint that the gentiles' opportunity is coming (15:25–26).

J. P. Meier ("Matthew 15:21–28," *Int* 40 [1986]: 397–98) points to the law of threes in interpreting this story. The reader would normally expect the climax to occur in the third scene (as it does, for example, in the parable of the talents). Consequently, the reader assumes that the mother's attempt to obtain help from Jesus has fizzled. Three strikes and you are out. But the incident is not terminated. In a fourth appeal the mother accepts Jesus' assessment, "Yes, Lord," but with quick wit rejoins that "even the dogs eat the crumbs that fall from the table of their masters" (15:27). The mother's logic is clear: the scraps are not thrown down to the dogs but fall from the table in the course of the meal and therefore do not take food away from the children. Jesus then relents, "O woman, great is your faith, let it be done for you as wished" (15:28; see 8:13).

Neither the miracle nor its effect is developed; the emphasis falls on the mother's faith (*not* her cleverness that traps Jesus in his own words). (a) She is an exemplar of faith (15:28). Faith is unshakable confidence in Jesus, and her faith in this Jewish messiah is tenacious. It is like that of the centurion (8:10), and it contrasts with the total lack of faith exhibited by the synagogue of Nazareth (13:53–58) and the little faith of Peter (14:31) and the disciples (16:8). (b) She also is one who is poor in spirit. Pride goes out the window when one is truly desperate. She acknowledges the difference between Jew and Greek, but she acts on her conviction that the barriers that separate her, a gentile, from Israel are not impregnable. (c) Her will is also emphasized (contrast 8:13; 9:29). She ardently wants only healing for her daughter, which contrasts with what others want or do not want in the Gospel. The scribes and Pharisees "want" to see a sign (12:38). Herod "wants" John the Baptist dead (14:5, 17:12). James and John "want" premier positions in the kingdom (20:21); Judas "wants" money (26:15); the crowd "wants" Barabbas (27:15,17, 21). The servant does not "want" to show mercy to his fellow servant (18:3); and the rich young man does not "want" to be perfect because he will not heed Jesus' admonition (19:21). The son does not "want" to go into the vineyard (21:29); the invited guests do not "want" to attend the marriage feast (22:3); and Jerusalem does not "want" to be gathered (23:37).

Matthew was apparently oblivious to the problems in the story, which so jar modern sensitivities. Jesus' brusque treatment of this Canaanite mother has and continues to trouble. Why does he give a frantic mother the cold shoulder when she pleads for her demonized daughter? Why does he speak about throwing bread to dogs as if a sick child could be compared to a dog? In the analogy, the children equal the Jews, the dogs equal the gentiles, and bread equals rescue and life. He seems to say that the only legitimate diners are members of the people of Israel. Others, no matter how deserving or needy, can expect nothing from him.

"Dogs" was a term of ultimate scorn for gentiles: "As the sacred food was intended for men, but not for the dogs, the Torah was intended to be given to the Chosen People, but not to the gentiles" (*Babylonian Talmud Ḥagiga* 13a; see *'Aboda Zara* 54b; *Pirke Rabbi Eliezer* 29; *Joseph and Aseneth* 10:13). Does Jesus share this same bigotry against gentiles? The text does not allow us to appeal to a gentle tone of voice or a twinkle in the eye to explain it away. One also cannot argue that the use of the diminutive form of "dogs" to refer to pet house dogs takes the sting out of what he says. A dog is a dog whether it is a pampered household pet or a street cur. There is no indication that Jesus was struggling over the scope of his mission and mulling things over in his mind as he speaks to the woman, or that he withheld his help to test her faith or to evoke a more strenuous effort of faith. If this were a test of faith, what would have happened if she failed the test? What if she had weak faith like the father of the epileptic (Mark 9:24)? It also does not help to trace this story back to the bias of the earlier Jewish Christian church that was resisting the mission to the gentiles. The story reflects the real distance between the Jew and the heathen, and perhaps a socio-psychological explanation offers the best explanation for understanding Jesus' response (G. Theissen, "Lokal — und Sozialkolorit in der Geschichte von der syrophönikischen Frau (Mk 7.24–30)" *ZNW* 75 [1984], 202–25). Rich Tyre was perceived as posing a threat against Galilee as a permanent aggrandizer. Economically, Tyre took bread away from Galilee. Jesus may have shared the prejudice of the underprivileged against the privileged. What he might be saying is: "Let the poor people in the hinterland be satisfied first for once. It is not good to take the bread of the poor people and throw it to the rich heathens in the city" (Theissen, 217).

The scandal remains, but possibly our modern sensitivities are mistaken. We assume that Jesus is obligated to respond to every request and to heal everyone. We tend to dejudaize Jesus and are offended by the particularity of God's election. During the ministry of Jesus, the boundary between Jews and gentiles is very real. On the one hand, this incident affirms the priority of Israel as children (Deut 32:6; Isa 1:2; Jer 31:9; Hos 11:1; *Jubilees* 1:24, 28; *Mishna 'Abot.* 3:15). Our prejudice is that gentiles are just as important as Israel, if not more so, because we know that many in Israel will reject the messiah while gentiles will respond in greater numbers. In Matthew's day, the church was becoming predominantly gentile; and this incident makes it clear that they are not included because Israel was rejected capriciously. Jesus restates the limitation of his mission to Israel, and a gentile expresses the faith of Israel by recognizing Jesus as the son of David and acknowledging the priority of Israel as the children. The miracles of the loaves and fishes preceding and following this incident make it clear that divine provision for Israel can be extended to gentiles and that Israel will still have no lack. The children are filled and there are abundant leftovers.

On the other hand, this story brings to the fore the issue of faith and foreshadows the response of the gentiles to the gospel. Even though Jesus has been sent only to Israel, membership in Israel does not guarantee salvation. The key will be faith, and "faith is not a national privilege" (Sand, *Matthäus,* 315). This woman's faith has not removed the barrier; it has only overcome it (Donaldson, *Jesus on the Mountain,* 133). The barrier will be removed only after the death and resurrection of Jesus when he commands his disciples to go to all the nations (28:16–20).

(3) The departure to the sea of Galilee, ascending the mountain, and healing and feeding the crowds in 15:29–39 recapitulates much of what has already happened between Jesus and the crowds. Jesus sitting on the mountain recalls 5:1. The healing of the lame, blind, maimed, deaf, and many others recalls 11:5 (Isa 35:5–6; and other healing summaries, 4:23–24, 8:17; 9:35; 12:15, 22; 14:14; see 19:2; 21:14). The crowds marveling at what they see (but not hearing) recalls 9:33, and their glorifying the God of Israel recalls 9:8 and the emphasis on the election of Israel emphasized in 10:6, 23; 15:24, 31 (see 19:28). This second miraculous feeding of the crowds takes place on a mountain where the gathered sheep of Israel are to be fed (Jer 31:10–14; Ezek 34:14, 26–27).

(4) In the last unit (16:1–12), the Pharisees join forces with a new, if perhaps improbable (see Acts 23:7–8), ally in their clash with Jesus. The Sadducees, who are never mentioned outside of Judea elsewhere in the Gospels and Acts, collude with the Pharisees in asking Jesus for an authenticating sign from heaven (=from God). One need not infer from this unusual partnership that Matthew is unaware of the fundamental differences between the two camps. His interest is only in their shared blindness. They have in common a hostile attitude toward Jesus, which is the feature of their teaching that is so deadly (16:6, 11).

This second request for some heavenly validation of Jesus' ministry (see 12:38–39) is described as an attempt to put him to the test. These sworn enemies take up where Satan left off (4:3). The Pharisees have already twisted the evidence of Jesus' miracles to construe them as the workings of the prince of demons. They are as unable to interpret the signs of the times as they are unable to speak good – because they are evil (12:34). They consequently do not glorify God as the crowd does (15:31) when they witness the works of the Christ (11:2, 5). Labeling the Pharisees as "a wicked and adulterous generation" links them to the mutinous wilderness generation that tested God (Exod 17:2, 7; Ps 78:41, 56).

The earlier reference to the sign of Jonah (12:38–39) is repeated here. If these Jewish teachers repented as the Ninevites did at the preaching of Jonah (12:41; see 3:8), perhaps they might see some sign of what they claim to be seeking. Otherwise, God does not give command performances; and Jesus abandons these who are already wedded to their own evil opinions about him.

This testing incident spurs Jesus to warn his disciples about the corrupting effect of the teaching of his theological rivals. Unfortunately, the disciples are too worried about an empty bread basket to be able to comprehend. The warning to beware of the leaven of the Pharisees and Sadducees frames the paragraph (16:6, 11). The saying validates the wedge that already divides the disciples (the church) from these false interpreters of Judaism. There can be no ties with them. The disciples' chatter about bread, however, reveals that their minds are focused only on material needs and that the significance of the miracles of the loaves and fishes has not yet sunk in. It is described as another manifestation of their little faith due to bad memories and a lack of understanding. One must have complete trust in Jesus to provide for material needs (6:30); otherwise, one may be reluctant to sever relationships with those who hold the reins of economic prosperity in society.

BUILDING THE CHURCH
ON BEDROCK

16:13-20

The large division (4:17–16:20) that began with the summoning of "Simon, who is called Peter" (4:18), now ends with his confession that Jesus is the messiah, the son of the living God, and a word-play on his nickname. Jesus intended to gather the lost sheep of the house of Israel into a new messianic community — "my church." The phrase "my church" (*ekklēsia*) is significant because it implies that what God was to the *ekklēsia,* Israel, in the Old Covenant, Jesus is to the *ekklēsia,* Christians, in the New Covenant. This section has to do with the church: (a) its foundation on bedrock; (b) its potency as a bulwark against the powers of the abyss; and (c) Peter's authority for the church.

Peter's confession takes place in a predominantly non-Jewish area as far away from Jerusalem as one could possibly get and still be in Israel. It follows Jesus' stock-taking of his ministry: "Who do people say the son of man is?" The answers of the run of the general public suppose Jesus to be some kind of recycled prophet (see 21:11). When he asks the disciples, "Who do you [plural] say that I am?" Simon Peter articulates their earlier confession, "You are the Christ the son of the living God" (16:16; see 14:33). Three major christological titles in the Gospel are brought together: son of man, messiah, and son of God. The vague "son of man" has been used before by Jesus (8:20; 9:26; 10:23; 11:19; 12:3, 32, 40; 13:37, 41), and this confession clarifies for the first time precisely who he is. He is the Christ, the son of the living God.

While Peter speaks for all the disciples, he is singled out as blessed for having received special revelation from heaven (see 4 Ezra 10:57; *Joseph and Aseneth* 16:14). His answer is not someone's best guess. Jesus declares that his identity has been revealed to Peter by the heavenly Father, and the confession tallies with the voice from heaven in 3:17 and from the bright cloud in 17:5. The Pharisees and the Sadducees demanded a sign from heaven and will receive nothing

(16:1-4); Peter demanded nothing and receives a revelation from heaven. What is hidden from the wise and understanding is revealed to babes (11:25-27).

Jesus' celebrated response to this confession consists of three promises: (a) that the church will be built upon "this rock"; (b) that it will prevail against the gates of Hades; and (c) that the keys of the kingdom of heaven and the authority to bind and loose will be given to Peter.

(a) The first promise, "And I say to you that you are Peter [*Petros*] and upon this rock [*petra*] I will build my church," occurs only in Matthew, and its meaning has long been disputed. Are Jesus and Peter merely exchanging plaudits? Does Jesus bestow on Simon the new nickname Peter at this occasion? I would give a negative answer to both of these questions. If Jesus were renaming Peter, one might expect it to read: "You shall be called Peter" (compare Gen 17:5, 15; 32:28; *Joseph and Aseneth* 15:7). Simon already has been identified as Peter (4:18; 10:2; 14:28-29; 15:15, although only by the narrator). It is possible that he was given the Aramaic nickname Cephas (translated into Greek as *Petros*) shortly after following Jesus (see John 1:42; Luke 6:14), since the name Simon was so popular that some other identifying feature was needed to distinguish one Simon from all the others (for example, Simon the Cananaean, 10:4; Simon the leper, 26:6; Simon from Cyrene, 27:32; Simon Iscariot, John 6:71; Simon Magus, Acts 8:23; and Simon the tanner, Acts 9:43). The nickname Cephas was also not unknown before this time.

The vital question is, how does the statement "You are Peter [*Petros*]," relate to the declaration "upon this rock [*petra*] I will build my church"? Many readers interpret the rock to be Peter himself. A supposed Aramaic original is assumed to have used the same word for Cephas and rock: "You are *kepha'*, and upon this *kepha'* I will build my church." Some draw an analogy between Peter and Abraham, who is "the rock" from which Israel is hewn (Isa 51:1-2). In the Dead Sea Scrolls, the Teacher of Righteousness is also regarded as the bastion of the community:

> [7]Thou hast made me strong before the battles of ungodliness, and in the midst of all the calamities which they have brought on me. Thou hast not permitted me cravenly to desert Thy Covenant. [8]But thou hast set me up as a stout tower, as a steep rampart, and hast established [9]my fabric upon rock and everlasting foundations serve me for my ground and all my walls are a tried rampart which nothing can shake. (1QH 7:7-9)

The rest of the New Testament reveals Peter's eminence in both the Jewish Christian (Acts 2–12; 15:6–11) and gentile Christian sectors of the early church (the Galatians and the Corinthians apparently both know and esteem him). Peter is a prominent figure in all four Gospels. He is the first called (Matt 4:18–19; Mark 1:16; Luke 5:1–11), the first in every listing of the disciples (Matt 10:1–4; Mark 4:16; Luke 6:12–16), the first witness of the resurrection (1 Cor 15:5; Luke 24:34), and he is singled out in the Fourth Gospel as the one who is to feed the sheep of the Jesus' flock (21:15–19). Paul may be vying with the Petrine mystique in Galatians 1:15–16 ("I did not confer with flesh and blood") and in 1 Corinthians 3:11 ("For no other foundation can anyone lay than that which is laid, which is Jesus Christ").

C. C. Caragounis's study of this passage carefully argues, however, that the rock refers to something other than Peter. The demonstrative pronoun "this" logically should refer to something other than the speaker or the one spoken to and would be appropriate only if Jesus were speaking about Peter in the third person and not speaking directly to him. If Jesus were referring to Peter, it would have been clearer to have, "You are Rock, and upon you I will build my church" (Caragounis, *Peter and the Rock,* 89). *Petros* usually meant a free-standing "stone" that could be picked up; and *petra* usually was used to mean "rock," "cliff," or "bedrock." But the two terms could reverse their meanings, and no clear-cut distinction can be made between the two (Caragounis, *Peter and the Rock,* 12, 15). If the two words were intended to refer to the same thing, *petros* could have been used in both places since it could be used to mean both stone and rock. The use of two different terms in the saying, *petros* and *petra,* implies that the two were to be distinguished from each other. The appeal to a hypothetical Aramaic saying is not decisive. Caragounis contends that if an Aramaic word lay behind the Greek *petra,* it was probably *tnra* (compare the Syriac version). According to Caragounis, each of the two words in the word-play has a separate referent and a separate meaning (Caragounis, *Peter and the Rock,* 90). The word-play (*Petros, petra*) has two foci, similarity and dissimilarity. *"Petros* has given utterance to a *petra,* but the *petra* is not *Petros."* The similarity is "in the sound and general sense." The dissimilarity is in the meaning or specific reference. *Petros,* a man's nickname, refers to a stone; *petra* refers to bedrock, the content of his confession (Caragounis, *Peter and the Rock,* 109). The assertion "you are Peter" is a solemn affirmation formula to introduce what follows: "As sure as you are [called] *Petros,* on this rock of what you have just said I will build my church" (Caragounis, *Peter and the Rock,* 108-13).

One may also argue that there is no indication elsewhere in Matthew that Peter was regarded as the foundation rock of the church. Peter is not idealized as a disciple. The fifteen incidents in the Gospel that specifically involve him portray him as rash, confused, desirous of reward, overconfident, faltering, and cowardly – in other words, he represents a normal disciple. He is, nevertheless, unique as the spokesman for the disciples who voices their questions and doubts as well as their faith. To recognize that Peter was a prominent leader of the early church does not entail that he was its foundation. The rock upon which Christ's church is built is the confession, revealed by the Father, that Jesus is the Christ, the son of the living God. The answers of others about who Jesus is offer him nothing on which to build. Peter's confession does. This confession alone provides the church a secure, defensive position from which it can repel attacks from the powers of the abyss. It is the foundation for strong faith as opposed to little faith.

This interpretation satisfactorily allows the pronoun "this" to refer to what Peter said. It also fits the context, which concerns the identity of Jesus, not the significance of Peter. Jesus first raises the question of his identity, and Peter provides the correct answer. The concluding words in 16:20 enjoin the disciples to say nothing about what has been revealed to them, namely, that Jesus is the Christ, not that Peter is the rock upon which Christ's church will be built. Just as the disciples are to build on the bedrock (*petra*) of the authoritative teaching of the Christ (7:24), so Christ will build his church on the disciples' confession in response to God's revelation. This interpretation does not lessen the significance of Peter. Weak and mixed-up as he sometimes might be, he is the leader in faith. He was also probably revered by Matthew's church as the guarantor of the tradition about Jesus (see Paul's visit to him, Gal 1:18) that leads others to recognize and confess Jesus as the Christ, the son of God.

(b) Jesus also assures Peter that the gates of Hades will not prevail against the church (16:18). Hades was conceived as the abode of the dead and of the demonic agents of death and destruction, and the "gates of Hades" personify that world of death and its rulers that are determined to break loose and to destroy Christ's church. The church is not exempt from Satan's onslaughts – the boat will be rocked by storms (14:24) – but this saying assures the disciples that the assault will never prevail. A similar sense of security was expressed in the hymn scroll from Qumran:

> [And I wa]s like a sailor on a ship. In the fury [23] of the seas were their waves and their billows roared against me; a wind of confusion (blew) [and there was no] breeze to restore the soul and no [24] path to direct the way on the face of the waters. And the Abyss resounded to my groaning and [my soul went down] to the gates of Death. And I was [25] like a man who entered a fortified city and sought refuge in a steep wall awaiting deliverance, And I lea[ned on] Thy truth, O my God, For it is thou who [26] wilt set the foundation upon rock and the frame-work on the cord of righteousness and the plumb-line [of truth] to [test] the tried stones in order to build a [27] stout [building] such as will not shake, and that none who enter there shall stagger. (1QH 6:22-27)

If the church confesses that the son of the living God can repel the powers of death, it also means that death does not hold any power over the church (see Rom 6:9). Disciples may lose their lives (10:38-39), but the gates of death's prison will have been breached once for all by Jesus' resurrection.

(c) The heavenly Father gave to Peter the revelation of Jesus' identity; Jesus now bestows on Peter the keys of the kingdom (16:19). To give the keys to someone meant to confer authority on that person (Rev 1:18; 3:7). The keys are an image for stewardship of God's affairs on earth (*2 [Syriac] Apocalypse of Baruch* 10:18; *4 Baruch* 4:3-5; *Babylonian Talmud Ta'anit* 29a; *Leviticus Rabba* 19:6). This image does not represent Peter as the porter at the gates of heaven, as he is portrayed in popular humor, but is related to his authority to interpret and teach so that he opens up the kingdom of heaven to others. Later, Jesus will accuse the scribes and Pharisees of shutting access to the kingdom of heaven to others (23:13; the verb "to shut" in Greek is similar to the noun for "keys"). They do not have the power to keep persons from entering into heaven, but they can dissuade people from responding to Jesus with their deadly teaching (16:6, 11). The woe against the scribes and Pharisees is related to their function as interpreters of God's will to the others (in *Sipre Deuteronomy* §321, the locksmiths listed in the company of those exiled in 2 Kings 24:16 are presumed to be teachers). Giving the keys of the kingdom to Peter implies that the teaching office has been taken from the scribes and Pharisees (and Sadducees) because of their malfeasance (compare Isa 22:15-22). This saying divinely legitimates the teaching authority of the church over against that of the church's opponents.

The keys of the kingdom are connected to the authority to bind and to loose, to make decisions about what is forbidden and permitted, what is binding on disciples and what can be loosed (see *Babylonian Talmud 'Aboda Zara* 36a-b). With the keys of the kingdom, Peter will be authorized to lay down rules, grant exemptions, and promulgate authoritative decisions on the basis of Jesus' teaching. He is able to determine what actions are permissible or not. Perhaps that is why Peter is portrayed as asking questions concerning such crucial issues as food regulations (15:15), the temple tax (17:24-27), and forgiveness (18:21-22). He can assume the role that the earthly Jesus played for his disciples when he defended them for not fasting, for presumably breaking the sabbath, and for eating with unwashed hands. An example of this authority to bind and loose is the decision to admit uncirmcumcised gentiles into the church (see Acts 15:6-11).

This interpretation of binding and loosing is commended by 23:4, where Jesus castigates the Pharisees for binding heavy burdens upon the shoulders of men and not lifting a finger to move them, and the warning in 5:19 that anyone who "looses" one of the least of these commandments and teaches men so shall be called least in the kingdom of heaven. These references from Matthew suggest that binding and loosing have something to do with how one interprets commands, whether from Moses or from Jesus (see Paul's treatment of divorce in 1 Cor 7:15, "the brother or sister is not bound"). The authority to interpret may be extended to include the tasks of discipline, governing, condemnation, and acquittal. As the revelation is not given alone to Peter (11:25-27), neither is the confession (14:33) or the blessing (13:16), and Matthew will later refer to the authority of binding and loosing residing in the entire church (18:18).

Matthew 16:21–28:20

JESUS' PASSION
AND RESURRECTION

INTRODUCTION

16:13-20

Peter's confession in 16:16 prompts the first of four predictions of Jesus' passion and resurrection, which begins the third and final division of the Gospel: "From that time Jesus began to show his disciples that he must go to Jerusalem and suffer many things from the elders and high priests and scribes and to be killed and on the third day to be raised" (16:21). The promise of building his church that will withstand invasion by the powers of the abyss will be fulfilled only after Jesus himself suffers death and is resurrected. That death has been foreshadowed by the massacre of the innocents (2:16), the image of the bridegroom being snatched away and causing the disciples to mourn (9:15), the warnings about arrest, betrayal, persecution, and death (10:17-39), the murderous intent of the Pharisees (12:14), the cryptic sign of Jonah explained as the son of man being three days and three nights in the heart of the earth (12:40), and the execution of John the Baptist (14:3-12).

For the first time Jesus unambiguously forecasts his death at the hands of the Jewish leaders, and it marks a turning point in the story. If the textual variant in 16:21, "Jesus Christ," is to be accepted, it is also the first time that the name and title have been used since the beginning of the Gospel in 1:1, 18. This final large division of the Gospel presents Jesus as the messiah who will undergo death and be resurrected by God, and the recurring passion/resurrection predictions (16:21; 17:22-23; 20:17-19; 26:1-2) will take the place of the summaries of Jesus' teaching and healing ministry that were sprinkled throughout the preceding division (4:23-25; 9:35; 11:1; 12:15; 14:34-36; 15:29-31). No longer will Jesus retreat in the face of peril (12:15; 14:13); he now plunges headlong into the dragon's lair. The one who has demonstrated power over disease, demons, and storms becomes powerless as he takes on the role of the suffering servant who gives his life. The disciples may salute Jesus as the Christ, but they can proclaim it only when they fully understand the necessity of his suffering and all that it entails for them.

The previous large division of the Gospel (4:17–16:20) opened with the announcement that Jesus "began" to preach the kingdom (4:17), the calling of disciples ("come after me," 4:18–22), a statement that gives the gist of what is to come (Jesus' teaching, preaching and healing, and the response of the crowds, 4:23–25), and Jesus ascending a mountain, Moses-like, to teach (5:1). This last division opens similarly. Jesus sounds the basic theme: "he began" to disclose to his disciples the necessity of his passion and the promise of his resurrection (16:21–23). He renews the call to his disciples "to come after me" and spells out what that entails. He again ascends a mountain (like Moses; Exod 24, 34) where his transfiguration confirms that the suffering that is to come is not incompatible with his glory. The crowds are no longer the center of Jesus' attention as he prepares the disciples for his coming death and resurrection.

While this final division primarily presents Jesus' passion and resurrection, it will also provide instructions about the timing of the destruction of Jerusalem and cautions about the coming judgment. The warning about the son of man coming to judge each one according to his or her work (16:27) prepares for the teaching about the end of the age and the parables of judgment appearing in chapters 24–25. This teaching has particular relevance for Matthew's church living in the in-between time, after the resurrection and before the final vindication and judgment. It must pass through the anxiety of the middle of the way, having left worldly supports but not having yet reached the final goal.

This last division begins with the prediction of Jesus' passion and resurrection and the affirmation that the disciples will not taste death until they see the son of man coming in his kingdom (16:28). It ends with the resurrected Jesus appearing to them on the mountain with all authority in heaven and earth. The instruction in 16:20 to tell no one that he is the Christ is countermanded in 28:19–20 when they are commanded to tell all the nations. The division divides into three sections: (1) final mission and instructions in Galilee and the region of Judea beyond the Jordan (16:21–20:16); (2) the approach to Jerusalem, confrontation with Jewish leaders, and warnings to the disciples (20:17–25:46); and (3) the passion and resurrection (26:1–28:20). Each of these sections begins with a passion prediction.

THE SHADOW OF DEATH
AND THE PROMISE OF GLORY

16:21-17:23

The first section, 16:21-17:23, is framed by two predictions of Jesus' passion and resurrection (16:21; 17:22-23). In between are (1) Peter's reaction to Jesus' announcement of his impending suffering (16:22-23); (2) Jesus' teaching on the implications of his suffering for discipleship and gaining life (16:24-26); (3) a warning about the coming judgment (16:27); (4) assurance of Jesus' vindication (16:28); (5) the transfiguration (17:1-8); (6) clarification about the coming of Elijah and the resurrection from the dead (17:9-13); and (7) an episode that underscores the need for faith during Jesus' physical absence (17:14-23).

The passion/resurrection predictions indicate that Jesus does not want his disciples to have any illusions about where following him will lead. They alone have discerned who he is and are judged ready to be given another, even deeper, mystery of the kingdom – the necessity and significance of his suffering and death as messiah (16:21). The "must" in classical Hellenistic literature frequently referred to blind, impersonal fate that had to be played out. In Matthew, as in the rest of the Gospels, it refers to the purpose and will of God. As the suffering servant (12:15-21), Jesus has been sent by God to take away the sins of the people through his death (1:21; 20:28; 26:28), and he now makes ready to fulfill that mission.

(1) Conveying the mystery of the ways of God to the disciples who look at things only from a human angle of vision will be challenging, as Peter's reaction to Jesus' announcement reveals (16:22-23). When Peter hears mention of suffering, he dares to rebuke Jesus: "Far be it from thee Lord!" His perception of what "Christ" meant was probably shaped by Jewish traditions of an earthly ruler with charismatic powers who would restore Israel and launch an abiding earthly kingdom (*Psalm of Solomon* 17:32; *1 Enoch* 52:4; 4 Ezra 12:32; 1QS 9:11).

179

He may have reasoned, if the church is to be invincible even against the gates of Hades, should not its Lord be exempt from suffering and death? Perhaps this reflex reaction comes from an inkling that death for his Lord may mean death for him as well, and Peter gives voice to the human penchant to want to skip on to advanced glory and bypass the course on elementary suffering (see Rom 8:17).

(2) Jesus' sharp response to Peter, "Get behind me Satan" (*hypage opisō mou*), may seem at first glance to echo his dismissal of Satan in 4:10 ("begone [*hypage*] Satan"). The key phrase, however, is "behind me," which was part of Jesus' first words to him when he called him ("come after me" [*deute, opisō mou*]; 4:19; see 10:38, 16:24). Peter is recreating Satan's part by trying to direct Jesus' path with a vision of earthly triumph. Instead of following behind in the way of Jesus, he tries to take the lead and plants himself firmly in Jesus' way. Because he thinks in terms of human aspirations, he stumbles over the ways of God (1 Cor 1:23; Gal 5:11). This blunder gives Jesus the opportunity to clarify further the role of the disciple.

Crying, "Lord, Lord," or simply hailing Jesus as the Christ, the son of God, is not enough for a disciple (see 7:21-23), who must become like Jesus in obedience. If one wants to be a disciple, to find life, and to be confirmed in the judgment, one must be centered on Jesus, centered on the cross, and centered on others. The following are prerequisites.

(a) Denying self. The disciples must deny the self. Self-denial is not to be confused with the denial of things to the self as expressed in asceticism or self-discipline, which sometimes are done for quite selfish reasons. It means putting oneself in submission to the will of another (see 26:39), and it rules out all attempts to try to save one's life by seeking refuge in the false securities of this world (16:25-26). "It is the opposite of self-affirmation, of putting value on one's being, one's life, one's position before man or God, of claiming rights and privileges peculiar to one's special position in life or even of those normally believed to belong to the human being as such" (E. Best, *Following Jesus: Discipleship in the Gospel of Mark* [Sheffield: JSOT, 1981], 37). Discipleship requires a radical commitment (4:18-22; 9:9) that allows no conflict of interest (6:33; 8:18-21).

(b) Taking up a cross and following Jesus. It is one thing to be fascinated by Jesus; it is another thing to follow one who will be killed. An unwelcome fate awaits anyone who faithfully follows a suffering leader. Taking up Jesus' yoke (11:29) means taking up a cross as well, the instrument of one's own execution. The cross was described by

Cicero as a cruel, disgusting penalty, the worst of extreme tortures inflicted on slaves (*Against Verres* II.v.64, 165; v.66, 169). It was something to be dreaded (*Pro Rabiro* 5.16). Disciples cannot be repelled by the cross and need to understand that it is necessary not only as a means of redemption but also as a way of life that they are to share if they are followers. True disciples are those who stake their lives on the confession that Jesus is the son of God and who accept the cross as the only valid way of life. They learn from Jesus' example (11:29) and become like him (10:24-25). Meaningful life is to be found only in giving one's life for others.

(3) This is not the first time that Jesus has spoken to his disciples of the necessity of bearing a cross (see 10:38), but now there is also mention of resurrection and judgment. What shall those who flinch at this demand give as a price for their souls in the judgment (16:26-27; see Ps 49:8-11)? For Matthew, the only acceptable ransom is Christ (20:28); and those who give their lives to and for Christ are assured that they will have life given back to them in the resurrection. The certainty of Jesus' ultimate vindication and of a future resurrection and judgment when each one's work shall be judged (16:27; see 18:23-35; 22:11-14; 24:45-51; 25:1-46) should govern all decisions in this present life.

(4) Jesus solemnly promises that some of the disciples will not taste death before they see him appearing in his kingly role (16:28). This assurance picks up on the phrase "raised on the third day" (16:21, 17:23), and shows that his suffering is not incompatible with his final glory. Matthew is apparently unworried by the problem of fulfillment of this promise in the lifetime of first-generation believers. To what does the son of man coming in his kingdom refer?

It may refer to the transfiguration that immediately follows (17:1-8; see 2 Pet 1:16-18), the resurrection scene (28:16-20), or the second advent (see 24:3; 25:31), which is assumed to be swiftly approaching. Perhaps one should see precursory fulfillment of this prediction in the transfiguration and resurrection, which point to the glory of the second advent. The parallels between 17:1-8 and the resurrection appearance in 28:16-20 suggest that the transfiguration is a preview of Jesus' resurrected glory when he is given all authority over heaven and earth. Both scenes have a mountain setting. In both Jesus "comes" to the disciples (17:7, 28:18), the only time the verb is used in Matthew with Jesus as subject. Both record the disciples' response of awe and the emphasis on hearing/obeying Jesus. In the transfiguration, Jesus' face is said to shine like the sun — like the righteous resurrected ones "who will shine like the sun in the kingdom of their Father" (13:43). A parallel in *2 (Syriac Apocalypse of) Baruch* 51:3 on the vindication of the righteous who will be "changed" (51:1) in the resurrection is pertinent:

> As for the glory of those who proved to be righteous on account of my law, those who possessed intelligence in their life, and those who planted the root of wisdom in their heart — their splendor will then be glorified by transformations, and the shape of their face will be changed into the light of their beauty so that they may acquire and receive the undying world which is promised to them. (see also Dan 12:3; 4 Ezra 7:97; *1 Enoch* 104:2)

Jesus' clothes also are said to become "dazzling white" like those of the angel at the tomb (28:3; see *1 Enoch* 62:15-16, the resurrected ones shall wear "garments of glory"). The transfiguration of Jesus therefore anticipates his resurrection, and it, in turn, is a preview of the eschatological glorification and vindication of the son of man that will be fully realized in his return.

(5) The account of the transfiguration (17:1-8) is rich in biblical imagery and provides divine confirmation of Jesus' status as the son of God and is a precursor of his heavenly glory. This milestone contains five points that are theologically important to Matthew.

(a) The first has to do with the appearance of Moses and Elijah, notable biblical figures who both spoke with God on a mountain (Exod 24; 1 Kgs 19:8-19). What is the point of their presence? Although they may represent the law and the prophets (5:17; 7:12; 11:13; 22:40), it is their eschatological significance that is key. Moses prophesied that God would raise up a prophet like him who would reveal the divine will (Deut 18:15-19), and Elijah was believed to be the forerunner of the great and terrible day (Mal 4:4-6; see *Deuteronomy Rabba* 3:17: "God told Moses: when I will send Elijah, the prophet, you are to come both of you together"). Here they materialize giving ear to Jesus and are bathed in his glory. It is a sign that the end has drawn near.

(b) Peter interrupts this scene by deferentially offering to erect dwellings for all three. The purpose and background of this desire remains a mystery, but one thing is sure: he is still reacting to things from a human perspective. He is checked in midsentence by a bright cloud that overshadows them and a voice proclaiming: "This is my beloved son in whom I am well pleased. Hear him!" (a combination of Ps 2:7; Isa 42:1; Deut 18:15). The bright cloud signifies the presence of the Lord (Exod 16:10; 19:9; 24:15-18; 40:34; 1 Kgs 8:10-11; Ps 97:2; Ezek

10:3-4; 2 Macc 2:8; Josephus, *Antiquities* 3.12.5 §290; 3.14.4 §310) and clarifies the identity of the voice. It confirms Peter's confession in 16:16 while gently censuring him. The transfiguration is to be only a fleeting glimpse of Jesus' glory and not yet a permanent state of affairs. The bright cloud, the voice, the figure of Moses and Elijah will all vanish as suddenly as they appeared. The golden moment cannot be prolonged because Jesus still must go his way to death and cannot dally on holy mountains.

(c) The chiastic structure of this scene indicates that what is most vital is what the disciples hear from the cloud, not what they see (Davies and Allison, *Saint Matthew,* 2:684):

a   Narrative introduction (17:1)

   b   Jesus is transfigured (17:2-3)

      c   Peter's response (17:4)

         d   The divine voice (17:5)

      c′   The disciples' response (17:6)

   b′   Jesus speaks (17:7)

a′   Narrative conclusion (17:8)

The voice decrees that they are to listen to Jesus. The disciples' great fear is a typical reaction to a theophany (Gen 17:3; Josh 5:14; Ezek 1:28; Dan 8:17; 10:9-10; Acts 26:13-14; Rev 1:17). In Mark, they fear immediately after the transfiguration of Jesus and the vision of Moses and Elijah (Mark 9:6). In Luke, they fear at the descent of the cloud (Luke 9:34). In Matthew, fear comes upon the disciples when they hear the voice (17:6) that affirms Jesus' as the supreme teaching authority.

(d) Jesus comes to the trembling disciples, touches them, and says, "Be raised" (see 9:25); "do not fear" (precisely what the angel and Jesus say to the women followers after the resurrection, 28:5, 10; see also Ezek 2:1-3; Dan 10:5-12). The use of these terms makes this scene a foreshadowing of the disciples' own resurrection.

(e) The parallels between this private epiphany with the public spectacle of Jesus' crucifixion are both striking and significant (see Davies and Allison, *Saint Matthew,* 2:706-7). Here Jesus is surrounded by two celebrated saints of old; on the cross he will be surrounded by two criminals (27:38). On the mount of transfiguration, Jesus' garments glisten in his glory; at Golgotha, his garments will have been taken from him in his humiliation (27:35). In both scenes, there is mention of Elijah (27:47-49) and of great fear at divine manifestations (27:54). In the first, Jesus is confessed as the son of God by a divine voice; in the second, by his executioners, Roman soldiers (27:54). Both scenes are witnessed by his followers: the first by the inner circle of disciples; the second, by women from afar. These parallels reveal that, for Matthew, Jesus' suffering and glory can been seen properly only as two sides of the same coin.

(6) The next scene (17:9-13) further connects the transfiguration to the resurrection and the resurrection to suffering. Coming down from the mountain, Jesus commands these disciples to say nothing about the vision until after he is raised from the dead. The disciples think in terms of a general resurrection and query about the scribes' belief that Elijah must come first (before the resurrection). Jesus partially concurs with this conviction. The scriptural expertise of the scribes may be relied upon when it comes to details such as where the messiah is to be born (2:4-5) and the timetable for Elijah. Otherwise, they are untrustworthy guides who will be party to the death of the messiah (16:21). Jesus must add the definitive interpretation ("but I say to you"; see 5:21-48), and the disciples must listen to him (17:5). Elijah has already come; they did not know him and did to him as they wished (11:14; 14:3-12; 21:24-27). The disciples have already been told that John the Baptist was Elijah (11:14), and fulfilling Elijah's role meant martyrdom (14:10). They can infer from this fact that the messiah can expect to be treated no differently; he too will die. Only after his resurrection can the disciples relate what they have just experienced with clear understanding. His suffering was part and parcel of his glory.

(7) In Matthew's account of the exorcism of the possessed boy when Jesus descends the mountain (17:14-21), the concern is not to demonstrate once again Jesus' power over the demonic since that has long been established. As the reader has come to expect, the demon exits the lad without a whimper as soon as Jesus speaks. The issue is what the disciples are able to do in Jesus' absence, and the story is directly applicable to the situation of the church after his death and resurrection. Jesus had given his disciples the authority to cast out demons (10:1, 8), and he reproaches them for their failure to exercise that authority as another sign of their little faith. Worse, they are in danger of becoming like the faithless and perverse generation that will be judged (11:16; 12:39, 45; 23:36). The image of moving mountains is a hyperbolic figure for doing the impossible (Isa 54:10; 1 Cor 13:2; *Babylonian*

Talmud Soṭa 9b; *Baba Batra* 3b; *Sanhedrin* 4a). If they have even the smallest amount of faith, they will have access to the power of God that will enable them to fulfill Jesus' commands in his absence.

The passion and resurrection prediction that concludes this section takes place after the disciples have assembled in Galilee (17:22–23). Instead of protests, it now elicits from them great sorrow. Their distress means that they have grasped only half of the statement about Jesus' death and resurrection. They may be too distracted by the prospect of suffering to hear Jesus' promise of victory, or they may assume that resurrection on the third day is simply an abstract reference to a remote day of divine deliverance (see Hos 6:2). They will not fathom the literal truth of this statement until the next time they assemble in Galilee – after Jesus has been raised on the third day (26:32; 28:7, 10, 16). Even then their awe will be mingled with doubt (28:17). Resurrection on the third day, however, will become a part of the church's proclamation of Jesus' vindication by God (Acts 10:40; 1 Cor 15:4).

LIVING TOGETHER
AS THE FAMILY OF GOD

17:24–18:35

The discourse in chapter 18 is introduced by a discussion about Jesus' obligation to pay the temple tax (17:24–27). The half-shekel tax (substituted by two *didrachma*) was levied annually on all Jewish males over the age of twenty (Exod 30:11–16) to fund the daily sacrifices in the temple. Some in Jesus' day argued that they were free from the tax (priests, according to *Mishna Šeqalim* 1:3–5) or that they need pay only once in a lifetime (Qumran, 4Q*159*). When the collectors ask Peter if his teacher pays the tax, he responds, without hesitating, "Yes." Jesus then confronts Peter in the house with a parable about the tax liability of the sons of earthly kings.

Because of Peter's previous misunderstandings (16:22–23; 17:4), the reader is primed for him to be corrected once again: Jesus is not obligated to pay the tax and will not. The parable would seem to confirm this expectation. The immediate family of kings are spared the tax burdens placed on others; so Jesus, as the confessed son of God (14:33; 16:16; 17:5), is not obliged to pay taxes for God's temple. It is perhaps surprising then that Jesus fully intends to comply with the custom to avoid causing offense (contrast 13:57; 15:12). Jesus, in effect, foregoes his rights for the ways of peace, a well-known principle applied in later Rabbinic rulings to prevent strife among the people and to reduce potential friction with non-Jews. Peter's "yes" can therefore remain a "yes" (5:37). The incident ends with what seems to be a whimsical fish story and a highly unusual solution to any cash flow problems. Peter is told that he will find the precise amount to pay the tax for Jesus and himself in the mouth of the first fish he catches.

How does this account fit into Matthew's story? (a) First, the incident provides a theological object lesson. Jesus' concern for the feelings and needs of others lays the groundwork for the discourse that follows on how the church is to live together as a family. The reason that Jesus will

186

comply is not because of any obligation or loyalty to the temple but to avoid giving offense to others. "The sons may be free, but they are not free from the claims of love" (D. E. Garland, "Matthew's Understanding of the Temple Tax (Matt 17:24–27)," *SBLSP* [1987]: 205).

(b) Second, it is further confirmation that Jesus is God's son (17:5). The miracle, although not reported, shows him to have divine fore-knowledge as one who rules over nature and the sea (14:28–33).

(c) Third, it underscores the fact that the disciples as Jesus' "broth-ers" (12:49; 25:40; 28:10) are also "sons" and are also exempt from the tax by virtue of their relationship to him. As they share in his author-ity to cast out unclean spirits and to heal every disease (10:1, 8), they also share his authority to make governing decisions for the church (18:18–20; 16:19).

(d) Fourth, it prepares the reader for the rejection of the temple that will follow later in the narrative. Jesus will declare the temple to be a den of robbers (21:13) in a defiant demonstration in the outer court. His last words in the temple pronounce its abandonment (23:38), and he will predict its complete destruction as he exits (24:1–2). Matthew omits the touching story that commends a widow for donating all that she had to the temple treasury not only because it would interrupt the mood of judgment that connects 23:37–39 with 24:1–2 but because it implicitly sanctions support for the temple (Mark 12:41–44; Luke 21:1–4). Prior to Jesus' execution at the instigation of the temple authorities (16:21), the blood money for Jesus' betrayal winds up in the sanctuary (27:4–7); and at his death the veil of the sanctuary is split from top to bottom (27:51). The reader has already been told that something greater than the temple is here (12:6), and this division presenting Jesus' passion and resurrection spells that out more clearly. "The children's" exemption from the temple dues indicates their freedom from its sacrificial cultus. The temple tax was associated with sin atonement provided by the sacrifices it funded. It is called "atonement money" and a reminder of "the ransom given for your lives" in Exodus 30:16 (see *Tosepta Šeqalim* 1:6). The death and resurrection of Jesus, however, will replace temple sacrifices for the forgiveness of sin (18:32; 20:28; 26:28; 27:42).

The sayings collected in the following discourse (18:1–35) have to do with living together as the family of God (see Mark 9:50, "be at peace with one another"). They candidly anticipate that the church will include those who arrogantly look down their noses at others, those who cause scandal, those who stray, those who defy admonition, and those who are unforgiving – a tangled assortment of sinners. The structure of this discourse divides into two units: (1) concern for the "little ones" (18:1-14), and (2) reproof and forgiveness of fellow members of the church (18:15-35). Both units contain three paragraphs concluding with a parable: unit 1: (a) the significance of the child in the kingdom (18:1-5); (b) a dire warning against causing offense to little ones that makes them stumble (18:6-9); (c) the parable of the lost sheep (marked off by an inclusio with the term "little ones," 18:10-14). Unit 2: (a) procedure for reproving and gaining a fellow member (18:15-18); (b) an affirmation of the community's disciplinary decisions (18:19-20); (c) the parable of the unmerciful servant (marked off by an inclusio with the reference to forgiveness, 18:21-35).

(1) The first paragraph (18:1-5) has to do with eminence in the kingdom of heaven and is touched off by the disciples' question about who is the greatest. In Matthew's account, the disciples do not appear to be absorbed in establishing their own pecking order in the kingdom (contrast Mark 9:33-34; Luke 9:46) but want to know where they rank on the scale of things. Jesus turns the question on its head. The disciple is not to be concerned about a hierarchy of status as many in the ancient world were (see 20:25). Society under the reign of God is to be of a totally different nature; and disciples, who are all equals (23:8-10), are not to worry about their own or others' individual status.

Jesus uses a child as an object lesson to convey the point. He has no romanticized notions about the qualities of children (see the parable of the children's games, 11:16-17) and is *not* setting up the child as a model to be imitated. To "turn and become as children" in 18:3 is clarified in 18:4 as "humbling oneself as this little child." Children were generally regarded as insignificant. They, along with women, did not count (see 14:21), which explains the disciples' reflex reaction to the children in 19:13-15. If the saying in 18:3 refers to any inherent quality of children, it is that they are weak and defenseless and have no security in themselves, which means that they must always look to others. Jesus is calling his disciples to be self-effacing like Solomon when he ascended the throne. He prayed: "And now O Lord my God, thou hast made thy servant king in place of David my father although I am but a little child; I do not know how to go out or come in" (1 Kgs 3:7).

To become as a child is basically to recognize one's status of insignificance and absolute dependence. What hinders genuine repentance is the presumption that one is great. What makes repentance possible is the recognition that one is "as small and slight as a child before God" (R. Schnackenburg, *Moral Teaching of the New Testament* [London:

Burns and Oates, 1965], 30). As in 25:31–46, Jesus identifies himself with the weak and seemingly insignificant. Those who receive children also receive him, and it is the humble who will best care for the humble. Those who want to become great are tempted to give themselves to more dazzling occasions of service, such as prophesying, casting out demons, and working mighty miracles (7:22); and they overlook the basic task of receiving and ministering to the nobodies.

The second paragraph cautions against causing offense to "the little ones who believe in me" (18:6–9). This qualification of the little ones as believers makes it clear that Jesus is not talking about children but Christians. The little ones are little esteemed by others either because they seem negligible according to the world's rating system (see 10:42; 25:35–36, 40, 45; 1 Cor 1:26–29) or because they seem to be of marginal worth to the church (as recent converts, catechumens, or untutored Christians who are on the fringe of the community).

The illustration of the child points out that all should be acutely conscious of their insignificance before God. Paradoxically, it also reveals that none are actually insignificant in the kingdom of heaven. The second paragraph grimly threatens that it would be better to have a large (literally, "donkey powered") mill stone hung around one's neck and be dropped in the deepest part of the sea with no hope of escape than to face what lies in store for the one who leads a little one into sin (18:6). It would seem that leaders and teachers in the church (the scribes instructed in the kingdom, 13:52) are particularly in view.

The third paragraph contains the parable of the lost sheep (18:10–14). Since most readers are more familiar with the Lukan version of this parable (15:3–7), it is helpful to detail the differences. In Luke's Gospel, the parable is occasioned by the indignant grumbling of the scribes and Pharisees about Jesus' habit of receiving sinners and eating with them (15:1–2). It is linked with two other parables, the lost coin (15:8–10) and the man with two sons (15:11–32), to justify Jesus' association with sinners. The parable implies that the action of the shepherd in seeking out the lost sheep is what God is doing through Jesus' ministry.

The Matthean context of the parable is entirely different. It is not directed to opponents who have challenged Jesus but to disciples whom he is preparing to become leaders of the church. While Luke's parable emphasizes the heavenly joy in recovering the lost sinner (15:5–7), Matthew's parable emphasizes the heavenly will. It begins with the command: "See that you do not despise one of these little ones, for I tell you that their angels always see the face of my Father who is in heaven," and concludes with the words: "Thus it is not the will of your Father in heaven that one of these little ones be destroyed." The "little ones" have just been identified as those who believe in Jesus (18:6). In Luke, the sheep has been lost (15:4); in Matthew, it goes astray (18:12). The other ninety-nine are not likened to righteous ones not needing repentance as in Luke (15:7) but as those "who did not go astray" (18:12). Matthew's parable also hints that the stray sheep may not be recovered ("if he finds it," as opposed to Luke's "when he finds it"), and the teaching that follows (18:15–17) reveals that erring members may not always accept correction.

The parable of the lost sheep in Matthew has in view a quite different situation from its counterpart in Luke. The church confessed that God loved sinners, sought to save them, and rejoiced when they repented. This belief, however, did not always translate into a loving, accepting brotherhood that was marked by similar acts toward one another (E. Schweizer, "Matthew's View of the Church in his 18th Chapter," *AusBR* 21 [1973]: 12). Matthew's parable anticipates the situation in the church when little ones who believe in Jesus (18:6) go astray and no one in the church cares about it or goes after them. They are in danger of being lost in the shuffle because they are viewed as superfluous as "little ones."

The parable begins by affirming that the angels of these so-called little ones always behold the face of God (see the angels of the Face [Presence] who continually serve God, Tob 12:15; *Jubilees* 2:2, 18; 31:14; 1QSb 4:25–26; Luke 1:19; Rev 8:2). The argument moves from the greater to the lesser. If the elite of heaven are actively interested in these little ones, how much more should the shepherd, who is, after all, only a shepherd, watch over them and stubbornly seek to restore those who stray? When one is dealing with things, it is impressive to maintain a 99 percent average. But the statistical approach does not work when one is dealing with persons. God is never willing to say, "We have most of them." In a family, the one who is missing is never compensated for by the ones who are present. Polycarp's letter to the Philippians (6:1) captures the sense of this section in commenting that presbyters must be "compassionate, merciful to all, bringing back those that have wandered, caring for all the weak, neglecting neither widow, nor orphan, nor poor."

(2) The second section (18:15–35) begins with specific instructions for reproving a fellow member (18:15–18). It is not accidental that it is preceded by demands to be humble as a child, to purge one's

own sins (see 7:1-5), and to seek urgently after the one who strays, and that it is followed by a demand for unlimited forgiveness. The structure of the first paragraph (18:15-18) is determined by four conditional sentences: (a) "if your brother sins [against you]"; (b) "if he does not listen to you"; (c) "if he ignores them"; (d) "if he ignores the church."

The procedure for reproving one's brother is strikingly similar to what is found in the Qumran literature (1QS 5:25-6:1; CD 7:2-3; CD 9:2-8, 9:16-22; see also *Testament of Gad* 6:3-5). Both deal with reproving a fellow member who has offended. Both refer to a three-step process and with reproving the fellow member before witnesses. Both refer to a final step of taking the matter to the full assembly or judging body that will make some kind of judgment of the offender.

T. R. Carmody ("Matthew 18:15-17") carefully compares these parallels with 18:15-17 to show their important differences. Leviticus 19:17 and Deuteronomy 19:15 are linked in the Qumran literature so that reproving is simply part of a judicial process against the offender. The problem addressed in CD 9:17 is how to get a legal conviction when only one witness finds another guilty of breaking the law since the law required two witnesses. The accuser was required to reprove the offender on the same day before witnesses prior to bringing the case to be heard by others. In Matthew, the visit to the offender is not to initiate prosecution; and the securing of witnesses is not to insure that the reproof was legally executed. It is aimed at persuading the offender of the sin with the minimum embarrassment and to win him or her. The one who considers himself or herself sinned against bears the responsibility of initiating reconciliation and mending the breach. The one sinned against is not to sit back and wait for the other to do his or her Christian duty and apologize (see 5:23-25, "if you remember that your brother has something against you . . . "). Approaching the brother or sister is a gesture of reconciliation; and the outcome will be forgiveness, *not* judicial action, if the offender listens and repents.

The enlistment of witnesses is a second attempt to persuade and to win the guilty party. Deuteronomy 19:15 is cited (18:16) to make the point that the legal number of witnesses establishes that the offender should listen and repent (to "convince" the offender, not to "convict" him or her, Carmody, "Matthew 18:15-17," 154). The involvement of the entire community is a last effort to get the offender to listen and confess the sin. The church is to exercise its moral influence, not its disciplinary muscle (see W. G. Thompson, *Matthew's Advice to a Divided*

Community: Mt. 17, 22–18, 35, AnBib 44 [Rome: Pontifical Biblical Institute, 1970], 176–88). In the parallels from the Qumran literature, the assembly gathers to try the case and pass judgment. Carmody concludes: "The Essene attempt to be completely legal in convicting an offender is replaced in Matthew by the attempt to surpass the legal and be completely thorough in trying to bring the offender back" ("Matthew 18:15–17," 155).

The primary concern in the Qumran literature is for the accuser. The rules are designed to prevent the one who has been made angry by another from incurring guilt through his anger by requiring him to bring his hostility into the open (Lev 19:17–18; see Sir 19:13–17; 20:1–2). Matthew 18:15–18 differs in that no mention is made of the anger or the feelings of the one sinned against. The focus is only on reclaiming the errant member and rescuing that one from sin. Just as the shepherd seeks the stray sheep to bring it back into the fold, so the church tries to bring the offending member back into fellowship.

If wrongdoers refuse to listen to the entire community, however, the church is instructed to cut all ties with them (see 1 Cor 5:1–8). The key phrases are "if he does not listen," and "if he ignores," which imply that the church is not so much breaking off fellowship with an offender as recognizing that there is no fellowship to break (F. Stagg, "Matthew," *The Broadman Bible Commentary* [Nashville: Broadman, 1969], 8:184). Treating someone as a gentile and a toll collector does not mean that the church is to wash its hands of the person but that it distinguishes between dealing with a member who is out of sorts and dealing with one who is not a member. Since Jesus eats with toll collectors (9:10–11), is berated as a friend of sinners and toll collectors (11:19), and later affirms that the prostitutes and toll collectors will enter the kingdom of God before the temple authorities (21:32), and since the gentiles who appear in this Gospel display exceptional faith (the magi, the centurion, the Canaanite woman, and Pilate's wife), one may assume that the church is now to relate to the offender as one who is to be evangelized.

Disputes among church members are not to be settled by outsiders; the church itself is to be the final arbiter of conflict. The focus of the next saying in 18:18 has to do with the church's authority to pronounce judgment on what is or is not sin (see 1 Cor 7:36). The subject of the verbs, binding and loosing, is plural. The object of the binding and loosing is neuter ("whatever," not "whoever"). They are not to bind or loose persons. The community is to do whatever is necessary to see that a little one does not perish, but it can make pronouncements on what is or is not sin with confidence. The final judgment of the individual, however, is still left to God.

These instructions picture a community where every member watches over another, the whole church assumes responsibility for every member, and every member is accountable to the whole church (Stagg, "Matthew," 184). This may seem unduly intrusive to modern readers imbued with the spirit of rugged individualism, but a sense of household solidarity offered the early Christians security in a hostile world.

The second paragraph (18:19-20) is frequently interpreted as having to do with the efficacy of prayer (see Ignatius, *Ephesians* 5:2), but this interpretation is problematic. It does not fit the context, which has to do with reproving one who sins (18:15-17) and forgiving a fellow member who sins against you (18:21-35). Does this saying imply that for prayer to be granted or, perhaps, to insure that it will be granted, one has to find one or more to agree with one? What if two pray for something, and three pray for the exact opposite? Why does the church need to be assured that Christ is in the midst of two or three who pray? In 28:20, the risen Christ promises the disciples that he will be with them at all times whether they are praying or not.

A reference in the *Mishna 'Abot* 3:2, 6 to the Divine Presence attending scholars who gather to study Torah has been uncritically applied as a parallel for understanding 18:19-20. It is assumed that these verses teach that no matter how small the gathering of disciples, Christ, who replaces the Divine Presence in the minds of Christian believers, is present. The Rabbinic tradition, however, originally applied to judges judging; and the *Mishna* switched it to Torah scholars because it was compiled when current practice required three judges, not one or two, as a minimum for judging cases (see *Mishna 'Abot* 4:8; *Sanhedrin* 1:1). The earlier tradition is preserved in *Mekilta Baḥodesh* 11 (to Exod 20:24):

> And how do we know that He is also with three people holding court? It says: "In the midst of the judges He judges." [Ps 82:1b]

> And how do we know that He is also with two? It is said: "Then they that feared the Lord spoke one with another, etc." [Mal 3:6]

> And how do we know that He is even with one? It is said: "In every place where I cause My name to be mentioned I will come unto thee and bless thee." [Exod 20:24]

The saying in Matthew reflects this earlier tradition about two or three judges who gather to arbitrate in a dispute. It affirms that Christ is present to shepherd their decisions (see J. Sievers, " 'Where Two or Three . . . ': The Rabbinic Concept of *Shekinah* and Matthew 18,20," *Standing Before God,* ed. A. Finkel and L. Frizzel [New York: Ktav, 1981], 171–82).

The final paragraph contains a parable about forgiveness (18:21–35). Just as 18:10 and 18:14 bracket and interpret the parable of the lost sheep, 18:21–22 and 18:35 bracket and interpret the parable of the unmerciful servant. In 18:21, Peter asks for clearly defined limits for the obligation to forgive another. He generously suggests forgiving his brother up to seven times for sins against him. It is generous because no mention is made of the offender's repentance. It is biblical, because that is the limit of transgressions God allowed Israel (Amos 2:4, 6). Jesus' response consciously counters the Lamech principle of measureless blood vengeance (Gen 4:24). One must forgive seventy-seven times (or seventy times seven). One has learned nothing if one keeps a tally of the number of times one has forgiven another so that when the magic number is reached, one can stop forgiving and mete out punishment. Under Lamech there was no limit to hatred and revenge; under Moses it was limited to an eye for an eye, a tooth for a tooth, a life for a life; under Jesus there is no limit to love, forgiveness, and mercy. The concluding sentence warns of severe punishment if one does not forgive the fellow member from the heart (18:35).

The necessity of a forgiving heart is illustrated by a parable of a king's cancellation of a monumental debt. A servant of the king owes his master ten thousand talents, a deliberate exaggeration. Ten thousand was the highest figure in arithmetic (like our billion), and the talent was the highest currency. If one talent equaled ten thousand denarii, as some suggest, the debt would be equivalent to a hundred million working days for the day laborers mentioned in 20:2. To no one's surprise, the servant is unable to pay off his account. When he and his family are about to be sold into slavery to defray the king's losses, the servant gives homage to his king and begs: "Lord, have patience with me, and I will repay you everything." The bankrupt servant audaciously believes that he can make up this incredible deficit and avoid punishment by rescheduling his payments. He refuses to become as a little child and admit that he is irredeemably insolvent.

The king had requested payment of what was due him, but his compassion goes far beyond the frantic appeal of his servant. The servant asked for patience; the king shows him compassion. He does not let him go out to try to raise the money within a month or put him on a time payment plan. The debt is written off entirely, something the servant never dared to ask. It would seem that the debt becomes a gift with no strings attached, but as the story unfolds there is an unspoken condition. The parable expresses Matthew's view of grace. God does not give to human beings their due but forgives. God's mercy is not cheap grace, however; it requires an appropriate response.

In the second act of the parable, the servant happens upon a fellow servant who owes him a comparatively paltry one hundred denarii. The pleas of the second servant for more time parallel those of the first. There are two significant differences: the staggering amount of the debt – a hundred million denarii as opposed to one hundred – and the opposite responses – mercy versus ruthlessness. The servant does not forgive the debt but has his debtor thrown in prison.

In the final act, the king is informed of the heartless actions of his servant. The king, formerly moved to compassion, is now moved to anger. He declares: "Evil servant, I forgave you all that was owed by you since you appealed to me. Was it not necessary that you have mercy on your fellow servant as I had on you?" The reader can only share the outrage of the king because the servant had been shown such extravagant mercy and responded to another with extravagant mercilessness.

The parable intones that mercy requires mercy. If one has received mercy, how can one still insist on coldly asserting one's rights and claims over others? The debtor, however, apparently took his pardon as a personal beneficence that made him a favorite of the king. He was thus emboldened to start throwing his weight around and was brazen enough to insist on having his petty debt paid by a man who was about to settle accounts with his sovereign. His lack of charity is the epitome of proud insolence and stupidity.

The parable turns from one of grace to one of judgment (like 22:11–14), and the hard-boiled servant is turned over to the torturers until he pays all that he owes — which will be never. "The wrath of God is kindled against the hard and relentless more than against the weak and foolish" (Manson, *Sayings,* 213). The parable complements what is prayed in the Lord's Prayer, "forgive us our debts as we forgive our debtors" (6:12), and reinforces the warning that follows it: forgiveness can be forfeited (6:14; see Sir 28:1–7). Disciples should know themselves as forgiven and therefore are to be forgiving. The miserly balance sheets that are used to keep mental tabs on the slights of others are to be torn up lest they come back to haunt us in the judgment (7:1–5).

This discourse gives us a glimpse of Matthew's view of the church. It is a household whose special relationship to God (17:25–26) derives from their intimacy with Jesus as his brothers and sisters (12:50). They believe in him and worship him as the son of God, gather in his name, and observe God's law as it is clarified by his authoritative actions and words. They ascribe to him divine attributes, incorporate others into the community by baptizing in his name (28:19), and make disciplinary decisions in his name (18:18). They also consider themselves to be free from the Jewish system of animal sacrifice because of his atoning death. A church that is so centered on Jesus has broken away or has been banished from the sphere of influence of the Jewish synagogue.

Matthew does not present the church as a perfect community immune to the problems caused by human sinfulness, pride, arrogance, obstinacy, ruthlessness, and little faith. For that reason, Matthew emphasizes the need for the church to be infused with a spirit of care, tolerance, and kindheartedness as well as regulated by high standards of conduct. All are to be treated as equals (23:8) regardless of past history, race, or social station; and all should regard themselves humbly as "little ones." The church whose primary reason for being is to be a light to the world cannot take a gospel message of reconciliation to the nations while being unreconciled to one another.

WHAT'S IN IT FOR US?
THE DEMANDS AND REWARDS
OF THE KINGDOM

19:1–20:16

The suffering that Jesus forecast (16:21) draws nearer as he leaves Galilee and moves toward Judea. The crowds again follow in his train as he continues to heal them. But the emphasis in this section falls on teaching that further illustrates the greater righteousness and the self-denial required of those who want to follow him as disciples (16:24; 19:27–28). Themes from the Sermon on the Mount resurface: the issue of divorce (19:3–9=5:31–32); the low worldly status of those who will receive the kingdom of heaven (19:14=5:3–10); the commandments of Moses (19:18–19=5:17–48); the command to be perfect (19:21=5:48); treasure in heaven (19:21=6:19–21); the danger of mammon (19:22=6:24); the obstacles to entering the kingdom of heaven (19:23–24=7:13–14). The promise of reward (19:27–20:16=5:3–10) culminates the section.

The difference between Matthew's account of the passage on divorce (19:3–12) and Mark's (10:2–12) is significant for discerning the structure of this section. Jesus' assertion that divorce and remarriage is adultery (19:9) forms part of his public declaration about divorce and is not, as it is in Mark 10:10–12, a private clarification for the disciples ("in the house"). The saying about becoming eunuchs for the kingdom of heaven (19:10–12), which appears only in Matthew, is introduced as the private explanation for the disciples. The rearrangement fits Matthew's reshaping of the whole section, "which is concerned with the distinction between what the gospel explicitly requires from all and the specific demands which for reasons of personal vocation or sheer spiritual prudence it may make on individuals" (Green, *Matthew,* 167). This observation provides a helpful pointer to the structure of the seven paragraphs in this section. They oscillate between what is applicable

197

to all and what is pertinent only to some: (1) the prohibition of divorce, applicable to all (19:3-9); (2) the renunciation of marriage, applicable to some (19:10-12); (3) childlikeness and the kingdom, applicable to all (19:13-15); (4) the renunciation of wealth, applicable to some (19:16-22); (5) the vain hope of salvation from human resources, applicable to all (19:23-26); (6) the rewards awaiting the twelve and those who deny themselves for the sake of Jesus' name, applicable to some and to all (19:27-30); and (7) the lack of distinction in the rewards, applicable to all (20:1-16).

(1) The first paragraph concerns the issue of marriage and divorce (19:3-9). The Pharisees, who refuse to submit to the teaching of Jesus, attempt to ensnare him in some way with a test question on divorce (see 16:1; 22:18, 35) — the issue that ultimately led to the death of John the Baptist (14:3-4). They ask: "Is it lawful to divorce one's wife for any cause?" (Matt 19:3). The phrase "for any cause" was a catchword (see Philo, *On the Special Laws* III:30; and Josephus, *Antiquities* 4:253) in a debate on how to apply Deuteronomy 24:1: "if a wife finds no favor in her husband's eyes because she is guilty of a matter of indecency" (literally, "the nakedness of a thing," 24:1). The *Mishna* presents two schools of thought on this issue (*Mishna Gittin* 9:10). The school of Rabbi Hillel placed stress on the word "matter." Any matter that provoked the husband's displeasure with his wife, such as ruining a dish or finding a prettier woman (exceptional cases used only to make a legal point), could be legitimate grounds for divorce. Josephus apparently favored this view because he says that he had been married three times and sent away his second wife because he was "displeased at her behavior" (*Life* 426-27). The school of Rabbi Shammai, however, emphasized the word "indecency." One may not divorce his wife unless he found some indecency in her. One should not take this condition to refer to adultery. That automatically led to divorce since most believed that the husband should not continue to cohabit with his wife after she had defiled herself. Instead, "some indecency" refers to other violations of propriety such as conversing with men, spinning in the streets with bare arms (*Mishna Ketubot* 7:6), loosening the hair in public (*Babylonian Talmud Gittin* 90b), as well as deliberate transgressions of the law.

Jesus ignores the exegetical debate about the valid grounds for divorce and raises the question to the level of the unconditional will of God for marriage. Once again, the opponents have misread the Scripture. In Mark 10:3, Jesus asks his interrogators, "What did Moses *command?* They respond, "Moses *permitted* a man to write a bill of divorce and put her away" (Mark 10:4). Jesus then counters by citing texts from the first book of Moses, Genesis 1:27 and 2:24, and implies that they contain Moses' real command as well as the unadulterated will of God for marriage. In Matthew 19:7, it is the Pharisees who ask Jesus, "Why did Moses *command* one to give a certificate of divorce and to put her away?" Jesus counters by saying that Moses did *not* command this but *permitted* it because of human hardness of heart. The stipulations in Deuteronomy 24:1-4 are therefore only a concession to the obstinacy of humans and do not sanctify divorce. What God intends for marriage is not to be found in Deuteronomy 24:1-4 but in the beginning, in Genesis 1-2. The opponents treated marriage as a contract that could be canceled at the will of the husband, but the Creator intended it to be a lifelong commitment that took precedence over all other human relationships: "What God has joined together let not a man put asunder." Since God had joined the couple together, God is the Lord of the marriage. Consequently, the husband may not usurp God's role and dispose of his wife as if he were the lord of the marriage (G. Friedrich, *Sexualität und Ehe. Rückfragen an das Neue Testament* [Stuttgart: KBW, 1977], 128).

In Sirach 25:26, one finds the advice that if your wife does not go as you would have her go, you should cut her off from your flesh. Jesus claims that one can never disentangle the one flesh unity created by marriage, and the spouse can never be considered a disposable appendage. His teaching undercuts all those who thought that a husband could consider himself righteous before God if he put away his wife according to the proper procedures. With the advent of the kingdom of heaven, one can no longer deal with God on the basis of what Moses may have "permitted." God's will, as it is now fully revealed by Jesus, invades all areas of life, including what is culturally accepted and legally sanctioned.

(2) The second paragraph (19:10-12) is evoked by the dumbfounded response of the disciples to Jesus' insistence the marriage is to be permanent: "It is better not to marry!" Jesus' answer contrasts those who are literally eunuchs because of circumstances beyond their control with those who figuratively make themselves eunuchs for the sake of the kingdom. The reasons for their renunciation of marriage have nothing to do with the desire to avoid getting stuck with a lemon (the disciples' worry), a concern for cultic purity and a general suspicion of women (the motive at Qumran according to Josephus, *Antiquities* 18.1.5. §21; Philo, *Apology for the Jews* 11.14-18), or the wish to at-

tain a higher spiritual plateau (the goal of some at Corinth, 1 Cor 7). While marriage originates in the divine purpose of creation, some may choose to forego it because of their devotion to the kingdom of heaven (see 6:33; 1 Cor 7:32-35). Jesus' blessing of that choice once again goes against the grain of societal norms. The Jews took God's command to marry and to procreate seriously (Gen 1:28), and Rabbis were not to forsake this commandment even to devote themselves to the study of the Torah (*Tosepta Yebamot* 8:4; R. Eliezer argued: "Any Jew who does not have a wife is half a man," *Babylonian Talmud Yebamot* 63a). By contrast, Jesus allows for a variety of stances of how the disciples may live out the calling to follow him.

(3) The third paragraph (19:13-15) finds the disciples shooing away those who brought their children to be blessed by Jesus. The disciples have not yet mastered the lesson in 18:1-5. Little ones are to be received, not despised (18:10), because the kingdom of heaven belongs to such as these. The children represent the weak, the dependent, and the vulnerable of the beatitudes. The scene reinforces that childlikeness and humility is required of all (18:3-4) and that it will receive the gift of blessing.

(4) The fourth paragraph (19:16-22) addresses the particular situation of the wealthy. One who has many possessions comes to Jesus as a trustworthy teacher to inquire: "What good shall I do that I might have eternal life?" (19:16). Jesus responds curtly by asking, "Why do you ask me concerning the good? Keep the commandments!" (see Mic 6:8: "He has told you, O mortal, what is good; and what does the Lord require of you but to do justice, and to love kindness, and to walk humbly with your God?"). When the man asks for specifics, "Which ones?" Jesus starts with the second table of the ten commandments that have to do with human relationships and caps them off with the addition of the love command: "You shall love your neighbor as yourself" (see 5:43; 7:12; 22:39).

Jesus does not set himself up over against the commandments (5:17), but he has warned that unless one's righteousness exceeds that of the scribes and Pharisees (5:20) one will not enter the kingdom of heaven (=life). Could the young man have brashly claimed that he had kept the commands had he known how Jesus interpreted them (5:21-48)? One must do more than obey commandments; one must follow Jesus and Jesus' interpretation of them. The key for interpreting and obeying the commandments is the love for the neighbor. Obedience that follows only the letter of the law does not suffice. Obedience that is suffused with the spirit of love alone will open the way to life.

The command to sell all and to follow Jesus to become perfect is like a bolt from the blue. Jesus has challenged disciples to give to those who ask (5:42), to lay up treasures in heaven and not on earth (6:19–20), and to be generous (6:22–23). He has warned of the risk of trying to serve both God and mammon (6:24). But nowhere else has he insisted that selling one's possessions and giving to the poor was a condition of discipleship. For many, hostility to wealth was an important ideal (Seneca wrote: "No one is worthy of God unless he despises wealth," *Epistles* 14.18). Few actually lived out this ideal, and most would have found the demand to sell all to be unduly rash. Modern readers would probably consider the later Rabbis' charity cap of 20 percent of one's wealth more reasonable. It was designed to protect an overly generous person from becoming penniless (*Jerusalem Talmud Pe'a* 1:1, 15b; *Babylonian Talmud Ketubot* 50a; *Ta'anit* 21a).

Jesus' demand to sell all springs from the observation that the man has many possessions. The wealthy may have considered their bounty to be a sign of God's blessing. The oppressed considered it to be a sign of unrighteousness because it was assumed to be obtained through violence and oppression. B. J. Malina has argued that economic perspective in the Mediterranean world was colored by the belief: (a) that the supply of all things was limited; (b) that everyone could have the necessities of life without overexertion if others did not have too much ("Wealth and Poverty in the New Testament," *Int* 41 [1987]: 361). In an overpopulated area like Palestine with meager land resources, limited even more by the confiscation of lands by conquest, all goods were in short supply. The goal of economic life for the vast majority was not to get ahead but simply to maintain one's inherited status, no matter how humble it might be, by keeping food on the table, making payments to the landlord and other creditors, and paying tributes and tithes. The peasant had little or no buying power for anything except necessities. To try to get ahead in a limited goods economy meant that someone else had to go without. Malina writes:

> Since all good exists in limited amounts which cannot be increased or expanded, it follows that an individual, alone or with his family, can improve his social position only at the expense of others. Hence any apparent relative improvement in someone's position with respect to any good in life is viewed as a threat to the entire community. Obviously, someone is being deprived and denied

something that is his, whether he knows it or not. And since there is often uncertainty as to who is losing – it may be me and my family – any significant improvement is perceived not simply as a threat to other single individuals or families alone, but as a threat to all individuals and families within the community, be it village or city quarter. (*The New Testament World: Insights from Cultural Anthropology* [Atlanta: John Knox, 1981], 75–76)

For the small-time farmer, the landless tenant, the day laborer, and the village craftsman, it was next to impossible to accumulate wealth except through dishonorable means. If one were able to accumulate wealth, it was assumed that one had taken more than one's proper share and that another would not only have to suffer with less but might not be able to survive.

From this perspective, the rich created social disharmony and suffering for others (see Neh 5:1–13; Isa 5:8–10; Amos 5:11–12; Sir 13:3–4; 34:20–26; *1 Enoch* 92–105; Jas 5:1–6). "One was presumed to have become rich by depriving others, defrauding and eliminating others, prospering by having others become wretched, pitiable, ill, blind, and naked" (B. J. Malina, "Wealth and Poverty in the New Testament," *Int* 41 [1987]: 357). If one were born into wealth, it was presumed that one's ancestors were guilty of this. The wealth of the rich had been attained by impoverishing the peasant farmers who, as a result, led a marginal existence or became totally destitute.

The man who comes to Jesus is a special case because he is rich. When Jesus asks him to sell all that he has and give to the destitute, however, he is not asking him to impoverish himself but to redistribute his wealth among those who were deprived of what was rightfully theirs and who lacked the basic necessities of life. What he would be doing is simply returning to them their fair share of the pie and fulfilling the command to love the neighbor. A Rabbinic story expresses the general sentiment. A Roman governor of Judea asked Rabbi Akiba: "If your God loves the poor, why does He not support them?" Rabbi Akiba replied that helping the poor was a means for the rich to be saved from the punishment of hell (*Babylonian Talmud Baba Batra* 10a). God the Father of both the rich and the poor wants the one to help the other, and thus to make the world a household of love.

On the other hand, the rich man is not a special case. The demand to be perfect is made of every disciple and is not considered as something optional for extra credit (5:48). In contrast to the Greek idea of perfection, it "is not an ideal which we are to approach step by step, without ever reaching it; rather, it is a total surrender to God which we as Christ's disciples must perform, and by which we are to structure our life in the world, each according to his vocation" (R. Schnackenburg, *Christian Existence in the New Testament* [Notre Dame: Notre Dame University Press, 1968], 177–78). If the rich man is to become perfect, he must show his radical trust in God and his love for others by divesting his goods and following Jesus.

He balks at this command apparently because he counts his many possessions dearer to him than life. His thumbs down on Jesus' proposal reveals that he wanted from him only some reassurance that would allow him to live out his days comfortable in the knowledge that eternal life had been added to the many other goods he had ("What must I do *to have* eternal life?" 19:16). He will not deny himself to follow Jesus, and his many goods will fail to ransom his soul (16:24–27).

(5) In the fifth paragraph (19:23–26) Jesus solemnly announces to his disciples that the rich will enter into the kingdom of heaven only with difficulty and illustrates his point with the cartoon of a camel trying to squeeze through the eye of a needle. Despite the attempts of wealthy Christians to vitiate the force of this saying with interpretations that shrink the size of the camel or expand the opening of the needle's eye, the imagery pictures something extraordinary. The eye of the needle is the smallest opening imaginable, and the camel is the largest animal in Palestine (compare 23:24 where camels are contrasted with gnats and *Babylonian Talmud Berakot* 55b; *Baba Meṣiʿa* 38b, which contrast an elephant, the largest animal in Babylonia, and a needle). The key point, however, has to do with the more general issue that is raised by the disciples' astonished question, "Who then can be saved?" (18:25). Jesus' answer is that salvation does not come from human resources but from God alone. The young man asked, "What good thing shall *I* do?" (19:16) and insisted, "All these things *I* have observed, what do *I* still lack." He assumes that entering into the kingdom of heaven is something that he can bid for and pull off on his own (see 8:19). Whether one is rich or poor, salvation does not come from human achievement but is a gift from God to those who follow Jesus. Only God's gift of a new heart (Jer 31:33; Ezek 36:26) will enable radical obedience.

(6) The sixth paragraph (19:27–30) raises the issue of rewards. Peter and the disciples are a positive contrast to the rich man, but Peter expresses their concern about what they shall receive for having forsaken everything to follow Jesus (compare Philo's admiration of the Therapeutae for divesting themselves of their possessions and

family, *On the Contemplative Life* 18). No glory awaits them in this present world, but Jesus gives them a particular promise: "In the new age [*paliggenesia*=rebirth, regeneration], when the son of man sits on his throne in glory [see 25:31], you will yourselves sit upon twelve thrones judging the twelve tribes of Israel" (19:28). A general promise of a hundredfold reward is given to all those who have left houses and family "because of my name" (19:29).

(7) The seventh and last paragraph contains a parable that is bracketed by the saying, "the first shall be last, and the last shall be first" (19:30; 20:16). This saying should be taken as a word of warning to disciples who are the spiritual firsts and are in jeopardy of becoming presumptuous, because the parable makes clear that the reward does not come for services rendered and that there will be no differentiation among the recipients.

The parable describes a vineyard owner who hires workers for one hour and pays them the same wage as those who have toiled through the scorching heat of the day. The seeming unfairness of this largess sparks immediate protests from the outraged sunrise-to-sundown laborers. The motives behind the quizzical behavior of the owner are left unexplained, and it is best to accept the paradox of the parable that, like so many of the parables in Matthew, begins in an ordinary way only to turn to the fantastic. Appeals to the urgency of the harvest or to the social compassion of the owner lead the reader away from the point that is intended to shock the sensitivities of just about everyone.

(a) It confounds those who expect justice from God. Most understood the theme of reward and punishment thus: within the context established by gracious election and assured atonement, God is absolutely faithful to reward obedience and punish transgression since God is just. Justice is not the opposite of mercy, for God elects and forgives out of mercy. Justice, rather, is the opposite of caprice (E. P. Sanders, "Jesus, Paul and Judaism," *ANRW* [Berlin/New York: Walter de Gruyter, 1982], 25/1:398). If God is to remain a just and not a capricious God, God will render to each one's due (Ps 62:12: "Steadfast love belongs to you, O Lord. For you repay to all according to their work"; see Matt 16:27; Prov 24:12; Sir 35:22, LXX).

(b) The parable frustrates those who considered themselves to be especially pious and looked forward to preferential treatment from God. A Rabbinic parable in *Midraš Psalms* 37 reflects that expectation:

With whom may David be compared? With a laborer who worked all his days for the king. When the king did not give him his hire, the laborer was troubled and said: "Am I to go forth with nothing in my hands?" Then the king hired another laborer who worked for the king but one day, and the king laid meat before him, gave him drink, and paid him his hire in full. The laborer who had worked all his days for the king said: "Such reward for this one who did no more than work but one day for the king? For me who has been working for the king all the days of my life, how much more and more my reward!" The other laborer went away, and now the one who had been working all his days for the king was glad in his heart. (See also *Sipra Behuqotai* 2 on Lev 26:9; and *Mishna 'Abot* 2:14: "Be assiduous in the study of the law; . . . and know before whom you toil, and faithful is your employer, who will requite you the reward of your labor"; 2:16: " . . . if you have studied much in the law much reward shall be given you, for faithful is your employer who shall requite you the reward of your labor, and know the bestowal of the reward upon the righteous will be in the time to come.")

The acceptance of sinners with no clear signs that they had repented (9:10–11) and the inclusion of prostitutes and toll collectors in the kingdom (21:31–32) on an equal level with the pious was too much for some to accept.

(c) The parable jolts those who would draw a connection between those last called into the vineyard and the gentiles. The implication is that they are given the same status as Israel, who was first called and whose long covenant relationship with God earns them no favored treatment from God. Gentiles, who had no covenant, promises, messiah, sacrifices, or obedience to the law to their credit (Rom 9:3–4; Eph 2:12), and who had a long history of idolatry and immorality, are accepted as equal partners with Israel (Eph 2:19; Rom 9:30–31). Many Jewish Christians had difficulty accepting gentile converts who did not first become Jews.

(d) The parable also goes out of its way to show that no one will have seniority in the kingdom. All will be treated equally, including the disciples who left everything to follow him, those who may have sold all their goods and given them to the poor, and those who have renounced marriage to concentrate their energies on serving God. All their sacrifices give them no advantage over others when the rewards are bestowed. This parable therefore offends anyone who believes that hard work pays off and who looks at salvation as a payoff.

The owner's defense to the grumblers makes clear that no one re-

ceives less than their due. The only one worse off in the deal is the owner
who chooses to be generous with his money, and the hired hands have
no right to tell him how he may spend it. They are said to suffer from an
evil eye (=stinginess) because they begrudge the windfall that comes
the way of the other workers who are in the same economic pinch.
They would have been satisfied only if they received a bonus or if the
other workers received far less. Their outcry betrays the fact that they
want justice only for themselves and mirrors our own irritation when
God is just as good to other people who do not deserve it as God is to us
(see Luke 15:29–32). In their mercenary spiritual world, they work to
earn status over others and deny any solidarity with them. It is a world
where love has grown cold (24:12) and where one maneuvers to get
the upper hand. The next day, if there were one, they would employ a
different strategy and not sign on until the eleventh hour. If the owner
then pays them one-twelfth of a denarius, they would complain bitterly
that they were supposed to get a full day's wage.

Matthew is a Gospel that emphasizes the doing of righteousness;
but this parable shows that Matthew also understands the scandalous
nature of God's grace. God is the one who calls all who labor and
are heavy ladened to come and offers them all the same rest (11:28).
Although the wage comes only to those workers who heed the call,
they are not treated according to their individual merits but according
to their needs. Most of us are fortunate that God does not deal with us on
the basis of strict justice and sound economics and that "God pays his
servants neither by time nor piece-work but by grace . . . " (G. V. Jones,
The Art and Truth of the Parables [London: SPCK, 1964], 117, citing
W. A. Curtis, *Jesus the Teacher,* 1943, 90). The parable underscores a
Matthean theme that salvation does not come from human resources
but from the mercy of God alone.

JERUSALEM MEETS ITS KING

20:17–21:22

J esus pushes on to Jerusalem knowing full well that death by crucifixion awaits him there. This section begins with him on the way and giving his disciples a third and even more precise forewarning of coming events (see 16:21; 17:22-23): "The son of man will be handed over to the high priests and scribes; they will condemn him to death; they will hand him over to the gentiles to be mocked, scourged, and crucified, and he will be raised on the third day" (20:18-19). The section ends with him on the way to the city for the last time (21:18). The prediction of his passion and resurrection (20:17-19) is followed by five scenes. First, there are two petitions: (1) a request for positions of glory for two brothers (20:20-28); (2) a request to see again from two blind men (20:29-34). These are followed by three symbolic actions of messianic consequence: (3) Jesus' royal entry into Jerusalem (21:1-11); (4) Jesus' entry into the temple, the overturning of the tables of the money changers and the seats of the dove vendors (21:12-13), and the healing of the blind and lame cheered by the adulation of the children (21:14-15); and (5) Jesus' condemnation of a barren fig tree (21:18-22). The first and the last scenes involve only the disciples. The first begins with a request (20:20-23), and the disciples' reaction leads to a lesson on discipleship and servitude (20:24-28). The last begins with the cursing of a fig tree (21:18-19), and the disciples' reaction leads to a lesson on making requests with believing prayer (21:20-22). The episodes in between hail Jesus as the son of David. Two blind men cry out to the son of David (20:29-31). The crowds lining the road into Jerusalem hail him as the son of David (21:9). Blind persons reappear, and the acclamation is repeated in the temple (21:14-15).

(1) The disciples have been promised thrones (19:28), and it is not long before they itch to get the top thrones (20:20-28). That the mother of the Zebedee brothers airs this request for her sons mitigates its total inappropriateness after Jesus' prediction of his death. She has not

been privy to Jesus' teaching to his disciples; and, like other mothers before her (Rachel, Bathsheba), she harbors ambitions for her own children. Jesus' answer, however, is directed entirely to the two disciples. He has promised disciples who follow him only suffering in this life (10:23; 16:24–27), and they have yet to learn that to share in his kingdom they must also share his passion (see Rom 8:17 and Rev 1:9, 20:4).

When the other disciples fume because James and John beat them to the punch and may have gained an edge on the power slots, Jesus reiterates his teaching on humility (18:1–4) using different imagery. The way to make it to the proverbial top as a disciple is to get down low as a slave. In the heathen world, the great ones were those who could best bend the wills of others to conform to their own. The goal is to dominate others. Disciples, however, are to serve others as if they belonged to them – as slaves. Those who are primarily interested in achieving status and honor for themselves will not be ready to drink Jesus' cup or bear a cross.

Jesus' own subservience to his Father's will (it is the Father who will choose the ones who sit with him) is eloquently expressed in his taking on the role of servant for others (see 8:17 citing Isa 53:4; 12:18–21 citing Isa 42:1–4, 9). His death is to be an atoning death that delivers others from a desperate plight (1:21; Isa 53:6, 10, 12). The idea of an atoning death would have been familiar to Jewish ears from the accounts of righteous martyrs (4 Macc 17:20–22, "And through the blood of those devout ones and their death as an atoning sacrifice, divine Providence preserved Israel that had been previously mistreated"; see also 2 Macc 7:37; 4 Macc 6:29). Gentiles would also have understood its significance (C. E. Lutz, *Musonius Rufus* [New Haven: Yale University Press, 1947], xxix: "One who by living is of use to many has not the right to die unless by dying he may be of use to more").

(2) The healing of the two blind men on the road from Jericho (20:29–34) is the twin of the healing of two blind men in Galilee (9:27–31). Both sets of blind men cry, "Have mercy on us son of David" (9:27; 20:30), address Jesus as "Lord" (9:28; 20:33), and are healed when Jesus touches their eyes (9:29; 20:34). The emphasis in the second account is on Jesus' compassion as the son of David, which contrasts with the callous attitude of the crowd (see 9:36; 14:14; 15:32), but the theme of discipleship also surfaces. The first blind men followed Jesus along the way and pursued him into the house pleading for mercy (9:27–28), but they disobeyed Jesus' command to keep quiet about the miracle

(9:30–31). The second blind men "follow Jesus" after their eyes have been opened, which implies that they follow as disciples. With his touch they recover their sight in time to witness his helpless suffering on the cross.

(3) Jesus' royal entry into Jerusalem (21:1–11) is framed by references to the city of Jerusalem: drawing near it (21:1) and entering it (21:10). The question of the inhabitants of the city, "Who is this?" (21:10), governs the scene.

Jesus arrives at the outskirts city, Bethphage, probably to be located on the summit of the Mount of Olives. From there, he dispatches two disciples (James and John, who wanted seats of power?) to commandeer a donkey and a colt. The special arrangements all point to careful staging by Jesus to present himself publicly as the son of David, the king of Israel. It is not a triumphal entry. Nothing associated with triumphal processions is mentioned, no military trappings, no trophies of war, no captives, no white horse. It is, however, a royal entry. The heir of David who was to be anointed as king rode a donkey to his coronation. When Absalom's hair got caught in the branches of a large terebinth, he was riding a donkey, which was symbolic of his claim to kingship (2 Sam 18:9). Mephibosheth rode a donkey as a symbol of his royal claim that he would make for the old house of Saul had the insurrection of Absalom succeeded (2 Sam 19:27). David, anxious to secure Solomon's claim to the throne over that of Adonijah's, instructs his comrades to mount Solomon on his donkey to ride to his anointing as king (1 Kgs 1:32–40; see also 2 Kgs 9:13). Jesus' approach to the city from the east, from the Mount of Olives, is also suggestive, since some expected that the messiah would come from the east, from the Jordan valley (see Josephus, *Antiquities* 20.8.6 §169; *Jewish War* 2.13.5 §261; *Genesis Rabba* 98:9; *Qoheleth Rabba* 1:9; *Babylonian Talmud Sanhedrin* 98a; 99a; and Zech 14:1–5).

Matthew turns again to the Scripture to amplify the significance of this event with a fulfillment quotation: "Say to the daughter of Zion, Behold your king comes to you, meek and mounted upon an ass [*onos*] and upon a colt [*pōlon*], the son of a beast of burden [*hypozygios*]." Most of the citation is from Zechariah 9:9, but the opening line comes from Isaiah 62:11. Both of these passages are addressed to the daughter of Zion and mention the coming of a savior or king. The end result of Matthew's blending of the two passages is telling. First, the splicing of the excerpt from Isaiah 62:11 supplants "rejoice greatly, daughter of Zion" in Zechariah and turns the quotation into a command, "deliver

a message to Jerusalem!" Jesus' arrival is not to be a time of rejoicing for the city. It is instead a challenge to recognize its king. Second,
the quotation from Zechariah with its reference to a coming king (instead of "savior" in Isaiah [LXX]) omits the phrase "he is righteous
and saving." This omission is perhaps surprising since it would fit ad-
mirably with Matthew's presentation of Jesus. It suggests that, from
Matthew's point of view, Jesus does not come to rescue the city from
its enemies but to confront it with its sins. His concluding words to
the city will announce its doom because of those sins (23:37–39; see
24:2).

Matthew's specific mention of Jesus entering the city with two
animals is perplexing. Is this another example of his doubling (two
demoniacs, 8:38; two blind men, 9:27; 20:30)? Is the mother brought
along to steady the young colt? The text reads that the disciples put the
garments on "them," and he sat upon "them" (21:7). Does the Evangelist want the reader to think that Jesus rode into Jerusalem riding
on both animals? Or should this be dismissed as clumsy expression?
Matthew meant that Jesus sat on the garments. The Evangelist is not
a clumsy writer, and the explanation for the two animals is probably
related in some way to the citation from Zechariah. Some argue that
Matthew misinterpreted the Hebrew parallelism (the repetition of the
same idea in different words) and took the two descriptions of the same
animal to be a reference to two different animals. Some contend that
he failed to understand because he was a gentile; but the Fourth Gospel
manifests a similar method of interpreting Scripture (see John 19:23–
24), and the assumption that each word has an application can also
be found in Rabbinic interpretation. It is more likely that Matthew had
some specific theological motive for referring to the two animals and
flexed the grammar to serve that purpose.

Justin's allegorical interpretation of this passage is congenial with
Matthew's mind-set if not his meaning. Justin read Genesis 49:11,
"He tethers his donkey to the vine, his purebred ass to the choicest
stem . . . ," into the story of the entry (see also *Genesis Rabba* 98:9). He
interpreted the donkey allegorically as a symbol of the Jews yoked to
the law and the colt as a symbol of the unharnessed gentiles (*Dialogue*
53:1–4). For Matthew, however, the two animals may have represented
two dimensions of Jesus' identity. Mounted on a donkey, a coronation
animal, Jesus enters Jerusalem as the royal son of David, the messiah.
Mounted on the son of a pack animal, he comes as the meek, suffering servant who will take away our weaknesses and bear our diseases

(12:19). The king messiah of Israel will rule by virtue of his humble suffering and death.

Those who go with Jesus into the city take their cue from the blind men of Jericho in crying aloud from the Psalms, "Hosanna to the son of David," "Blessed is He who comes in the name of the Lord" (21:9; Ps 118:26). Psalm 118 was a royal psalm recited on the annual enthronement of the king. Its association with Zechariah 9:9 is, according to J. A. Sanders, an "explosive fusion." "It would have been all right to recite it as one among many psalms in celebration of a festival, but it would have been blasphemous to reenact it with its original royal meanings to those not otherwise convinced of the claim" (Sanders, "Psalm 118," 180). The psalm was not to be read and enacted that way until the messiah came (Sanders, "Psalm 118," 190).

The reaction of the inhabitants of the city, who are distinguished from the crowds, is therefore not surprising given the messianic drama. They do not rejoice; instead, the narrator notes that "all the city was shaken" (21:10, compare 1 Kgs 1:40) and was perplexed as to who this one might be. The crowds announce Jesus to be "the prophet from Nazareth in Galilee" (16:14; 21:46; 2:23). Their perception of Jesus' full identity is muddled because it has not been given to them, but it is portentous. The city that has been called the "holy city" (4:5; see 27:53) and "the city of the great king" (5:35) will be soon be identified as the city that murders prophets (23:37).

(4) The temple was the ceremonial and cultural center of Judaism as well as the headquarters for the spiritual and political leadership. Jesus executes an even more daring act than his royal entry by disrupting the temple routine in 21:12–13. According to *Psalm of Solomon* 17:30, the son of David will "purge Jerusalem (and make it) holy as it was even in the beginning." It is questionable, however, whether Jesus' actions in the temple should be viewed as an attempt to resanctify it. Nothing in the text suggests that Jesus' attack was provoked by his pique at dishonest business practices or profiteering. He throws out buyers as well as sellers (21:12). There is also no hint that Jesus is angry that such activity was taking place within the temple precincts, nor does he impugn the moral or ritual impurity of the priests (contrast *Psalm of Solomon* 8:12; CD 5:6–8). "Those who write about Jesus' desire to return the temple to its 'original,' 'true' purpose, the 'pure worship of God,' seem to forget that the principal function of any temple is to serve as a place of sacrifice, and that sacrifices *require* the supply of suitable animals" (E. P. Sanders, *Jesus and Judaism* [Philadelphia: For-

tress, 1985], 63). A monetary exchange was also required for pilgrims to purchase animals for sacrifice and to pay their half shekel dues (see on 17:24–27) in the proper coinage (see *Mishna Šeqalim* 1:3). Jesus' prophetic protest is not directed against any so-called abuses but against the normal functioning of the temple as a place of sacrifice. If sacrificial victims cannot be purchased, then sacrifice must end. If money cannot be exchanged into the holy currency, then monetary support for the daily sacrifices that effect atonement between Israel and God (*Tosepta Šeqalim* 1:6) must end.

Jesus "does not merely lament like a prophet, he takes action. He does not call down judgment, he exercises it" (W. Trilling, *The Gospel according to St. Matthew* [London: Burns and Oates, 1969], 2:140). The action is interpreted by a combination of quotations from Isaiah 56:7 ("My house shall be called a house of prayer for all nations") and Jeremiah 7:11 ("Has this house, which is called by my name, become a den of robbers in your sight"). The context of Jeremiah 7:8–10 is vital for understanding this latter saying:

> [8]Here you are, trusting in deceptive words to no avail. [9]Will you steal, murder, commit adultery, swear falsely, make offerings to Baal, and go after other gods that you have not known, [10]and then come and stand before me in this house, which is called by my name, and say, "We are safe!" – only to go on doing all these abominations? (NRSV)

The den is not the place where bandits do their robbing; it is the place of security and refuge where they retreat after having committed their crimes. Jesus rails against the temple for not being a house of prayer and for becoming a sanctuary for religious knaves who believe that they can find automatic absolution from sin and fellowship with God through the sacrificial cultus (see the emphasis on mercy over sacrifice in 9:13; 12:7). Jesus is to be the ransom for the people (Exod 30:12–13) for the forgiveness of sins (26:28) whose death will make the cult of animal sacrifice obsolete, and the temple will lie desolate (23:38). The *locus* of salvation and the hope of the nations is not to be the temple in Jerusalem (which is why the phrase "for all nations" is omitted from the quotation from Isa 56:7). It is so corrupt that it has lost its capacity to bring the unholy into communion with the Holy God. That power will shift to Jesus through his death and resurrection. Prayer and faith (in Jesus), not animal sacrifice, will be the way to fellowship with God.

This fact is highlighted by Jesus' healing of the outcasts in the temple and the response of the lowly. The blind and lame, who were barred access to the sanctuary of God's presence (see Lev 21:18-19; 2 Sam 5:8 [LXX]; 11QTemple 45:13; *Mishna Ḥagiga* 1:1), come to Jesus and are healed. On the one hand, this healing is a fulfillment of Micah's prophesy that the lame and rejected will be gathered and restored (4:6-7). On the other hand, it is another token of the inadequacy of the temple. The temple and its purity system failed to make these people whole and only promoted social injustice by stigmatizing them and excluding them according to purity classifications. Jesus embraces all who are weak and burdened and renews them.

The high priests and scribes, who have been singled out as the ones who will be responsible for Jesus' suffering and death (16:21; 20:18), have their first face-to-face encounter with Jesus in this scene. Annoyed by what "children" are yelling out, "Hosanna, to the son of David," they want Jesus to repudiate them. Instead, Jesus endorses their adulation as a fulfillment of Scripture. The praise God prepared for himself does not come from the priests and elders of the people but from babes (see 11:25), because the childlike, the nobodies, are closest to the kingdom of heaven (18:3; 19:13).

Jesus' first appearance in the temple is fateful. He (a) denounces the place of worship as a den of thieves, (b) dismisses the type of worship (sacrifice instead of prayer), and (c) degrades the leaders of the worship who are supplanted by suckling infants.

(5) Jesus' run-in with a fig tree on the way back to Jerusalem the next day is a bizarre conclusion to this section of dramatic signs (21:18-22). He resisted the temptation to turn stones into bread when he was hungry in the wilderness, but now he lays waste a fig tree for not providing him fruit to assuage his hunger. This action can be properly understood only when it is seen as an enacted parable that helps interpret what Jesus has done in the temple and what will happen to the temple. The tree that has not borne fruit is not pruned or fertilized but condemned and destroyed. Likewise, the temple will also be destroyed (24:2; see Jer 7:14; Mal 3:1, 4:6).

What amazes the disciples, however, is not that Jesus did such a thing or its prophetic symbolism but that the fig tree "withered immediately" (21:20). When Matthew wrote, the temple already lay in ruins; and this fact was construed as God's just punishment on a sanctuary that was indelibly defiled by the blood money for Jesus' death (27:5). The symbolism of the withered fig tree is muted in favor of learning how this miracle applies to the church. It becomes a lesson on the power of faith. The disciples will be able to do wonders through believing prayer (21:22), and the church will take the place of the temple as a house of prayer (21:13).

JESUS LORD IN THE TEMPLE

21:23–22:46

T his section finds Jesus teaching in the temple and challenged from all sides by enemies. It falls neatly into two parts. (1) The first part (21:23–22:14) begins with the high priests and elders of the people crossing swords with Jesus over his authority. Jesus deflects their challenge with an embarrassing question of his own and routs them with three slashing parables. The units are interconnected. The high priests' inquiry (21:23–27) and Jesus' first parable concerning the two children (21:28–32) are linked by the issue of believing and responding to John's preaching (21:25, 32). The parable of the two children (21:28–32) and the parable of the wicked tenants (21:33–44) have in common a reference to a vineyard and a reference to "the kingdom of God" (21:31; 21:43). An interlude apprises the reader that the chief priests and Pharisees recognize that the parables allude to them and that they want to seize Jesus (21:45–46). The parable of the wedding invitation and the guests (22:1–14) follows and is related to the parable of the wicked tenants by the mention of a son (21:37; 22:2), the sending of servants who are abused and murdered (21:35–36; 22:3–6), the destruction of the perpetrators, and the transfer of favor to another group (21:41, 43; 22:8–10). This first part exposes the culpability of the high priests as wayward leaders of Israel and highlights the judgment that they will incur on themselves and the nation.

(2) The second part (22:15–46) exposes the inadequacy of the teachers of Israel as the Pharisees and Sadducees take center stage in futile attempts to entrap or humiliate Jesus with three challenges: (a) a question about paying taxes to Caesar (22:15–22); (b) a question about the resurrection (22:34–30); and (c) a question about the greatest commandment (22:34–40). Jesus successfully parries their verbal jabs and, in the final scene, silences the Pharisees with his own question about the messiah. They correctly acknowledge that the messiah is the son of David but have no answer to the riddle, "If David calls him Lord, how can he be his son?" (22:45). The result is that the embarrassment

of Jesus' opponents frames the entire section. The high priests can only answer, "We do not know," to Jesus' question about the divine or human origin of John's baptism (21:26-27). The Pharisees who hoped to snare Jesus in his talk (22:15) also end up outmatched, unable to answer him a word (22:46).

(1) The first part begins with the chief priests and the elders of the people questioning Jesus' authority to do "these things" (see Acts 4:7). "These things" refers to the royal entry into Jerusalem, the fracas in the temple, the healing of the blind and lame, as well as his teaching in the temple, which has been mentioned in passing (21:23; see 7:28). For the reader, the narrative has already furnished the answer. The Father has given all things to Jesus (11:27); and Jesus' presence is something greater than the temple (12:6). These leaders get no direct answer from Jesus as he keeps them at bay with a counter question about the origin of the baptism of John: Was it divinely sanctioned or not?

The divine authority of John is linked to what Jesus is doing. The connection is found in the similarity of their mission to Israel. Both John and Jesus sought the eschatological restoration of Israel, demanded that the people do what God requires, and warned of certain judgment if they failed. The reader is let in on the quandary of the authorities as they mull over the possible answers about John's authority and is able to witness their basic dishonesty. They cannot say that John's commission came from heaven because that would incriminate them for having ignored him (and his testimony about Jesus). They cannot say that his commission was *not* from heaven because that would imply that he was a fraud and cause them to lose more respect from the people who venerated him as a prophet. Controlled by their fear of the people (see Acts 5:26), they decline to commit themselves one way or the other. The three parables that follow implicitly condemn them for their refusal to heed the call of John and for the violence they will do to Jesus. The parables also outline what God requires: (a) belief, repentance, and obedience (going to the vineyard); (b) rendering to God what is owed (providing the fruits of the vineyard); and (c) responding worthily to God's grace (wearing the garment of righteousness).

(a) In the first parable (21:28-32), one child appears to be disobedient by refusing the father's request to go into the vineyard; the other child appears to be obedient by politely addressing his father as "Lord" and giving a positive response to the request. The truth is to be found in the hard evidence of their actions (a Matthean leitmotif). The first child later repented and went into the vineyard; the second failed to follow through on the promise. When asked which child did the will of his father, the leaders condemn themselves by picking the first (the most likely of the textual variants).

In Matthew, it is not the one who merely says, "Yes," but the one who actually goes and works who does the will of the Father (see 7:21; 12:50; 23:3). Jesus goes on to make a daringly direct application of the parable. The leaders' disobedience contrasts with the belief and repentance of notorious sinners who would seem to be beyond the pale (see 9:9–11). It is possible to turn one's "no" into a "yes." The leaders, however, only said yes to the trappings of piety and never repented from the heart. Consequently, the despised toll collectors and harlots not only precede the chief priests, they dislodge them (see 8:11–12).

In a Rabbinic commentary on Deuteronomy 14:1, "You are the children of the Lord your God," Rabbi Judah remarks, "If you conduct yourselves like dutiful children, you are His children; if not, you are not His children." Rabbi Meir, however, speaks for the majority by countering that the verse means what it says, that you are children no matter what (*Sipre Deuteronomy* §96; see *Babylonian Talmud Qiddušin* 36a). John the Baptist first raised the question whether Jewish religious leaders could be counted as true children if they did not repent (3:9). In this parable, Jesus would side with the interpretation of Rabbi Judah: those who can be counted as children are only those who obey the Father (see Rom 9:6–9).

(b) The second parable reflects the world of absentee landlords. In Longus's novel *Daphnis and Chloe,* the protagonists receive word that the master of the estate where they kept sheep is coming. Preparations are made to make things as presentable as possible (4.1), but Daphnis is frightened at the thought of seeing the dreaded master who heretofore had been only a name (4.6). They become even more anxious when an enemy vandalizes their garden, thinking that the master might have them hanged (4.8); and they pray that he may never come (4.9). Then a messenger relays news that their master will arrive in three days but that his son is coming first and will be there the next day (4.9). Daphnis is presented to the master as doubling his flock, turning fifty she goats and two he goats into one hundred she goats and ten he goats (4:14). Jesus' parable presents a totally different picture of the reaction of the tenants to the authority of the master. It is pointedly addressed to an audience of aristocratic landlords, the high priests, who should naturally sympathize with the landlord in the story stuck with unruly tenants.

The description of the establishment of the vineyard with its hedge, winepress, and tower has no significance in the later development of the story. Therefore, it was included only to call to mind Isaiah 5:1-7. Isaiah contrasts the care that God lavishes on his vineyard, Israel, with the people's ingratitude and lack of fruitfulness. This pregnant introduction suggests to an informed reader that the parable is an illustration of God's troubled relationship with Israel. The unrealistic elements turn it into an allegory (see Llewellyn, *New Documents,* 6 §13). The servants are a transparent metaphor for the prophets who were sent by God ("thy servants, the prophets," Jer 7:25; Dan 9:6; Amos 3:7) and whose mistreatment, according to popular legend, was infamous (see Jer 7:25-26; Neh 9:26; 2 Chron 24:18-19; 36:15-16; *Jubilees* 1:12-13; Matt 5:12, 23:31-39; Luke 13:31-33; Acts 7:52; 1 Thess 2:15; Heb 11:36-38). Whether the "son" would have been a transparent metaphor for the messiah is debated, but, for Matthew, the association is clear.

The son, who is sent "later" (21:37), is on a different level from the servants; and the Gospels all agree that the motivation for sending him is that the tenants would "respect him." The tenants recognize the son immediately: "This is the heir." "Come let us kill him [see Gen 37:20a], and we might have his inheritance." This acknowledgment of the son does three things. First, it heightens the tenants' guilt: they deliberately killed one whom they knew to be the son. Second, it raises the question: to whom does the inheritance truly belong? Third, it illustrates the blind folly of evil.

In Matthew, Jesus again invites the high priests to provide the conclusion to a parable with the loaded question, "What will the Lord of the vineyard do to those farmers?" Again, they condemn themselves from their own mouths: the wretched tenants will meet a wretched end and the vineyard will be taken away from them by the landlord and given to other farmers who will render to him the fruits in their seasons (21:41). This is what they as landlords have done with their tenants in the countryside (see M. Goodman, *The Ruling Class of Judaea* [Cambridge: Cambridge University Press, 1987], 55-60); and the implication is clear that God, as landlord, will do no differently.

The tenants live in a self-centered world and want to be the lords, not the servants, of the vineyard (20:26-27). God, however, stands in the way of their plans; and they will kill the messengers who remind them of that reality. When they slay the heir, however, they have not won. They still have to deal with God. The prolonged refusal of the owner to come in judgment becomes a symbol of God's patience and the blessed idiocy of God's grace (see Rom 2:4; 2 Pet 3:9). God has every intention of collecting the rent, however; and the owner suddenly changes from one who is seemingly impotent to one who is able to wreak vengeance on those who foolishly thought that they could have things all their own way. The additional conclusion to the parable in 21:43, unique to Matthew, develops the idea of the transfer of the stewardship of the vineyard to new, ideal tenants and is significant for Matthew's ecclesiology. The fact that "nation" is not plural means that it does not refer to non-Jews, "the nations" (contrast 5 Ezra 1:24). The "nation" consists of those who will produce the fruits of the kingdom (21:41, 43). This criterion means that the new stewards of God's vineyard will not hold their position by inheritance as the priests did. They can come from all walks of life, including ex-fishermen, toll collectors, and harlots. They need not be limited to the heirs of Abraham. They can come from every tribe among the nations.

Matthew also specifies that it dawns on the high priests *and the Pharisees* that the parables apply to them (Matt 21:45, compare Mark 12:12; Luke 20:19). They fully understand the implications of the parables (contrast 13:10–17) including the insinuation that Jesus is the "son," an issue that will resurface in the trial before the Sanhedrin (26:63). That they moved ahead with their plot to have Jesus killed in spite of being forewarned means that they did so with malice aforethought. Real life will imitate art, and the guilt and folly of these leaders is magnified.

The inheritance, however, still belongs to the one heir, the son. The imagery in Psalm 118:22–23 of the rejected stone that originally applied to the nation Israel is here transferred to Jesus (21:42). He is the stone rejected by the builders (an epithet for the temple leadership? see CD 4:19; 8:12) who will be vindicated by God in his resurrection and established as the keystone of a new structure. Matthew understands the church to be the continuation of Israel (see 8:10–12; 19:28) and discounts those who reject its Lord as a counterfeit Israel. God's vineyard, Israel, is no longer represented by the temple and its leadership. The church is something new and separate. It is made up of former outcasts and rejects who have repented and have been gathered in by the son, the true heir of the vineyard. They have welcomed the invitation, honored the rejected cornerstone, and complied with the demands that come with God's gracious acceptance of them. Those who hold cheap God's gracious offer will be judged because one cannot string God along, but those who accept that offer cannot take God's grace for granted, as the next parable makes clear.

(c) The third parable, the parable of the wedding feast (22:1–14), bears some resemblance to the parable of the banquet in Luke 14:15–24, but the dissimilarities are substantial. Matthew's parable concerns a royal feast, and the details are especially unrealistic. Why would anyone kill a king's servants simply for bringing them an invitation? How can a wedding feast still be ready for other guests after the king has mobilized an army and burned a city to the ground? Why is a man bound hand and foot and thrown into the outer darkness where there is weeping and gnashing of teeth – hints of eternal damnation – simply for not showing up in a proper garment? The punishment seems incommensurate with the crime. How does one explain such fanciful details?

Again, we have an allegory. The feast is a transparent image for the eschatological culmination of history (see 8:11, 25:10; see Rev 19:7–9; *2 [Syriac] Apocalypse of Baruch* 29:3–8) that has been *prepared* by God (22:4, 8; see 20:23; 25:34, 41). Like the previous parable, servants are sent and rejected. A son is also mentioned; but, unlike the previous parable, he is not sent and does not otherwise figure in the story. The best explanation for this feature is that the son represents the son of God, the bridegroom (9:5; Rev 21:2, 9), who is assumed to be "already with his father in glory" (Meier, *Matthew*, 247). The allegorical parable looks back on the sweep of the history of salvation from the sending of the prophets to the final judgment.

The servants who are sent to summon those who had been invited to the feast are ignored by some and abused by others. The disregard of the invitation (22:3) fits Jesus' complaints against both Galilee (11:16–20) and Jerusalem (21:24–26; 23:37, "you would not"). They dismissed both John and Jesus. The brutality fits Jesus' remarks about how the prophets were received (5:11–12; 23:29–31, 37) and his warnings about what will happen both to him (16:21; 17:22–23; 20:18–19; 26:2) and to his disciples (10:7–25; 20:23; 23:34). The incongruous detail of setting out on a military campaign to kill the murderers and to burn their city (22:7) could have been omitted without effecting the point of the parable: those who were invited first were not worthy and others will be invited to take their place (22:8–9). The fact that the *Blitzkrieg* against the city is mentioned at all is therefore suggestive. While it may be a stock motif in vengeance stories (Lev 26:31; Judg 1:8; Isa 1:7; 1 Macc 5:28; *Testament of Judah* 5:6), after 70 C.E., Matthew and his readers could hardly see it as anything other than an allusion to the destruction of Jerusalem that has already taken place. The murderers (the Jewish leaders) and their city (Jerusalem) have been destroyed.

The parable does not end with the destruction of the city. The privileged who rejected the invitation are declared to be "unworthy" (see 3:7-10; 10:11, 13, 37, 38), and the servants are sent out once again to invite the unprivileged who do accept. The camera pans to a hall that is packed with both evil and good. As Jesus' disciples include one who is a betrayer (10:4), so his church that has cast its net far and wide will mirror the world and will also be composed of a mix of evil and good. The final separation will not occur until the last judgment (13:24-30, 36-43, 47-50), and this last scene depicts it taking place as the king comes to inspect his guests. All are arrayed in their wedding garments except for one who represents a category of persons with rumpled and soiled garments.

While modern readers may be troubled by what seems to be the unfair ejection of a man for failing to have the proper attire when he has just been pulled in off the street, his silence is an admission of guilt. The garment must be interpreted allegorically, and the man is assumed to be as responsible for providing himself with clean, suitable clothing for the banquet as the maidens are for providing oil for their lamps (25:1-13). A similar point is made in a parable attributed to Rabbi Joḥanan ben Zakkai interpreting Qoheleth 9:8, "Let thy garments be always white, and let not thy head lack ointment":

> This may be compared to a king who summoned his servants to a banquet without appointing a time. The wise ones adorned themselves and sat at the door of the palace ["for"] said they, "Is anything lacking in a royal palace?" The fools went about their work, saying, "Can there be a banquet without preparations?" Suddenly the king desired [the presence] of his servants: the wise entered adorned, while the fools entered soiled. The king rejoiced at the wise but was angry with the fools. "These who adorned themselves for the banquet," ordered he, "let them sit, eat and drink. But these who did not adorn themselves for the banquet, let them stand and watch." (*Babylonian Talmud Šabbat* 153a; see also *Mishna ʾAbot* 4:16: This world is like a vestibule before the world to come: prepare thyself in the vestibule that thou mayest enter into the banqueting hall.)

Clothing is frequently used as a metaphor in the New Testament (Rom 13:12, 14; Gal 3:27; Eph 4:22-24; Col 3:9-11) and particularly as an apocalyptic image for moral worthiness (Rev 3:4-5, 18; 6:11; 7:13-14; 22:14-15). In Revelation 19:8, the fine linen represents the righteous deeds of the saints. This meaning fits an emphasis found throughout Matthew: grace does not cancel the reality of the judgment; each one will be judged according to their works (16:27; see 7:15–27 and the three parables in chapter 25). God's summons requires a changed life that results in fruit (3:8), and a righteousness that surpasses conventional norms of behavior (5:20).

The first part of the allegory portrays the failure of Israel to heed the summons of God's servants. They rejected the prophets and the disciples of Jesus, and the destruction of their city is the consequence. One cannot trifle with God and get away with it. The addition of the man without a wedding garment, however, prevents the reader from gloating over the presumed fate of Israel. It introduces a new motif of the final assessment of those who do respond to the invitation that went out indiscriminately to one and all – the members of the community. Matthew's ecclesiological and ethical interests once again emerge. The vineyard is to be turned over to tenants who are expected to produce the ethical fruits of the kingdom (21:43), and the wedding garment expresses the same requirement using different imagery. This allegory is a warning to disciples who may ignore doing what God requires: they are not exempt from the same judgment that befell the leaders of Israel who ignored God's invitation.

Throughout his Gospel, Matthew uses the threat of judgment to motivate disciples to do good works (G. Barth, "Matthew's Understanding of the Law," 60). The theme of the coming judgment of God appears in some sixty units (for example, 5:21; 7:2, 22–23; 10:15; 11:22–24; 12:36, 41; 13:36–42, 47–50). Many of these are salted with vivid imagery: being pitched out into the outer darkness where humans will weep and gnash their teeth (8:12; 22:13; 25:30; see 13:42); being burned in fire (3:10; 7:19), an unquenchable fire (3:12), a fiery furnace (13:42, 50), eternal fire (18:8, 9; 25:41), or a fiery Gehenna (5:22; 18:9, see 5:29); being delivered to the tormentors until the last penny is paid (18:34); being dismembered ("cut in two," 24:51); entering the way that leads to perdition (7:13); and being consigned to eternal punishment (25:46). This hell fire and brimstone imagery is unwelcome if not repugnant to a modern generation that has lost a sense of sin and that does not give credence to God's recompense for sin. God is supposed to be more obliging. In Matthew's Gospel, God is obliging in forgiving sins (9:2–7; 18:27), in graciously offering a full day's wage to those who deserve less (20:1–15), and in extending the invitation to the wedding feast to one and all. This parable makes clear that one need not possess the garment to be invited to the party – both good and bad are brought in – but one needs it to stay (Bruner, *Churchbook*, 2:777). God's grace may not be taken for granted. God requires obedience, which does not merit salvation but is evidence of it (Gundry, *Matthew*, 439).

A church that is composed of good and evil, of false prophets (7:15), of those who cause others to sin (18:6), who refuse to listen to correction (18:15–17), who are unmerciful (18:23–35), whose love has grown cold (24:12), and who abuse their fellow servants (24:49) needs to be warned. God's standard bearers in the world must live up to God's standards (5:16).

The final punch line of the parable (22:14) seems to suggest on first reading that God has chosen only a few for salvation. The "many" and "few," however, reflect a Semitic idiom that basically means that all are called but not all are chosen (see 4 Ezra 8:3, 41; B. F. Meyer, "Many (=All) are Called, But Few (=Not All) Are Chosen," *NTS* 36 [1990]: 94–96). "Called" refers to the invitation (20:3, 4). "Chosen" is an adjective in the Greek text and does not mean that some are chosen to participate while others are chosen not to participate. The ones who were originally invited were deemed unworthy because they chose not to come (see 7:13–14). While some spurn the invitation, others respond unworthily. The chosen ones are those who respond to the invitation worthily; they are "choice" (see 1 Thess 2:12, "to walk worthily of your calling").

(2) The second part of this section (22:15–46) presents religious teachers challenging Jesus. (a) In 22:15–22 a delegation from the Pharisees first attempts to disarm Jesus with flattery and then snare him with a yes or no answer about the head tax paid to the Romans. Its establishment provoked the revolt of Judas of Galilee in 6 C.E. for placing God's own land at the service of pagans (Josephus, *Antiquities* 18.1.1 §1–10; *Jewish War* 2.8.1 §118), and so the question is fraught with danger. Jesus sets his own trap, however, by asking them for the coin used to pay the tax. A Roman coin, bearing the image of the emperor and conveying Roman ideology ("Tiberius Caesar, son of the divine Augustus and high priest"), is found in the temple. Jesus reminds them that they already acknowledge Caesar's authority by having in their possession Caesar's money. The decisive matter is rendering to God, Caesar's Lord, the things that are God's. "Render" means to pay a debt and is the same verb used in 21:41: the vineyard will be handed over to a nation that will render to God the fruits of the kingdom. Jesus therefore takes the issue out of the political crossfire and raises it to the level of the demands of the reign of God. Caesar is owed what bears his image and name – money. But God is owed what bears God's image and name – our very

selves (Gen 1:26; Prov 7:3; Jer 38:33; Isa 44:5; Tertullian, *On Idolatry* 15; *Against Marcion* 4.38.3, cited by C. H. Giblin, " 'The Things of God' in the Question Concerning Tribute to Caesar [Lk. 20:25; Mk 12:17; Mt 22:21]," *CBQ* 33 (1971): 522–23.

(b) The Sadducees, who rejected what they perceived to be theological innovations not found in the Pentateuch, enter the fray to pose a mocking question to ridicule Jesus' belief in the resurrection (22:23–33; see 16:21; 17:22–23; 20:17). They present him with a conundrum involving the custom of levirate marriage (Gen 38:8; Deut 25:5–10). The goal of the levirate marriage was to ensure that a man who dies without children will have descendants. Death is thwarted by the production of heirs. In their case study, seven brothers have married the same woman, and all have died without providing heirs for the late brothers (like Sarah whose seven husbands had each died on the marriage night, Tob 3:8; 6:14). They gleefully ask, "In the so-called resurrection, whose wife will she be, since they all had her?" (22:23–28). The assumption behind their lampoon is a crude, materialistic view of resurrection and the mistaken conviction that family is all there is to life here and now and in any life to come.

Jesus' responds to the riddle by charging that they do not know the Scriptures or the power of God (22:29). His answer does not start with anthropology but with the biblical view of God that was voiced thrice daily in prayer by devout Jews in the first and second of the Eighteen Benedictions (D. Daube, *Appeasement or Resistance and Other Essays on New Testament Judaism* [Berkeley: University of California, 1987], 6–8). The first benediction refers to "the God of Abraham, Isaac, and Jacob." God is not God in general but a God who binds himself to individuals who become a part of God's name, the God of Abraham, Isaac, and Jacob. Schweizer writes, " . . . it is not only true as long as this individual will be strong and good; it will also be true when he or she will be weak or low" (E. Schweizer, "Resurrection – Fact or Illusion," *HBT* 1 [1979]: 144). As God lives, they will live. The living God (Num 14:14:28; Josh 3:10; Ps 41:2; Isa 37:4, 17; 49:18; 4 Macc 7:18–19; 16:25) is therefore the God of the living (compare the Rabbinic answers to the question, "How is resurrection derived from the Torah?" in *Babylonian Talmud Sanhedrin* 90b–91a). The second benediction addresses God as the one "who revives the dead." The Sadducees have underestimated God. To deny the resurrection is to deny the basic confession of God as a God of power (Sand, *Matthäus*, 445; see 24:30; 26:64).

Jesus also corrects the Sadducees' misconception of resurrection.

It will not be a return to a more enjoyable and longer life on earth; the resurrected will enter into a new kind of existence with God to become like angels (see *2 [Syriac] Apocalypse of Baruch* 51:3, 10). Since death is no more, marriage is no longer needed to propagate the human species. Family relationships in the life to come will be transcended, which explains why Jesus has insisted that they cannot be regarded as the primary relationship in this life (see 10:37; 12:46–50; 19:29).

(c) The third and final questioner is identified as a lawyer from the Pharisees who regroup after the Sadducees have been silenced (22:34–40). In Mark 12:28, he approaches Jesus as a sympathetic observer. In Matthew, he comes with a test question that is presumably intended to expose Jesus' lack of mastery of the law. But Jesus' answer ultimately silences the Pharisaic expert in the law.

The lawyer's question has to do with the priority of the command-ments and assumes that the various laws have differing importance. Once more, Jesus' answer comes from the daily prayer life of the Jews, this time the Shema (Deut 6:5). The great and first commandment is this: "You shall love the Lord your God." But Jesus adds that a second "is like" or "equal to" it. The command to love neighbor is placed on the same level as the most basic obligation of religion, the command to love God. Love has nothing to do with feelings that come and go but refers to the covenantal commitment to God that is expressed in all conduct and relationships. The conclusion is that "the whole Law and the prophets hang on these two commandments" (22:40; see 7:12). They are the fundamental principles by which all other commandments in Scripture are to be interpreted and applied, as majestically demon-strated by Jesus' teaching in the Sermon on the Mount. The incident shows that Jesus' insight into God's law is more profound than that of his Pharisaic antagonist.

(d) In the final incident (22:41–46), Jesus turns the tables on the Pharisees and asks them a direct question (only in Matthew) about the relationship between the Christ and the son of David: "What do you think? The messiah, whose son is he?" The Pharisees' conven-tional answer — that he is the son of David (see 2 Sam 7:12; 1 Chron 17:11–14; Isa 11:1; Jer 23:5–6; 33:15; Ezek 34:23–24; 37:24; 4QFlor 1:11; 1QSa 2:11–12; 1QPB 3) — is met with two further questions that frame a quotation from Psalm 110:1 (21:44): "How does David call him Lord?" (21:43); "How is he his son?" (21:45). The issue is not whether he is one or the other but how he can be both Lord and son.

Matthew has provided the reader with the answer to this question in 1:18–25.

In Matthew, the Christ is also identified as the son of God (16:20; see 26:63), and the recognition of that provides the answer to the question that opened this section, "By what authority do you these things?" Jesus' prerogatives derive from the fact that he is both the son of David and David's Lord. He is David's son by virtue of his lineage, but, more importantly, by virtue of his healing and shepherding his people. He is David's Lord by virtue of his unique relationship to God as God's obedient son (3:17; 17:5). The title son of David appears for the last time in the Gospel as it is now implied that Jesus is not simply the son of David but the God of David (see Rom 1:3–4). He is the messiah who will ascend a heavenly throne.

This last scene contains two significant differences from its parallel in Mark. What is a monologue in Mark about what the scribes say concerning the Christ becomes in Matthew a dialogue between the Pharisees and Jesus. The statement that no one dared to ask him any more questions appears after the question about the greatest commandment in Mark 12:34. In Matthew, it occurs at the end of the discussion about the son of David when Jesus has bested the Pharisees in the debate. The expert Jewish teachers have not only been unable to prevail over him in verbal jousts, they are reduced to an embarrassing silence, unable to interpret the Scripture. Jesus stands over against the so-called authorized interpreters of the law as the authoritative interpreter.

FALSE TEACHERS
LEAD OTHERS TO RUIN

23:1-39

J esus is the clear victor in the debate with the various spiritual guides
of the nation, and next he is shown impeaching their personal character and false interpretations before the disciples and the crowds. The
crescendo of charges against the scribes and Pharisees in the temple
(23:1-39) leads into the discourse on the earthly and the cosmic judgment to come that is directed only to the disciples on the Mount of
Olives (24:1-25:46).

The abusive language found in this discourse ("hypocrites," "double sons of hell," "blind fools," "blind guides," "sons of murderers,"
"brood of vipers," who are guilty of all righteous blood poured out on
the earth) has caused many to regard it as evidence of a vindictive and
vulgar anti-Judaism that is hardly compatible with Jesus' own command
to love one's enemies. Three things need to be said in response. (a) The
venom in this attack should be assessed in light of the conventions of the
rhetoric of ancient polemic (see L. T. Johnson, "The New Testament's
Anti-Jewish Slander and the Conventions of Ancient Rhetoric," *JBL* 108
[1989]: 419-41). Similar language can be found in the rhetoric of rival
Hellenistic philosophical schools and almost everywhere in the frag-
mented Judaism of the first century to vilify opponents (Johnson, 441;
for some examples, see CD 1:18-2:1; 5:12-6:1; 6:15; 8:12-13, 18; 1QH
4:10-11; 1QpHab 8:8-13; 11:4-12:10; 4QpNah 3-4 II, 8; 11QTemple
64:1-12; *Psalms of Solomon* 4; 8:22; *Assumption of Moses* 7:3-10;
Babylonian Talmud Soṭa 22b). There are hints that what the other
side was saying about "Christians" was no less bitter (see 9:3; 9:34;
12:24; John 8:48). Johnson concludes that the use of such polemic
would have communicated "that these are opponents and such things
should be said about them" (Johnson, 441). As a consequence, modern
interpreters need not try to convict or to vindicate first-century Pharisees of the charges leveled at them in this discourse. It is designed to

defrock recognized authorities and is the outgrowth of a family row — frequently the most vitriolic. It is also no more anti-Semitic or anti-Judaism than the scorching denunciations found in the prophets and other Jewish literature that announce God's wrath on those who are judged to be false stewards. The problem that many have noted, however, is the "power of such language to shape hostile and destructive attitudes and actions toward Jews" (Johnson, 421). The story has since changed from the persecution of Christians by Jews in the first century (23:34; 1 Thess 2:14–16) to the persecution of Jews by Christians ever since. The preacher therefore must be extremely sensitive to this issue in interpreting this polemic for others. The opponents of Jesus and, later, of Matthew's community did not have a corner on hypocrisy, arrogance, and injustice. One should look within one's own life and one's own religious circle to see where these denunciations apply.

(b) This discourse is not simply polemic that impugns rivals who compete to make converts to their way of thinking and doing (23:15). The language is that of a prophet who chastises a stubborn people (see Jer 23:1; Ezek 34:1–6, 7, 9, 10; Isa 10:5–19). Jesus has identified himself as a prophet (13:57) and has been extolled as one by the crowds when he enters the city (21:11; see 21:46). He has acted like a prophet in the temple and linked his authority to that of John the Baptist, recognized as a prophet by everyone but the temple hierarchy (14:5–9; 21:23–26). Now, Jesus pronounces doom-laden woes like a prophet (Isa 5:8–23; Hab 2:6–20; Zech 11:17) and expresses the prophet's characteristic outrage at injustice (23:23) and greed (23:25; Mic 6:8; Zech 7:9–10). The ironic command to fill up the measure of your fathers' sins (23:32; Isa 8:9–10; Jer 7:21; Amos 4:4; Nah 3:14–15) and the concluding lament over the judgment that is to come on the city with its allusion to an apocalyptic visitation conforms to prophetic style. The accumulation of the sins of "this generation" (23:34) will result in the inevitable devastation of the temple (24:2).

Other Jews drew similar conclusions. The sacking of Jerusalem by the Romans was viewed as God's judgment for sins committed (see Josephus, *Jewish War* 6.2.1 §110; 6.4.5 §250; *Babylonian Talmud Berakot* 3a: "on account of whose sins I destroyed my house and burnt my temple and exiled them among the nations of the world"). This discourse offers a Christian explanation for that disaster. Not only was all of this foretold by Jesus, he is the one who pronounced the sentence for the rejection and murder of his messengers (see Justin, *Dialogue* 107).

(c) A third issue has to do with the question why this discourse is specifically addressed to disciples (23:1, 8-12) and not to those who are accused. Why do disciples need to be instructed about the scribes and Pharisees (see 16:1-12)? The answer is that this discourse has a didactic purpose. "The purpose of polemic is not so much the rebuttal of the opponent as the edification of one's own school. Polemic was primarily for internal consumption" (Johnson, 433; see also D. E. Garland, *The Intention of Matthew 23,* NovTSup 51 [Leiden: Brill, 1979], 37-41, 61-63). The scribes and Pharisees provide forbidding examples of sins that are a present danger to disciples, the "scribes of the kingdom" (Matt 13:51; 23:34), who have authority in teaching and discipline (13:52; 16:19; 18:18; 28:18). They are no less guilty of a desire for first places (23:6; see 20:20-28); a discrepancy between outer appearance and inner reality (23:25-28; see 7:15); hypocrisy (7:5; see 6:1-6, 16-18); the abuse of authority (24:45-51); a haughtiness that causes others to stumble and be shut out from the kingdom (23:13; see 18:6; 19:13); an inner lawlessness (23:28; see 7:23); and a lack of mercy (23:23, see 18:21-35; 24:12). Matthew's critique of these same ruinous trends within the Christian community is oblique and accords with the rhetorical strategy attributed to Demetrius of Phaleron:

> Since great lords and ladies dislike to hear their own faults [*hamartēmata*] mentioned, we shall therefore, when counseling them to refrain from faults, not speak in direct terms; we shall rather blame some other persons who have acted in the same manner. For example, in addressing the tyrant Dionysius, we shall inveigh against the tyrant Phalaris and the cruelty of Phalaris.... The hearer is admonished without feeling himself censured.... (*On Style,* 5.292, noted by R. H. Smith, "Matthew's Message for Insiders," *Int* 46 [1992]: 237)

The warning for the church is that they had better not be found false stewards like the scribes and Pharisees; for if God did not spare a defiant Jerusalem and its temple, God will just as surely not spare an unfaithful church.

The structure of this discourse falls into three units: (1) the failure of the scribes and Pharisees as leaders and warnings to the disciples (23:1-12); (2) the failure of the scribes and Pharisees as interpreters and the pronouncement of judgment (23:13-36); (3) a lament directed to all Jerusalem (23:37-39).

(1) Jesus begins his attack by conceding the authority of the scribes and Pharisees: they sit on the seat of Moses (23:2). The seat of Moses is an abstraction (unlike "the first seats" in 23:7) and refers to their

claim to be the rightful interpreters of the Mosaic tradition (see *Mishna 'Abot* 1:1; compare Sir 45:15-17). The counsel to obey what they say but not what they do (23:3) would seem to contradict Jesus' earlier warnings about them (12:33-37; 15:14; 16:5-12), but the whole point of this discourse is to discredit these opponents who are the title holders. This opening statement cannot be a blanket endorsement of their teaching authority (see 15:14; 16:5-12), and the second half drives home the basic point that teaching must square with practice. Those whose teaching does not correspond to their deeds are automatically disqualified (see 7:15-20).

The scribes and Pharisees discredit themselves by their behavior. (a) They say but do not do (23:3b). (b) They bind heavy burdens on the shoulders of others and will not lift a finger to move them (23:4). They make the law burdensome to others – "to define in ever more detail, to impose ever more precision, to formulate ever more rules, and thus to lay ever more burdens upon those who would conform to the will of God (cf. Acts 15.10)" (D. R. Catchpole, "Temple Traditions in Q," *Templum Amicitiae,* ed. W. Horbury, JSNTsup 48 [Sheffield: JSOT, 1991], 311). The problem is that they lack the quality of love and mercy when it comes to interpreting God's will for others (see 9:9; 12:7). (c) They flaunt their piety in the way they wear phylacteries and fringes (accounted as light commandments in *Sipre Numbers* §115; see Justin, *Dialogue* 46:5-6). (d) They seek out praise and honorific titles in a scramble for social rank (23:6-7). Their professional influence is used only for self-aggrandizement. They want to be exalted by others rather than serve them as their slaves (see 20:26-27; 18:1-4).

By contrast, all titles are rejected for the disciples as an encroachment on the prerogatives of Jesus and God, who alone are worthy of them. Disciples are not to make disciples for themselves who pay homage to them (perhaps a jab at what was going on in Rabbinic circles). The one teacher and personal tutor is Christ, who alone represents the true expression of God's will in the law, by easing its burdens (11:28-30), limiting the rules (12:1-13; 15:1-20), and highlighting its broad principles (7:12; 22:34-40; see Catchpole, "Temple Traditions in Q," 311). The one Father is God (6:9). The church that is envisioned is egalitarian with the only ranks being brother, sister (12:50, 28:10), and servant. Equality, not elitism, is its mark of distinction. True authority does not exalt itself or seek to dominate others (20:25) but is exercised by those who serve others as those without authority – as slaves.

(2) The rancor intensifies in the second unit with woes that denounce the scribes and Pharisees as false interpreters (23:13-36). They can be divided into three sets of two woes with a concluding announcement of judgment. (a) The first two (23:13, 15) have to do with gaining followers. On the one hand, the scribes and Pharisees are condemned for erecting a wall that keeps others from entering the kingdom (23:13; see 9:33-34; 12:23-24; 27:11-15). A similar woe is found in the *Gospel of Thomas* 102: "Woe to the Pharisees, for they are like a dog sleeping in the manger of oxen, for neither does he eat nor does he [let] the oxen eat." On the other hand, their hard-won converts to their point of view become doubly sons of hell (as opposed to sons of the kingdom, 8:12, 13:38; compare the story of the conversion of Izates of Adiabene in Josephus, *Antiquities* 20.3.4 §38-48).

(b) The next two woes (23:16-22, 23-24) expose them as blind guides whose fixation on the minutiae of the law leads them to neglect what really matters. Their casuistry regarding oaths (which Jesus rejects altogether, see above on 5:33-37) is based on fallacious reasoning that leaves God out of the equation (23:16-22). Their application of the law regarding tithes (see Lev 27:30; Deut 14:22) is an illustration of how they make the law more specific and obedience more exacting (23:4). The problem is that they substitute tithing mint, dill, and cummin for doing justice, mercy, and faith.

(c) The next two woes (23:25-26, 27-28) exploit Pharisaic purity concerns to pour scorn on the disparity between their ritually pure outside and their corrupt inside. The first woe takes for granted that if the inside of a cup is unclean, the whole vessel is unclean (which is the way most modern readers would also see things: a cup that is full of filth is unsuitable for use no matter how clean its exterior). The same thing may be said for the spiritual purity of persons. When it comes to spiritual matters, Jesus accuses the scribes and Pharisees of attending only to the outside, which is contrary to what they insist on in ritual matters concerning cups (H. Maccoby, "The Washing of Cups," *JSNT* 14 [1982]: 3-15; see 12:34; 15:18; Acts 15:8-9). It is no surprise that those who neglect justice and mercy have cups and plates full of food gained by extortion and greed (see Amos 2:6-8). They are scrupulous when it comes to cups but without scruples when it comes to persons. For Jesus, the whole question of the purity of cups is irrelevant if their contents are derived from gouging the poor. The second woe (23:27-28) ironically condemns those who would protect the people from the impurity of graves while being themselves a source of contamination because of their inner corruption. They are teachers of law who are filled with lawlessness.

(d) The seventh and final woe accuses the scribes and Pharisees of murder (23:29–33), and its expansion threatens them with certain ruin (23:34–36). As the number of martyred prophets grew in popular legend, tombs were built to honor them and perhaps to atone in some way for innocent blood. But how does this reverence for the prophets of old implicate the scribes and Pharisees? The next verses establish the connection with a bitter prophecy that they will harden their hearts against the Christian message. The full measure of their allotted sins (see Gen 15:16; Dan 8:23; 2 Macc 6:12–14; *Pseudo Philo, Biblical Antiquities* 26:13; 47:9) will overflow with the persecution and murder of those sent by Jesus (23:34; 1 Thess 2:15–16; see 2 Chron 36:15–16). The murder of the prophets of old was a thing of the past, but the murder of Christian prophets is not. The final straw is not the condemnation of Jesus but the persecution of his envoys who are sent once more with the message to repent. Shedding their innocent blood aligns them with all the murderous villains of the past who shed innocent blood (*2 [Syriac] Apocalypse of Baruch* 64:2) and makes them ripe for judgment since righteous blood cries out until it is avenged (Gen 4:10; Job 16:18; Isa 26:21; Ezek 24:7–8; Joel 3:19; Lam 4:13; 4 Ezra 15:22; *1 Enoch* 47:1–4; *Assumption of Moses* 9:6–7). Because the scribes and Pharisees are not poor in spirit (23:6–7), do not hunger and thirst to do what God requires (23:13), are not merciful (23:23), are not pure in heart (23:28), and persecute the righteous (23:34), theirs will not be the kingdom of heaven but the judgment of hell (23:32).

(3) The mournful lament over Jerusalem (23:37–39) concludes the discourse of woes (contrast its position in Luke 13:34–35) and is also the climax of Jesus' public ministry to Israel. Jesus concedes that the attempt to gather Israel has failed, and it will be abandoned to its chosen fate, having rejected the fulfillment of its messianic hopes. As the religious teachers have forsaken the weightier matters of the law (23:23), so God will forsake the temple and allow it to be destroyed (see 2 Macc 5:15–20; *2 [Syriac] Apocalypse of Baruch* 8:2). Jesus prophesies the devastation of Jerusalem, but what does the future hold for Israel?

The cry "Blessed be he that comes in the name of the Lord" (23:39) has been taken as (a) an unconditional promise of salvation (see Rom 11:25–27); (b) a begrudging recognition of the messiah that comes too late for salvation; and (c) a conditional promise of salvation: "when his people bless him, the Messiah will come" (D. C. Allison, Jr., "Matt

23:39=Luke 13:35b as a Conditional Prophecy," *JSNT* 18 [1983]: 75–84; see Acts 3:19–21). The last interpretation implies that this particular dull-hearted and murderous generation will suffer the consequences of its sins but that Israel is not abandoned without hope. It accords with a later Rabbinic homilist's connection between Psalm 10:1 and his analysis of Israel's sad plight in the world (*Midraš Psalms* 10.2). The Holy One said to Israel:

> Return, O backsliding children (Jer 3:14, 22), and *Seek ye the Lord while He may be found* (Isa 55:6), but not one of them was willing to turn to Him. Whereupon the Holy One, blessed be He, said: *I will go and return to my former place* (Hos 5:15). Then, when the children of Israel were surrendered to the kingdoms and to the principalities, they cried out to God: *Why standest Thou afar off, O Lord?* The Holy One, blessed be He, replied: "When I sought you, you did not heed me. Now that you seek Me, I will not hear you. Measure for measure!" Hence it is said, *It came to pass that, as He called, and they would not hear; so they shall call and I will not hear, said the Lord of hosts* (Zech 7:13). Will not hear for ever? By God's mercy, no! Only *Until a time and times and half a time* (Dan 7:25).

Israel may feel the sting of God's judgment for its sins, but God does not abandon repentant Israel forever.

This interpretation also accords with the spirit of Justin who, in the second century, held out hope for Israel in spite of his own grievances against certain Jews. He complains to Rabbi Trypho that the Jews continue to slander Jesus as a deceiver and his followers as a godless and lawless sect:

> In addition to all this, although your city has been taken, and your land laid waste, you do not repent, but dare even to curse Him and all them that believe on Him. And, as for us, we do not hate you, nor them that because of you accept such suspicions of us, but we pray that even now you may repent and find mercy from God the Father of the universe, who is tender-hearted and full of compassion. (*Dialogue* 108:3)

JUDGMENT IS COMING

24:1–25:46

Jesus' announcement of doom that crowns the torrent of woes in the temple (23:34–39) and his prophecy of things to come on the Mount of Olives are related whether one regards 24:3 as the beginning of a new discourse or the continuation of the discourse begun in 23:1 (see Syreeni, *The Making of the Sermon on the Mount*, 94–96: "Matthew could have it both ways"). The moving account of the widow who offers her last penny that precedes the eschatological discourse in Mark (12:41–44) and Luke (21:1–4) does not appear in Matthew to interrupt the dark mood of judgment that links the two speeches. Jesus prophesies the abandonment and desolation of "your house" (23:38); and as he quits the temple and moves on to the Mount of Olives, he gives notice to his disciples that it will be totally demolished (24:2). As "God with us," Jesus' exit betokens God's own abandonment of this supposedly sacred space (see Ezek 11:23).

The audience narrows to the disciples alone in 24:3 (compare 13:1–2, 36), but the subject of Jesus' teaching does not completely change. The topic still concerns the announcement of destruction as Jesus answers the disciples' question about "when these things shall be." The development of this theme is nudged along by the disciples' endeavor "to show" (see 16:21) Jesus the buildings of the temple. Jesus' response, "Do you not see all these things?" differs significantly from that in Mark 13:2, "Do you see these great buildings?" and in Luke 21:6, "As for these things that you see." In Matthew, "these things" are ambiguous and most likely refer back to the disciples' inability to understand (see 13:13, 16) the "things" that Jesus has just spoken about. They refer to the judgment that will come upon this house (23:36; 24:3; compare the use of the phrase "all these things" to refer to Jesus' words in 13:34, 51, 56) and not to the temple edifice. The disciples did not point out the buildings to Jesus as if he were a tourist who had never seen them before. They were calling his attention to them to ask how he could condemn such a "noble structure dedicated to the glory of God." Jesus' answer goes beyond repudiation of the temple to a prophecy of its total destruction: "Not one stone will be left upon another, that will not be thrown down" (France, *Matthew,* 336).

The disciples follow up with a further question when Jesus is seated on the Mount of Olives. In Mark 13:4, their uncertainty relates only to the destruction of the temple, "Tell us, when will these things be and what is the sign that all these things are about to be accomplished." In Matthew 24:3, their question is two-pronged, "When shall these things be, and what is the sign of your coming [*parousia*] and the end of the age?" The question implies that the disciples now understand the gravity of "these things" and assume that the destruction of the temple would usher in the end of the age. Jesus' answer corrects this misperception. The fate of the temple is a quite separate matter from the *parousia* of the son of man and the end of the age. Jesus then proceeds to warn the disciples not to be surprised by nor to get mixed up in the mayhem that will accompany the temple's ruin.

The key to the structure of this discourse on the Mount of Olives is the disciples' double question in 24:3. (1) The answer to the first half of the question, "When will these things be?" is given in 24:4-35. "These things" refer to Jesus' announcement about God's judgment on the temple and Jerusalem. This interpretation is only one of many ways to treat this much-disputed passage, but it best explains why everything in this section is described in terms of what the disciples are able to witness and experience (24:6, 9, 10, 15, 20, 23, 25, 26, 33) and why it concludes with the affirmation that "all these things" will be fulfilled before "this generation" passes away (24:34; see 23:36, 27:25). This first section consists of four units: (a) the prelude to the catastrophe (24:4-14); (b) warnings to flee before the eruption of hostilities (24:15-22); (c) the destruction of the city described in stereotyped images of a cosmic cataclysm (24:23-31); and (d) the assurance of the certainty of this prophecy (24:32-35). The terms "these things" and "all these things" from the disciples' question in 24:3 are repeated in 24:33, 34 to form an inclusio to this section.

(2) The answer to the second half of the disciples' question about the parousia and the end of the age is given in 23:36-25:46. In contrast to the preceding section, where there are clear portents pointing to the destruction of Jerusalem ("whenever you see," 24:15) and a sequence of events ("then," 24:9, 10, 16, 21, 23, 30, "immediately after," 24:29), Jesus avows that no one knows when the end of the age will be (24:36).

It remains classified information, hidden with the Father who has not revealed it even to the son to impart to others.

In this second section there is a switch from the plural "those days" (24:19, 22, 29) to the singular "that day" (24:36, 42, 50; 25:13). Matthew has in view a single event, the final judgment day, not a sequence of events as is the case in the first section. This is confirmed by a comparison of the phrasing of Luke 17:26, "the days of Noah . . . the days of the son of man," with Matthew 24:37, "the days of Noah . . . the parousia of the son of man." From Matthew's perspective, the day and hour of the parousia and the end of the age with its judgment are unknown; and there will be no prior signs to alert one to get ready. It is inevitable, however; and one must be perpetually ready by keeping one's eyes on the job and not on the stars. The five parables that follow expand on this theme from different angles: (a) the unready generation in the days of Noah surprised by the flood (24:37-41); (b) the unready householder surprised by a thief (24:42-44); (c) the faithful versus the wicked servant set over the Lord's household surprised by his sudden return (24:45-50); (d) the prepared versus the unprepared maidens who greet the bridegroom who has been delayed (25:1-13); (e) the servants who are productive with their Lord's resources versus the unproductive one (25:14-30). The sixth and last parable in this section shifts the scene to the final judgment day and depicts the separation of the nations using the imagery of sheep versus goats (25:31-46).

The concern of this discourse is quite practical for a community that lives in the time between the destruction of the temple and the coming of the Christ at the end of the age. God's people must always be on guard against false prophets who either fan false expectations or offer false security and sidetrack them from the mission to preach the gospel to the world. Jesus' prophecies concerning the temple were fulfilled as God permitted the destruction of the holiest of shrines. No one knows the time of the end of the age, however; and no one can rest secure. Therefore, the discourse emphasizes the need for individual preparedness and faithfulness to the commission to take the gospel to the world.

(1) The first part of this discourse addresses the issue of the destruction of the temple (24:4-35). (a) It opens in 24:4-14 with Jesus citing events that presage the destruction of the temple but that *do not* herald the end (24:6). There will be a rise of impostor messiahs (24:5), wars and rumors of wars (24:6); nation arising against nation, kingdom against kingdom (24:7a, the revolt against Rome?); famine and earth-

quakes (24:7b); the escalation of persecution of Christians by all nations (24:9); the apostasy of many (24:10); the appearance of false prophets who will deceive many (24:11); and spiritual decay within the church (24:12). The dire predictions resemble Tacitus's rueful description of the age:

> The history on which I am entering is that of a period rich in disasters, terrible with battles, torn by civil struggles, horrible even in peace. Four emperors fell by the sword; there were three civil wars, more foreign wars, and often both at the same time.... Italy was distressed by disasters unknown before or returning after the lapse of the ages.... Beside the manifold misfortunes that befell mankind there were prodigies in the sky and on the earth, warnings given by thunderbolts, and prophecies of the future, both joyful and gloomy, uncertain and clear. (*Histories* 1.2, 3)

Jesus' prophecy is gloomy, but the ones who persevere through this conflagration will be saved (24:13; see Dan 12:12; 4 Ezra 6:25). Through it all, the gospel is to be preached to the whole world (24:14; see Rom 15:19). This statement anticipates the great commission in 28:20 and implies that the church is not to circle the wagons until the danger passes but is to engage in active mission. In spite of the trauma, the community's responsibility to love and to proclaim the gospel of the kingdom remains in force.

(b) In 24:15-22, the disciples are warned to stay calm and to stay out of the pseudo-messianism that will inflame others. Compare the derision of Josephus for the gullibility of the large number of Samaritans who were duped by a false prophet to rally around Mount Gerizim to view the restoration of the sacred vessels Moses had supposedly buried there and who were subsequently slaughtered by a detachment of cavalry dispatched to the scene by Pilate (*Antiquities* 18.4.1 §85-87). They are not to fret over appalling events such as the abomination of desolation "in the holy place" (24:15). The punishment of this generation does not concern the Christians; it is only the signal to flee. This command to take wing cannot refer to the end of the age when escape will be impossible, but alludes to the horrible devastation to be wrought on Jerusalem. The breakout to the mountains whose caves provided traditional hideouts (Ezek 7:16; 1 Macc 2:16, 28; 2 Macc 5:27; 10:6; Josephus, *Jewish War* 5.10.1 §420-423; see Gen 19:17) makes sense only to escape the temporal dangers of a brutal war. The disciples need only worry about those things that might hinder flight – pregnancy and nursing children; winter, when the rains make the roads impassable and food becomes more scarce; the sabbath, when fleeing Christians would stand out like sore thumbs and would antagonize other Jews (G. N. Stanton, " 'Pray That Your Flight May Not Be in Winter or on a Sabbath' [Matthew 24:20]," *JSNT* 37 [1989]: 17–30). While it may seem to be the end of the world, the parousia of the son of man is not connected to these events. Do not listen to hearsay about hidden messiahs. When he returns, he will come from heaven in a way visible to all, like lightning (*2 [Syriac] Apocalypse of Baruch* 53:8–10), or like vultures circling in the sky around a corpse (24:23–28).

(c) The paragraph in 24:29–31 depicts the end of Jerusalem using the idiom of the Hebrew Scriptures and does not depict the end of the world. The prophets used sensational figurative language to describe the destruction of cities and political disasters:

> For the stars of the heavens and their constellations will not give their light; the sun will be dark at its rising, and the moon will not shed its light. (a reference to the fall of Babylon; Isa 13:10)

> All the host of heaven shall rot away, and the skies roll up like a scroll.... " (a reference to the fall of all the enemy nations, particularly Edom; Isa 34:4)

> When I blot you out, I will cover the heavens, and make their stars dark; I will cover the sun with a cloud, and the moon shall not give its light. (a reference to the fall of Egypt; Ezek 32:7)

> The earth quakes before them, the heavens tremble. The sun and the moon are darkened, and the stars withdraw their shining. (a reference to the divine visitation on Judah; Joel 2:10; see 3:15 [4:15])

This same kind of symbolic language (compare Acts 2:16–21) is used in 24:29–31 to describe the destruction of Jerusalem, which will be held accountable for "all righteous blood" (see R. T. France, *Jesus and the Old Testament* [Downers Grove, Ill.: Intervarsity, 1971], 227–39). The grim fate of the temple and city that many assumed to be inviolable as "the sanctuary in which God dwells" (23:21) and "the city of the great King" (5:35) was far more momentous than the divine judgment of Babylon and Egypt and at least worthy of the same rhetorical fireworks.

The allusion to Zechariah 12:10, 12–14 in 24:30b refers to the tribes of the land of Palestine (see 27:45) in national mourning over the destruction of the city. The sign of the son of man (24:30a) is perhaps some heavenly sign that appeared over Jerusalem as a portent of its destruction (Josephus claimed that before its ruin a star in the shape of a sword appeared over the city for a year, *Jewish War* 6.5.3 §289). Some early exegetes interpreted the sign to be the cross (A. J. B. Higgins, "The Sign of the Son of Man [Matt. xxiv. 30]," *NTS* 9 [1963]: 380-82). The coming on the clouds of heaven with power and great glory (24:30c) is a symbol of a mighty reversal of fortunes within history and at the national level (see France, *Matthew*, 344). The trumpet call and gathering of the elect (24:31) serves as a sign to start the gathering of all the peoples into the kingdom (see Exod 19:16; Isa 18:3; 27:13; *Psalm of Solomon* 11:1; in Deut 30:4, it refers to the gathering of Israel). The destruction of Jerusalem is therefore seen as a turning point in the mission of the church.

(d) The last unit of this first section (24:32-35) confirms the certainty that "all these things" will come to pass (24:32-35). The end of the holy city and its temple is only the end of Jewish nationalistic hopes and a portent that the end of the age is near (24:33). Matthew's community could look back in retrospect on these events as a confirmation of the eternal authority of Jesus' words (23:35) and could assume that whenever and wherever similar travail arises for disciples, the same instructions apply. The vital issue for Matthew, however, was not Jerusalem's fate but the readiness of Christians for the end that seems delayed.

(2) The second section (24:36-25:46) begins with a thematic statement that no one knows the hour or the day (of the end) except the Father (24:36). It introduces five parables that contain several interlocking themes. (a) The sudden arrival of something or someone that creates a crisis appears in all five parables (24:37, 39, 43, 44, 46; 25:6, 19). (b) A key figure is delayed in three of the parables (24:48; 25:5, 19). (c) The exhortation to watch (24:42, 43; 25:13) and be ready (24:44; 25:10) for the unknown time of arrival (24:37, 42-44, 50; 25:10) sets the tone for the first four parables. (d) The division of the characters into two separate categories (the wise, faithful, and good versus the wicked, foolish, and hesitant, 24:45, 48; 25:2, 21, 23, 26) appears in the last four parables. (e) The last three parables also contain a judgment scene in which the faithful and ready receive a joyous reward (24:46; 25:10-11; 21, 23), and the unfaithful and unready are banished and/or ruthlessly punished (24:39, 51; 25:10, 30).

From these themes it is clear that the Evangelist uses the threat of a sudden reckoning to warn against lax behavior among Christians who may be under the false impression that merely being a part of the community will entail a reward and make them exempt from future punishment. All are to be vigilant and to be ready during what may deceptively appear to be a pause in the progress of salvation history when the gospel is to be proclaimed to the nations (24:14). The sixth parable in this section (25:31–46) changes tack. It depicts the final judgment of the nations who have encountered Christ in the persons of those suffering Christians who have faithfully carried out their mission to the world. This second section of the discourse portrays the time in between the death and resurrection of Christ and the parousia of the son of man as a time of testing and vigilance for the church. For the nations, it will be a time of decision.

The first two parables address the second half of the disciples' question, "What is the sign of your coming and the end of the age?" (24:3). The answer is that there will be no sign. Unlike the ample warnings portending the destruction of Jerusalem, the final cataclysm will be as sudden and as unforeseen as the one that overtook the generation of Noah. It will burst in when it is least expected, and many will be caught completely off guard, blissfully unaware of their impending doom and preoccupied with the normal routines of life (24:38–39). It will come as unexpectedly as the break-in of a cat burglar. Thieves do not book appointments to rob homes; they target those who are unwary (24:42–44).

The parable of the thief (24:42–44) and the parable of the wise and foolish maidens (25:1–13) both emphasize the need to watch and be ready for an end that cannot be calculated by discerning the signs. The only safeguard against thieves is to stay on constant watch. In the parable of the wise and foolish maidens, however, both groups fall asleep while waiting for the delayed bridegroom. The fact that they are not faulted for falling asleep indicates that "watching" has nothing to do with being alert to the signs of the coming bridegroom. They are sufficiently alerted by "a cry" (25:6a). The issue is whether they will have enough oil for the lamps at that moment to be able to welcome the bridegroom and enter into the marriage feast.

One might think that the wise maidens should have shared their supply of oil with those who were ill-provided so that all might enter together into the feast, but the parable is an allegory about spiritual preparedness, not a lesson on the golden rule. Spiritual readiness is not something that can be transferred from one to another. The point is that one must take steps to furnish oneself with oil *before* going to sleep while one has the chance.

The oil in this parable represents something similar to the wedding garment (22:11–14), namely, evidential works of righteousness (K. P. Donfried, "Allegory of the Ten Virgins," *JBL* 93 [1974]: 415–28). The Rabbinic homilists argued that the study of the law must be "mingled with oil," that is, good deeds (*Numbers Rabba* 13:15–16; see also *Qoheleth Rabba* 9:8 §1, where the reference to white garments and oil on one's head in Qoh 9:8 are interpreted as pertaining to good deeds). Matthew's interest in works and obedience to Jesus' commands (see 5:15–16 and 7:21–27) is expressed in a variety of images throughout his Gospel, and the parables of the wedding garment and the wise and foolish maidens convey related warnings. The expulsion of the man without a garment (22:11–14) teaches that, "Those who respond to the invitation . . . must have something more to bring to the judgment other than having said, 'Yes, Lord.' They must be properly clothed with the deeds of Christian discipleship" (J. R. Donahue, *The Gospel in Parable* [Philadelphia: Fortress, 1988], 96). The exclusion of the maidens without oil for their lamps also teaches that those who expect to join in the wedding festivities must be prepared with something more than the cry "Lord, Lord" (25:11; see 7:21–22). If one hopes to be acknowledged by Christ in the judgment, one must do the will of the Father (7:21).

The parable of the wise and the wicked stewards (24:45–51) and the parable of the talents (25:14–30) give more precision to what it means to watch and be ready. Vigilance is not a passive waiting and watching but consists of active, responsible service. When Christ returns, he will not ask if one had the date right but "What have you been doing?" The faithful and wise servant who devotedly feeds the household spiritual bread need not worry about the timing of the parousia. The trusted servant, however, may turn out to be wicked and may foolishly bank on a long delay. That servant will inevitably be caught in the act of abusing his fellow servants and will be severely judged. Others will be trapped by their inaction, as the parable of the talents makes clear.

In the parable of the talents, a master entrusts three servants with his money while he goes off on a journey. "After much time," he returns and settles his accounts with them. The first two have made a profit and are rewarded. The last has done nothing except play it safe. He buried his silver – the best security against theft (see *Mishna Baba Meṣi'a* 3:10). Having taken this precaution, he will not have to pay out of his own pocket in case of loss or robbery nor spend sleepless nights worrying about an investment that might go sour. When he is called to task because he had nothing to show from his commission, he tries to excuse his behavior by shifting the blame to the master. The servant alleges that the master is a hard man who reaps where he did not sow and gathers where he did not scatter. He justifies his zero profit by claiming that he was too paralyzed by fear to act.

If the master concurs with the servant's image of him, then the servant condemns himself out of his own mouth. With a master who is as grasping as this, the servant should have done something – anything – to make some gain, however meager, on his deposit. Precaution is no virtue, because the master wants to make a profit, not simply preserve his equity. The first two servants took the risks and were rewarded. The last simply tried to protect himself and, as a result, lost everything (see 10:39).

On the other hand, the servant may have been operating under an illusion about his master as a petty tyrant. In the parable, the master acts generously by giving the additional talent to the first servant and by inviting the two faithful servants to participate in his joy (25:21, 23, 28). The servant's fear, which is the opposite of love and trust (1 John 4:18–20), dictated his actions and led to his downfall. Love is concerned about the good of the loved one. It does not ask, "How am I going to come out on this deal?" but "How am I to serve my Lord?"

This parable illustrates that the "delay" (24:48; 25:5, 19) is not a meaningless interval. It presents a window of opportunity for servants who love their Master to put to good use the resources given them for gain. In the situation of the Christian community, the resources that have been given it apply to its task of mission in the world (10:1; 24:14; 28:19).

The last parable in the eschatological discourse (25:31–46) uses the everyday image of a shepherd dividing his flock (25:32) to portray the final judgment of the nations when the son of man finally appears in his glory. The son of man can tell the true nature of those gathered before the throne as easily as a shepherd can tell the difference between a sheep and a goat (S. W. Gray, *The Least of My Brothers: Matthew 25:31–46: A History of Interpretation,* SBLDS 114 [Atlanta: Scholars, 1989], 352–53). Interpreters are not so all-knowing and disagree over who the sheep and the goats are who are to be judged. Do "all the nations" who are gathered (25:32) represent only non-Christians, only Christians, or all the people of the world – gentiles, Jews, and Christians? Who are "the least of these my brethren" (25:40, 45)? Are they all the needy and suffering people of the world, only Christians, or the needy Christians in the church?

In Matthew, "all the nations" (25:32) is never used to refer to members of the church but to the nations that Christian disciples are to evangelize (24:9, 14; 28:19). The parable assumes that the mandate to proclaim the gospel of the kingdom to the whole world (24:14; see 26:12; 28:19) has been fulfilled and portrays the judgment of the nations to whom they have gone (see Joel 3:2–3; 4 Ezra 7:37; *Testament of Benjamin* 10:7–9; *Babylonian Talmud 'Aboda Zara* 2ab, for other Jewish notions of the judgment of the nations). It does not depict "the least of these my brethren" as being judged along with the nations but implies that they stand with the son of man who is seated on his throne of glory. "Brothers" is a term that is reserved for Jesus' disciples in the Gospel (12:49–50; 23:8; 28:10). "Little ones" refers to those who believe in Jesus (10:42; 18:6, 12, 14; see 11:11), and "least" is used here for emphasis (see 5:19). The least of these refers to Jesus' followers. The parable corresponds to the conclusion of Jesus' first mission charge to the disciples in 10:40–42:

> [40]Whoever welcomes you welcomes me, and whoever welcomes me welcomes the one who sent me. [41]Whoever welcomes a prophet in the name of a prophet will receive a prophet's reward; and whoever welcomes a righteous person in the name of a righteous person will receive the reward of the righteous; [42]and whoever gives even a cup of cold water to one of these little ones in the name of a disciple – truly I will tell you, none of these shall lose their reward.

The picture of the judgment in this parable therefore does not reflect a "humanitarian ethic" of good works (salvation based on kindness to all in need) with no specifically Christian content (France, *Matthew,* 355). The nations are judged according to the way they treated Jesus' humble brethren who represented Christ to them.

A similar sectarian outlook on the world can be found in a Jewish apocalyptic work contemporary with Matthew: the nations will be judged according to how they have treated Israel (*2 [Syriac] Apocalypse of Baruch* 72:1–6). The difference is that the disciples have been sent out to the nations, as they were earlier sent to Israel (10:5–42), to confront them with the reign of God. The instructions that Jesus gave his disciples in their mission to Israel (10:7–42) are still applicable for the time when Jesus commissions them to go to the rest of the world in 28:18–20. Like Israel, the nations must either accept or reject the messengers. Their kindness to these envoys is a token of their acceptance of the message and their obedience to what Christ taught (see Acts 16:30–34, the Philippian jailer's care of Paul and Silas).

Four inferences can be made from this parable that reflect Matthew's view of the task of the church in the world. (a) The world meets Christ through his disciples. (b) The primary function of the disciples is to represent Christ to the world. (c) The solidarity between Christ, as God with us, and his disciples will be revealed to one and all only at the parousia. The humbleness of the son of man's presence in his oppressed disciples contrasts sharply with the glory of his future coming with all the authority of God. The time is coming when he will appear in "his glory" with "his angels" and sit upon "his glorious throne" and will judge the nations as "the king" and as "Lord" (25:31, 34, 37, 40, 44). The sheep are not surprised that they are admitted to the kingdom but that they had ministered unknowingly to this majestic son of man when they ministered to his messengers (25:37). In seeking out and extending love and care to Jesus' brethren in distress they did it to the one who would be the final arbiter of the fate of all humankind. The goats ignored the messengers and their message because they did not recognize in these seemingly insignificant little ones the son of man, the ruler of the world and their final judge. Consequently, they will receive the punishment prepared for the devil and his angels.

(d) The humble status of Christ's emissaries as the hungry, thirsty, strangers, naked, sick, and imprisoned — or, in Paul's words, those reviled as weak, dishonored, rubbish, and the dregs of society (1 Cor 4:9–13) — will be reversed at the final judgment as they stand with the one who sits on the glorious throne. The parable functions primarily as a word of consolation to a persecuted community sent out on a mission fraught with danger to a hostile world. The list of the sufferings of "the least of these" parallels Paul's catalog of hardships that he incurred during his missionary labors (1 Cor 4:9–13; 2 Cor 11:23–29; see also Did 4:1; 2 Clem 17:3; *Acts of Thomas* 145–49). In their mission to the nations, they will share the precarious earthly lot of their Lord as ones who will be "hated" (10:22; 24:9), "killed, crucified, scourged, and chased from city to city" (23:34; 10:23; see Heb 11:36). In the end, they will share in his triumphant vindication.

This parable has often been used to emphasize the Christian's obligation to the down and out in society. Our interpretation calls this ethical reading of the parable into question. It does not negate the imperative to attend to the needs of the hungry, naked, and imprisoned that resounds throughout the Scripture (Isa 58:6–7; Ezek 18:7; Tob 4:16; Sir 7:35; 4 Ezra 2:20) but argues that the intention of this parable lies elsewhere. The ethical interpretation of this parable looks at things primarily from a position of superiority, from the perspective of those who have the material resources and ought to help the poor and needy (see 19:21). Matthew looked at the world from the perspective of the down and out, as a member of a group that was oppressed and dishonored because of its commitment to Christ. The collective honor of Christians will not be made fully known until the judgment. Then, those who scorned and despised Christians will discover that they scorned and despised the son of man who has all authority in heaven and earth.

THE LIFE-GIVING DEATH
OF THE REJECTED MESSIAH

26:1–27:56

The formula that marks the conclusion of Jesus' final discourse differs slightly from the others in the Gospel with the addition of the word "all": "after he finished *all* these words" (26:1; compare 7:28; 11:1; 13:53; 19:1). It makes it reminiscent of Moses' final speech to Israel: "When Moses had finished speaking all these words to all Israel" (Deut 32:45; see 31:1–2). The difference is that Moses, at the end of his life, can only bless the people for their journey into the promised land and cannot go with them (Deut 32:48–52). Jesus takes the final step in the deliverance of his people alone, and it is they who break faith with him and prove themselves as yet unable to go with him.

Matthew's report of the events of Jesus' passion varies little from Mark's. The small differences in wording and the inclusion of traditions not found in any other Gospel, however, give his account a distinctive slant (26:1–2, 24–25, 52–53; 27:3–10, 24–25, 51b–53). Following the formal introduction (26:1–2), the passion narrative falls into three parts: (1) preparations for death (26:3–56); (2) condemnation to death (26:57–27:26); and (3) death (27:27–56). Several themes emerge: (a) the recollection of strains from the birth narrative; (b) a heightening of the majesty of Jesus who foreknows all that is to take place and who holds his divine power in check in obedience to his Father; (c) a clarification of what Jesus' suffering and death means; (d) a stress on the guilt of this generation for shedding innocent blood; (e) a tendency to relate what happens more closely to the Scripture through allusions and direct quotations (26:15, 24, 31, 54, 56; 27:9–10, 34, 43, 51–53; 57).

(1) The first component of the passion narrative (26:2–56) relates the preparations for Jesus' death. It begins with Jesus' final announcement of his death and the plot by "the high priests and elders of the people" (26:3–5) and ends with Jesus' arrest by the posse from "the

246

high priests and elders of the people" (26:47-56). In between, there are six scenes: (a) the anointing of Jesus "for burial" (26:6-13); (b) Judas's bid to betray Jesus (26:14-15); (c) the command to the disciples to prepare for the Passover (26:17-19); (d) the last supper, when Jesus forecasts his betrayal (26:20-25) and explains the meaning of his death (26:26-30); (e) the prediction on the way to the Mount of Olives that all the disciples will be scattered and that Peter will deny him three times (26:31-35); and (f) Jesus' preparation for death through prayer in Gethsemane (26:36-46). The key themes are Jesus' foreknowledge of what is to come and his acceptance of the divine plan for his death. He foretells his death by crucifixion (26:2; see 20:19), his dishonorable burial (26:12), Judas's treachery (26:21-25), the flight of the disciples (26:31), and Peter's denial (26:34). He also foresees his ultimate triumph in his resurrection (26:32), the preaching of the gospel in the whole world (26:13), and the joyous banquet with his disciples on "that day" at the end of the age (26:29).

(2) The second component (26:57-27:26) relates Jesus' condemnation to death and consists of two units. The first (26:57-27:1) is the hearing before the Jewish council and is marked out by an inclusio. Peter "enters into" the courtyard of the high priest (26:58), and the high priests and the whole council seek false witnesses "against Jesus in order to put him to death" (26:59). At the conclusion, Peter "went out" from the courtyard (26:75), and all the high priests and the elders of the people took counsel "against Jesus to put him to death" (27:1). The key theme in this unit is Jesus' identification as the Christ, the son of God (26:63, 68).

The second unit is the hearing before the governor (27:2-26) which begins when Jesus is "handed over" to Pilate (27:2) and ends when Pilate "hands him over" to be crucified (27:26). The themes of blood guilt (27:4, 6, 8, 24-25) and Jesus' indictment as the "king of the Jews" (27:11, 19) dominate. In this section, Jesus' interrogation and condemnation by the Jewish council and his hearing before the Roman governor surround reports of the downfall of two of his disciples. Peter's passionate denials of his master end the first unit of the section (26:69-75), and Judas's confession and attempt to rid himself of the guilt of innocent blood begin the second (27:3-10).

(3) The final component (27:27-56) records Jesus' death. It includes the soldiers' mockery of Jesus as king of the Jews (27:27-31), the mockery of him on the cross as both the son of God and the king of the Jews (27:32-44), Jesus' final prayer, death, vindication by God

through supernatural events, and the confession by the soldiers that he is the son of God (27:45–56).

(1) The conclusion to the discourse in 26:1 indicates that Jesus' public teaching ministry has come to an end, but one final lesson remains for his disciples: his obedient death (Senior, *The Passion of Jesus,* 50). The first part of Matthew's passion narrative (26:2–56) centers on Jesus' preparation of himself and his disciples for his death. Jesus sets things in motion with a terse announcement: Passover comes, and he will be delivered up to be crucified (26:2). The verb, "delivered up," tolls throughout the narrative sounding the betrayal by Judas (26:15–16, 21, 23–25, 45–46, 48), the prosecution by the Jewish leaders (27:2, 18), and Pilate's final disposition of the case (27:26). This solemn introduction highlights the stately majesty of Jesus that contrasts with the guileful conniving of the chief priests and elders of the people (Senior, *The Passion Narrative,* 22). Their "stealth" (26:4) recalls that of Herod and his stratagem to kill the newborn king (2:7–8). The gathering of Jewish leaders in the Gospel is always ominous (see 2:4; 22:34, 41; 26:57; 27:17, 62; 28:12); and Psalm 31:13 is apropos, "For I hear the whispering of many – terror all around! – as they scheme together against me, as they plot to take my life." The difference is that Jesus is not struck by terror but goes willingly to his death.

Unlike Jesus, the conspirators are oblivious to what is really happening in God's scheme of things. They resolve to postpone arresting Jesus until after the feast, not out of reverence for the Passover but out of fear of the people (see 21:26) lest it create a tumult. Presumably, they want to wait until the swarm of pilgrims have returned home; but what they determine to avoid is exactly what will happen. The perfidy of Judas opens a window of opportunity for them to seize Jesus during the festival. Therefore, Jesus will die just as he predicts – during the Passover. A tumult will also take place (27:24), but not as the leaders feared; the crowds will clamor for Jesus' death (27:23, 25). This opening scene reveals that it is not the devious plans of the Jewish leaders that are being worked out, but the hidden purposes of God that Jesus already knows and accepts.

In the next scene, Jesus' composure in the face of death again comes out as an anonymous woman pours out costly ointment on Jesus' head (26:6–13). The disciples, still heedless of Jesus' imminent death, complain bitterly about the lavish waste of something that could have been put to better use as alms for the poor (26:9; see 25:35). Jesus, however, knows what is in people's hearts and proclaims that she has done a good thing by anointing his body for burial. In Rabbinic catalogs of good works, burying the dead surpasses almsgiving, putting up strangers, and visiting the sick (*Tosepta Pe'a* 4:9; *Babylonian Talmud Sukka* 49b; see D. Daube, *New Testament and Rabbinic Judaism* [New York: Athlone, 1956], 315). What the woman has done is therefore better than almsgiving because she has seized the moment to minister to one who was as good as dead.

Unlike Jesus and the reader, the disciples are unaware of the plotting that surrounds this act of devotion and can see only the waste (26:8). Another question arises, however. Why waste Jesus on a cross? The answer is to be found in the sinfulness of these indignant grumblers, the treacherous leaders of the nation, and the traitorous false disciple. But the incident affirms that neither the precious ointment poured out for Jesus nor his blood poured for out the many is a waste. The scene ends on a triumphal note. What this woman has done will be related when the gospel of Jesus' death and resurrection is preached to the whole world. It was the appropriate response to Jesus.

The next scene shows Judas offering his teacher for sale (26:14–16). Every time Judas is mentioned in the story, Matthew provides more information than is found in the other Gospels. Here, Matthew presents him as crassly haggling over the price of betrayal. The "thirty pieces of silver" that are offered to him allude to Zechariah 11:12, where the shepherd is given the insulting wages of a slave (see Exod 21:32), and underlines the fact that the events of the passion all fit into a divine plan (Senior, *The Passion Narrative,* 47). Even the price of betrayal was foreknown by God. Judas's willingness to sell out his Master for a pittance contrasts sharply with the woman who was willing to pour out a fortune on Jesus' head to express her adoration.

The preparation for the Passover shows Jesus and Judas to be on a collision course. Judas is now looking for a "good time" (*eukairia*) when he can cash in on Jesus (26:16). Jesus is looking for the time set by God ("my time," *kairos*) when he is to give his life and fulfill his assigned work (26:18). He commands all the disciples to prepare for the Passover and, later, casts a pall over the meal by bringing up the subjects of his betrayal by one of the twelve and his death. He announces that the betrayer is one who dips with him in the dish (26:23), who, as a table companion, breaks a sacred trust (Ps 41:9).

> Every friend says, "I too am a friend"; but some are friends only in
> name. Is it not a sorrow like that for death itself when a dear friend
> turns into an enemy? (Sir 37:1-2, NRSV)

The disciples each ask, "I am not the one, am I, Lord?" fishing for the
answer, "No." After a fearsome woe pronounced on the betrayer, an un-
daunted Judas asks the same question, except he revealingly addresses
Jesus only as "Rabbi" (26:25; see 26:49). Jesus' cryptic acknowledgment, "You said it," leaves him with an out. Jesus goes as it is written
of him (26:24; 16:21; 26:54, 56), but there is still time for the betrayer
to repent. In Gethsemane, Judas' imminent betrayal only adds to Jesus'
"sorrow unto death" (26:38).

Jesus next explains the meaning of his upcoming death (26:26-30).
It is not a stroke of ill fortune but something whose purpose lies deep
within the providence of God. (a) It is, first of all, a self-offering ("This
is my body"). Jesus provides something that others are unable to supply
for themselves. (b) It establishes a covenant that is to be offered to all
(see Exod 24:3-8, 11; Zech 9:11; Isa 42:6; Jer 31:31-34). (c) His blood
poured out brings the forgiveness of sins (Lev 17:11; Isa 53:12; Heb
9:22).

After the supper, Jesus makes another sad prediction of the break-
down of all of the disciples (26:31-35). They will all be "scandalized"
and "scattered" when their shepherd is struck. As Judas has succumbed
to the lure of wealth like the seed choked by thorns (13:22), the other
disciples will wilt at the first sign of persecution like the seed that landed
in rocky soil (13:21). The citation from Zechariah 13:7 again confirms
that what will happen is foreknown by God, who remains in control.
As bad as their collapse will be, however, it is not final. Resurrection
is to follow suffering and death, and they can count on a reunion in
Galilee where it all began.

Peter refuses to accept this forecast as he swings from the earlier self-
doubt that he shared with all the other disciples (26:22) to a competitive
self-confidence that leads him to boast that he alone will prove faithful
(26:33). He and the others protest that if it is necessary, he will die
together with Jesus (26:35). Ironically, it *is* necessary. In the Pauline
literature, the verb "to die with" refers to participation in the saving
death of Jesus (see 2 Cor 7:3, 2 Tim 2:11; also Rom 6:8, Col 2:20). The
death that the disciples "must" undergo is not like that of the heroic
Zealots who died at Masada but a death to selfish ambition and self-
centered purpose, no matter how sincere and noble it might appear.

Peter's failure will be immortalized by the crowing of the cock, the epitome of foolish pride.

Throughout this section on the preparations for Jesus' death there is an emphasis on his being "with" his disciples and they being with him (26:18, 20, 23, 29, 38, 40, 51; see 26:69, 71). After the supper, Jesus goes "with them" to Gethsemane (26:36, contrast Mark 14:32). The ensuing events, however, will reveal that while Jesus is with his disciples, they are not truly with him. The disciples are therefore not present for moral support but to learn from Jesus' example. Through prayer, Jesus "thinks the things of God" (see 16:23), denies himself (16:24), and accepts the cup his Father has prepared for him.

Jesus takes aside the same three disciples who were with him on the mount of transfiguration (17:5) to pray with him on the Mount of Olives. In that past moment the disciples fell on their faces in awe when Jesus' glory was revealed (17:6). In this moment it is Jesus who falls on his face in humble prayer when his nearing suffering is revealed (26:39). Jesus returns three times to find them sleeping (26:40, 43, 45), but more importantly, he retreats three times for prayer (26:36, 42, 44) as he models the prayer he taught his disciples (6:9-13).

The urgency of Jesus' prayer in Gethsemane reveals that the cross was God's decision for him, which comes as a cup that he needs to drink in obedience. He neither relishes the conflict nor embraces martyrdom but greets the prospect of death with the outspoken lament of the suffering righteous one (see Ps 31:10; 40:11-13; 42:6, 9-11; 43:1-2, 5; 55:4-8; 116:3-4; Sir 51). In the Jewish lament, one's prayer is not to be "fully controlled, or strained with politeness. In a rush of emotion, complaint, and even recrimination, the believers pour out their hearts to God" (D. P. Senior, *The Passion according to Mark* [Wilmington: Glazier, 1984], 76). This tradition would not have been fully appreciated by gentiles, who may have expected a more stoical approach to death. Dio Cassius disdains the groveling of Vitellius, the governor of Syria, who begged the emperor Gaius for his life with "tears and lamentations" (*Roman History* 59.27.4-6). But Philo defends this Jewish perspective on prayer: "the man of worth has such courage of speech that he is bold not only to speak and cry aloud, but actually to make an outcry of reproach, wrung from him by real conviction and expressing true emotion" (*Who Is the Heir of Divine Things?* 19). Fortified by such bold prayer, Jesus rises to meet the hour when he is betrayed into the hands of sinners. The disciples, dazed by sleep, are thrown into chaos when the crucial hour suddenly strikes. One comes to betray his master with a kiss; one lashes out with a sword; all flee; and one will deny even being a disciple with oaths and curses.

Despite the high priests' secret plots, coded signals, and high powered weaponry, it is not their will that is being accomplished. The son of man is being handed over in accordance with God's will revealed in the prophets (26:54, 56). Only Jesus is aware of this fact. One of those "with him" draws his sword and provocatively "strikes" the ear of the servant of the high priest (26:51). But God's will is not accomplished through brute force (5:38–48), and Jesus rebukes him. Violence only begets violence and destruction (as the debacle against Rome in 66–70 c.e. could testify). In God's plan, it is the shepherd who is to be "struck" on behalf of others (26:31), not disciples striking out at others. Matthew alone records Jesus' declaration that even now he could call on his Father for an assault force of twelve legions of angels, which makes this desperate stab at the enemy by one disciple seem all the more hapless. But Jesus has already rejected the temptation to rely on the supernatural intervention of angels as one who is obedient to his Father (4:6–7). Celestial rescues are out of the question (Senior, *The Passion Narrative,* 141; contrast 1QM 13:10; 17:6 where the great angel is sent to aid the army of light in holy war against the army of Belial).

Jesus accepts his seizure as in accord with the divine plan revealed in the prophets, but the disciples, who had *all* promised that they would die with Jesus (26:35), *all* forsake him and flee (26:56). Previously, they had forsaken everything to follow Jesus (19:27); now they forsake their discipleship. It is not their rash vow of fidelity that is fulfilled but the Scripture (Zech 13:7) as Jesus predicted (26:31).

(2) The second component of Matthew's passion narrative (26:57–27:26) records Jesus' condemnation to death. It begins with the Jewish leaders once again gathered in the hall of Caiaphas, the high priest, where they first conspired to arrest Jesus (26:3). The principle complaint against Jesus is that he claimed to be able to destroy the sanctuary of God. Threats to the temple were taken seriously not only because it was the holy place where God dwelt but also because it provided the priestly caste with its livelihood and status. Josephus reports that prior to the war against Rome, the leading citizens of Jerusalem arrested one Jesus ben Ananias for persistently pronouncing woes against the city and the sanctuary. In hopes of silencing him once and for all, they brought him before the Roman governor who had him flayed to the bone (Josephus, *Jewish War* 6.5.3 §300–309). In the inquiry before the council the charge that Jesus claimed to be able to destroy the temple is

not characterized as perjury as it is in Mark (14:56–58). The testimony of the two witnesses, however motivated, is assumed to be true and highlights Jesus' power over even the temple and its fate ("I am able to," 26:61, instead of "I will," Mark 14:58; see Matt 26:53).

The high priest marvels at Jesus' silence rather than at the accusations against him (26:62) and abjures him to swear by the living God whether he is the Christ, the son of God (26:63). The question echoes the confession of Peter in 16:16, but it is asked in the spirit of Satan (4:3, 6). Jesus refuses to swear an oath (see 5:33–37); and since the question contains its own answer, he replies with the evasive, "You said it" — the only answer that he gives to hostile questioners (to Judas in 26:26, and to Pilate in 27:11). Jesus continues, however, with a quotation from Scripture that combines a royal psalm (110:1) that is associated with the messiah with an apocalyptic tradition about the son of man (Dan 7:13). The two traditions interpret one another with an explosive result. On the one hand, the one like a son of man is no longer a mysterious apparition as he is in Daniel 7 but a real man, a descendant of David, in whom the messianic prophecies are realized. On the other hand, sitting at God's right hand is no longer simply a symbol of temporal, royal dignity, as it is in Psalm 110; it is a reference to divine power that is exercised on the heavenly plane (see A. Vanhoye, *Structure and Theology of the Accounts of the Passion in the Synoptic Gospels* [Collegeville, Minn.: Liturgical Press, 1967], 25–27). Jesus' oblique "yes" ("you said it") affirms that he is indeed the Christ, son of God; but the mixed quotation discloses that his sonship surpasses any current conception about a messiah. The son of man who is to be crucified (26:2) is the same son of man will who will share in God's cosmic dominion over the world and who will be its final judge (25:31–32). "From now on" (after the crucifixion and resurrection), this divine status will become obvious to them. The high priest understandably deems this response to be blasphemy that mandates death (Lev 24:16; compare Josephus, *Antiquities* 20.5.2 §108, where a soldier is accused of blasphemy simply for exposing himself to the temple crowd) and rends his garments (see Lev 21:10). The reader, however, knows that Jesus' statement cannot be blasphemous because it accords with God's own view proclaimed from heaven (3:17; 17:5).

The mockery (26:67–68) that concludes the hearing, "Prophesy, Christ, who struck you" (see 26:31), may seem to be only a cruel game. A later Rabbinic tradition that the messiah will be able to judge by smell (see Isa 11:1–4) suggests, however, that something more was at play:

> Bar Koziba [Bar Kochba, the leader during the second ruinous revolt against Rome in 132–35] reigned two and a half years, then said to the rabbis, "I am the Messiah." They answered, "Of Messiah it is written that he smells and judges; let us see whether he [Bar Koziba] can do so." When they saw that he was unable to judge by the scent, they slew him. (*Babylonian Talmud Sanhedrin* 93b)

Jesus' prophetic foreknowledge is not apparent to his tormentors, who taunt him to divine who it was who was assaulting him, but it should be to the reader. His claims are legitimized as each of his prophecies come true (Deut 18:21–22).

As Jesus stands up to the intense pressure, Peter caves in under the groping suspicions of two maidservants and some bystanders. He had followed Jesus at a safe distance – no longer as a disciple – and sits with his captors "to see the end," not to die with him as he had promised (26:58). He ineffectually denies "before all" any relationship to Jesus (see 7:23; 25:12; 10:32–33). The denials escalate in intensity, beginning with an indirect oath formula, "I do not know what you are saying" (26:70; see *Mishna Šebuʿot* 8:3), followed by an oath (26:72), and finally by a curse and the swearing of oaths (26:74). Peter's capitulation serves as a warning example for those who may presume on the strength of the spirit and the flesh (see 1 Cor 10:12) and who fail to watch and pray (26:41; 6:13). It also demonstrates, along with Herod's oath that led to the death of John the Baptist, that anything more than a simple "yes" or "no" comes from the evil one (5:37).

The tragic denial of Peter (26:69–75) concludes the account of the council hearing and butts up against the tragic suicide of Judas (27:3–10), which prefaces the Roman inquiry. As the woes uttered against the scribes and Pharisees will find their fulfillment in the destruction of Jerusalem, so the woe that Jesus uttered against the one who will betray him (26:64) finds its fulfillment in Judas' suicide.

Matthew alone reports that Judas "changed his mind" (see 21:29, 32) when he saw that Jesus had been condemned to death. Judas first tries to rid himself of guilt by returning the payoff to the priests and confessing: "I sinned betraying innocent blood" (27:4). This betrayal places him under a curse (Deut 27:25). His partners in crime, however, disavow any connection with him and ironically admit that they have nothing to do with the expiation of sin, "What is that to us? See to it yourself." The only other recourse for Judas to remove the blood guilt is through his own death (see Num 35:33; 2 Sam 21:1–6). Like the criminal who prays on the way to the place of his execution, "May my death be an atonement for all my sins" (*Mishna Sanhedrin* 6:2; see *Babylonian Talmud Sanhedrin* 47a), Judas hanged himself in an anguished attempt to atone for his guilt under rules of the old covenant, a life for a life (Lev 24:21).

The parallels between Peter and Judas make an important theological point for Matthew. (a) Peter invoked a curse on himself if he were lying and on those who accused him of lying when he denied knowing Jesus (26:74, which explains the lack of a direct object for the verb *katathematizein*). Both Peter and Judas are therefore under a curse of their own making. (b) Both feel remorse. At the sound of the cockcrow, Peter remembered Jesus' prediction and wept bitterly (26:74–75). He rends his heart, not his garments (Joel 2:12–13, cited by B. Gerhardsson, "Confession and Denial Before Men: Observations on Matt 26:57–27:2," *JSNT* 13 [1981]: 62). When Jesus is condemned, Judas tries to make amends, perhaps also remembering Jesus' prophecy (26:24). (c) The treachery of both disciples was foretold before and after the last supper, which should cause the reader to remember that Jesus interpreted his death during the supper to be for the forgiveness of sins (26:28). The fact that Peter is among the eleven disciples who obediently regroup in Galilee to be commissioned by Jesus implies that he has repented and has been forgiven (see 14:30–31). Judas, on the other hand, makes a fatal mistake by returning to the temple to seek absolution through his co-conspirators when the temple is no longer the place of God's presence or the seat of forgiveness. He is turned away by the callous shepherds who have no regard for the sheep. By contrast, Jesus does not turn away sinners who come to him in repentance. Only with him will they find the forgiveness they crave.

The demise of Judas also brings into focus the issue of the guilt for shedding innocent blood. The term "blood" occurs three times in this section: "innocent blood" (27:4), "price of blood" (27:6), "field of blood" (27:8). It reappears in 27:24–25, "this righteous man's blood," and "his blood be on us." In Matthew, the death of Jesus is to be viewed as the shedding of innocent blood, which incurs terrible guilt and punishment from the avenger of blood (see 23:35). Each of the guilty parties – Judas, the high priests, and Pilate – try unsuccessfully to slither out from this liability.

When Judas threw the pieces of silver into "the sanctuary," the "blood money" for the betrayal of Jesus has landed in the heart of the temple. The chief priests and the elders implicate themselves by acknowledging that the money they paid out is the price of blood that would defile the temple treasury. Since cemeteries were already unclean, they use the tainted money to purchase a field in which to bury foreigners. Their question, "What does it have to do with us?" however, has been answered. It is almost as if the Passover requirement that the blood of the lamb be offered on "the threshold of the altar" (*Jubilees* 49:20) has been met, but in this case it produces an ominous foreboding of doom.

This incident leads to the last fulfillment quotation in Matthew (27:9–10). The quotation comes primarily from Zechariah 11:13; but Jeremiah, who mentions a potter, "the blood of the innocent," the renaming of a field, a burial ground (19:1–13), and the purchase of a field (32:6–15), is cited as the source. Zechariah 11:13 has been studied, touched up, and interpreted in light of Jeremiah's prophecy of doom for Israel (Jer 19:3, 7, 11; see 2:17). The latter is specifically cited perhaps to draw attention to the subtle allusions that might otherwise be overlooked (R. H. Gundry, *The Use of the Old Testament in St. Matthew's Gospel*, NovTSup [Leiden: Brill, 1967], 125) and perhaps because the name Jeremiah summons up an aura of judgment associated with his message (W. Rothfuchs, *Die Erfüllungszitate des Matthäus-Evangeliums*, BWANT 88 [Stuttgart: Kohlhammer, 1969], 43–44; see Josephus, *Antiquities* 10.5.1 §79; *Babylonian Talmud Baba Batra* 14b).

The scene shifts to Pilate's interrogation of Jesus (27:11–29), and he quickly concludes that Jesus is no insurrectionist. Like the high priest, he is also bewildered by Jesus' silence before the charges (26:61–62; 27:13–14; see Isa 52:14–15). Unlike the high priest, he thinks Jesus innocent; but his one ploy to release him fails. In a trial for one who was not a Roman citizen (a trial "outside the system"), the governor was free to make his own rules and judgments as he saw fit, to accept or reject charges, and to fashion, within reason, whatever penalties he chose. He offers the people the choice between two prisoners: "Jesus Barabbas or Jesus the one called Christ" (27:17). The variant reading giving Barabbas the same name as Jesus was probably suppressed for pietistic reasons. Origen, for example, rejects the reading because no one who is a sinner is called Jesus in all the Scriptures (*Commentary on Matthew*, PG 13:1772).

Matthew emphasizes the free choice that the people have between the two prisoners who both have someone lobbying for their release. The temple hierarchy campaigns for Barabbas; Pilate's wife steps in on Jesus' behalf. The difference is that Pilate's wife is constrained to intervene by a dream. For many modern readers, dreams may seem to be flimsy grounds on which to base decisions, but they have been a reliable source of divine guidance and warnings earlier in Matthew's story (1:20; 2:12, 13, 19, 22). Pilate's wife therefore intercedes because of a divine warning about "that righteous one" (27:19). The temple hierarchy, on the other hand, is said to be aroused only by envy (27:18). Once again, a gentile is shown to be open to God's lead, while Jewish leaders, consumed by their passions, plot death (see 2:1–12, 16–18). She is also the second woman in the passion narrative who has insight about Jesus (see 26:6–13).

As Matthew presents the scene, the Jewish leaders make a double demand. They persuade the people to call for both the release of Barabbas *and* the execution of Jesus (27:20; compare Mark 15:11, where they only demand Barabbas's release). The governor is totally ineffectual and ultimately cedes his authority to decide the matter to the crowds, "What shall I do with Jesus, called the Christ?" They *all* demand his crucifixion (27:22). When he asks for some grounds, the tumult only increases, forcing Pilate to relent.

The key issue of blood guilt resurfaces. In Luke and John, Pilate proclaims Jesus to be innocent (Luke 23:4, 14, 22; John 19:4, 6). In Matthew, he proclaims *his own* innocence by washing his hands, while Israel accepts responsibility for the judgment against Jesus (27:24–25, see *Gospel of Peter* 1). For Matthew, steeped in Jewish traditions, the background for Pilate's hand washing is probably Deuteronomy 21:1–9, which concerns the expiation of an unsolved murder when a body is found in the open country. The elders of the city closest to the body are to slaughter a heifer, to wash their hands as an affirmation of their freedom from guilt, and to pray that the innocent blood of the murdered victim not be put in the midst of the people (see Josephus, *Antiquities* 4.8.16 §220–22; *Mishna Soṭa* 9:1–9). Ironically, Pilate employs a ritual that was used to prevent any further calamity from coming upon the land of Israel to profess his own innocence and in so doing insinuates that the execution of Jesus is nothing less than murder. His response, "You shall see" (27:24), echoes the high priests' stony dismissal of Judas (27:4) in their attempt to dissociate themselves from guilt. But, like the high priests, Pilate is also no idle bystander. He disregards the warning of his wife and has Jesus scourged. He delivers him to be crucified (27:26; see 26:2) and later permits the leaders to seal the tomb as best they can (27:65). Expiation is not to be found in quasi-magic rituals (Ovid faults the ancient notion that sins can be wiped out by rites of purgation: "Fond fools alack! to fancy murder's gruesome stain by river water could be washed away," *Fasti* 2.45-46). Pilate shares in the guilt.

While Judas, the high priests, and Pilate have all tried to wriggle out from under the onus of shedding innocent blood, it is "all the people" who openly accept responsibility (27:25). Throughout the Gospel, "the crowds" seemed to have been on the brink of acknowledging Jesus as God's son, but they have not been won over to faith in Jesus. They followed, marveled, and praised; but their highest praise, that Jesus is the son of David (21:15-16), is inadequate; and he is never confessed as such by the disciples. Jesus is David's Lord (22:41-46). At no point in the Gospel do "the crowds" recognize Jesus as Lord or as the son of God as the disciples do. In the passion narrative, "the crowds" are no longer neutral witnesses but become the pawns of the high priests. These leaders of the nation are obviously more culpable for their web of intrigue, but the crowds will also be judged if they cast their lot in with the blind guides. Both will plunge together into the pit (15:14).

The "crowds" of 27:20 become "all the people" in 27:25, and Jesus' public ministry has run full circle. He began his ministry to Israel by healing "the people" (4:23). The term "the people" drops out of the narrative until now when they end his public ministry by demanding his death. The cry "His blood on us and our children" is the dramatic moment when the people fatefully choose to reject their messiah and accept full responsibility for his condemnation and execution (see Jer 26:12-15; Sus 41-49). As the plight of Judas sets the stage for the people's acceptance of the blood guilt, it also portends its grave consequences. From Matthew's perspective, it provides an explanation for the destruction of Jerusalem. This wicked generation represents Israel at the point when its guilt has finally reached the full mark (see 23:32) and brings down the judgment of God. But Matthew certainly does not consider it to extend "forever" (contrast 1 Kgs 2:33; *Babylonian Talmud Yoma* 87a) to later generations or even to those in the Diaspora. One should not forget that Jesus has declared his blood to be the sacrificial blood of the covenant poured out for the forgiveness of sins (26:28). The Evangelist, a Jew, let alone the one whose life he records, would be more than a little dismayed at the way this and other passages in his Gospel have been used to foster and to justify hatred of the Jews.

Matthew's perspective challenges the covenantal ideology that assumed that the nation Israel had special status and that belonging to Israel was sufficient for salvation. Only those who belong to Jesus as his disciples are the elect of Israel. In the passion narrative, the reader can see the way of salvation opening up to all peoples, both Jews and gentiles, through Jesus' death (Senior, *The Passion Narrative*, 260). In contrast to the crowds who cry for his death, Pilate's wife exhibits reverence for Jesus. In contrast to the high priests who mock him (27:41–43), a chorus of soldiers will confess Jesus to be the son of God (27:54). Jesus would have gathered Jerusalem's "children" as a hen gathers her brood under her wings, but they would not (23:37); now Rachel has all the more reason to weep for her children (2:18). Later in the narrative, "all the people" (27:25) become simply "Jews" (28:15). If the mission to "the nations" also includes Israel (28:19), then Israel according to the flesh has become merely another nation among all the others. No nation of people is written off; all are to be evangelized.

(3) The last component of this section (27:27–56) relates what seems on the surface to be Jesus' powerless death. The ridicule of Jesus before the council in 26:67–68 scorned his messianic pretensions as the Christ (26:63–64). The derision of the soldiers (27:27–31) scorns his royal pretensions as the so-called king of the Jews (27:11). They give Jesus the red cloak of a foot soldier for a royal robe, thorns for a royal diadem, a reed for a royal scepter and then offer mock homage. These things mimic the trademarks of pagan rulers who swagger about and lord it over others (20:25–27), but they are only bogus tokens of power. True power comes through loving service (20:28). Cloaks, diadems, and scepters (along with coins, taxes [22:15–21], and soldiers armed with swords and clubs [26:47]) are used by kings to intimidate and enslave others and so disguise their tenuous and fragile power. These badges of rule hardly compare with the ultimate power of love unleashed by Jesus' giving of himself on the cross and the power of God who validates this decision by rocking the land.

Jesus has been led away to Caiaphas (26:57), to Pilate (27:2), and finally to be crucified (27:31). The mockery that usually accompanied crucifixion continues (see *Genesis Rabba* 65:22). The three taunts revolving around Jesus' tacit claim to be the son of God (27:40, 43) and the king of Israel (27:42) provide an ironically accurate commentary on what is happening. The scoffers' notion of a messiah is one who vindicates himself through sensational acts of power. As the son of God, Jesus must fulfill a divine mission; and only God can vindicate him. Jesus will not be delivered from death by his own powers but through death by the power of God. Consequently, he will not come down from the cross (27:40) because he is obedient to God's will (4:6; 26:39, 42). He cannot save himself (27:42), precisely because his mission is to give his life to save others (1:21; 20:28; 26:18). He is the righteous sufferer (see Wis 2:12–3:9) who trusts only in God to deliver him (27:43). The last taunt from Psalm 22:8 prepares the reader for Jesus' poignant cry to God from Psalm 22:2 (27:46; see Sus 42–44). Jeered as one who trusts in God, he promptly displays that trust in a lament. God's answer to this prayer and to the taunt comes in the chain reaction of events that occurs immediately after his death (27:51–53; see Ps 22:24). These events reveal that Jesus' suffering is not an expression of God's displeasure with him (see 5:10–12).

Ancient readers would readily understand the darkness that covered the whole land during the crucifixion (27:45) to be a cosmic sign that typically attended the death of kings and other greats (see Philo, *On Providence* 2:50; Virgil, *Georgics* 1.461–468; Plutarch, *Alexander and Caesar* 69; Dio Cassius, *Roman History* 56.29.3; see also Josephus, *Antiquities* 17:167; and *Babylonian Talmud Moed Qatan* 25b). The phenomenal events that take place after Jesus' death, however, convey that what has happened is of far greater significance. They are introduced by the solemn "and behold," which appears elsewhere in Matthew to announce divine intervention (2:9; 3:17; 4:11; 8:24; 17:5; 28:2–3, 9). The temple veil splits in two from top to bottom, the earth shakes, the rocks split, the tombs are opened, and many saints are raised who proceed into Jerusalem after Jesus' resurrection (27:51–53). There is nothing subtle here. Matthew spells out for the reader that Jesus' death shakes the very foundations of the world. The confession of the centurion *"and those with him"* (contrast the single centurion in Mark 15:39) that Jesus was truly the son of God (27:54; see 14:33) is the only reasonable response to such spectacular events of power.

What do all these phenomena signify? (a) First, they provide confirmation from God (see 1 Kgs 19:11; Job 9:5–6) that Jesus is indeed the son of God (27:40, 43, 54). The earthquake was a common theme in theophanies when God judges his enemies in wrath and delivers his people and establishes his rule on earth (D. Hill, "Matthew 27:51–53 in the Theology of the Evangelist," *IBS* 7 [1985]: 76; see Judg 5:4–5; 2 Sam 22:8; 1 Kgs 19:11; Ps 68:8; Isa 13:13; 24:18–23; 29:6; Jer 10:10; Ezek 38:18–19; Joel 3:16; Nah 1:5–6).

(b) Second, they connote God's judgment for the rejection of God's son. Darkness can signify judgment (Exod 10:21–23; Isa 13:9–13; Joel 2:2, 10; Amos 5:20), and the splitting of the temple veil symbolizes God's judgment on the temple cult (see *Lives of the Prophets* 12:11–12, where Habakkuk is said to have prophesied that the veil of the sanctuary would be torn in pieces at the destruction of the first temple). The risen saints' appearance in Jerusalem may tie into this theme. They are God's witnesses against a faithless generation and city (see 12:41–42).

(c) Third, earthquakes (see Joel 2:10; Amos 8:8–9; Hag 2:6; *1 Enoch* 1:3–9; *Assumption of Moses* 10:4; 4 Ezra 6:13–16; 9:3; *2 [Syriac] Apocalypse of Baruch* 70:8; Rev 6:12; 8:5; 11:13, 19; 16:18) and resurrection (Isa 29:16; Dan 12:2; Ezek 37:12; Zech 14:4–5; *1 Enoch* 51:1–5; *2 [Syriac] Apocalypse of Baruch* 50:2) are stock apocalyptic motifs associated with the last days and salvation. A wall mural from a third century synagogue uncovered at Dura-Europos, a frontier town in Babylon, depicts a series of events related to prophecies from Ezekiel (see E. R. Goodenough, *Jewish Symbols in the Greco-Roman Period* [New York: Pantheon, 1964], 10:179–96; 11, plate 21 for the picture; and D. C. Allison, Jr., *The End of the Ages Has Come: An Early Interpretation of the Passion and Resurrection of Jesus* [Philadelphia: Fortress, 1985], 40–46). One panel has a striking affinity with what Matthew describes as occurring at Jesus' death. It shows a split mountain with an olive tree, possibly representing the Mount of Olives (see Zech 14:4), a fallen building, suggesting an earthquake (Zech 14:5; Ezek 37:7, LXX), and ten men dressed in white rising from tombs that have been opened ("the holy ones," see Zech 14:5; Ezek 37:1–14). Matthew projects this imagery of these end-time events onto the death of Jesus to signify that it is the salvific moment that marks the turning of the ages, the decisive "from now on" that is peculiar to Matthew's eschatology (23:39, 26:29, 26:64). But the quickening of the dead reveals that it also a life-giving death. As Ezekiel envisioned God breathing new life into dead bones to revivify the house of Israel (Ezek 37:1–14), that image is evoked by Matthew to signify God's formation of a new people, Jesus' church, against which even the gates of Hades cannot prevail (16:18).

(d) Fourth, these events signify that a new phase has begun in God's dealing with Israel and the nations. The confession of the group of soldiers augurs the fact that gentiles are able to come to full faith in the son of God. Matthew has carefully portrayed the messiahship of Jesus as being exclusively bound up in his mission to Israel. In 10:5–6, he instructs his disciples to go only to the lost sheep of the house of Israel; in 28:19, after Easter, he instructs them to go to all the nations. The turning point is Jesus' death on the cross, which nullifies the restrictions of the old aeon. The barrier between God and humanity has been broken down, and God may no longer be roped off in a Jewish temple. Christianity is to become a universal religion.

THE VICTORIOUS
BREAKTHROUGH

27:57–28:20

The structure of the concluding section of the Gospel forms a chiasm (see C. H. Giblin, "Structural and Thematic Correlations in the Matthean Burial-Resurrection Narrative [Matt xxvii.–xxviii 20]," *NTS* 21 [1975]: 406–20; and France, *Evangelist and Teacher*, 133):

a   Jesus dead and buried (27:57–61)

    b   The posting of guards (27:62–66)

        c   The appearance of an angel and the risen Jesus (28:1–10)

    b′ The report of the guards (28:11–15)

a′ Jesus living and sovereign (28:16–20)

The section is bracketed by the verb "to disciple" (27:57; 28:19). A reference to Jesus and his disciples appears in each segment, and the middle scene (28:1–10) mentions elements from each of the others. The first three segments have a time notice (27:57, evening; 27:62, the next day; 28:1, after the sabbath) that confirm the literal fulfillment of Jesus' prophecy that he would be raised on the third day (16:21; 17:23; 20:19; see 12:40).

The section opens with Jesus' burial by a "rich" disciple (see Isa 53:9–12), Joseph of Arimathea, who places him in the realm of the dead in hewn rock, both of which have already been breached by his death (27:51–53). The high priests and the Pharisees wish to forestall any rumors of a resurrection that might validate the claims of "that impostor," and they gather once again to urge Pilate to surround the tomb with maximum security (27:62–66). The Pharisees reappear because they are primarily associated with the responsibility for teaching, a theme that emerges in 28:15. The scene is ironic for two reasons. The

Jewish leaders seem to put more stock in Jesus' prediction of his resurrection than his disciples; and the powers of Rome and Israel combine to try to prevent the resurrection as best they can with a sealed stone and posted sentries – all to no avail.

An annunciatory angel appears at the beginning of the story (1:20-21), and one now reappears at the close (28:2-3). Both angels impart privileged information about divine activity that is otherwise inaccessible to the characters in the story. They provide news of Jesus' miraculous conception and of his resurrection and give specific instructions on what to do in response. The angel who comes to the tomb is described in the language of Daniel 7:9 and 10:6 (see *1 Enoch* 14:20) and descends amid a great earthquake to roll back the stone and sit upon it as a symbol of God's triumph over death (Meier, *Vision,* 36).

The ones guarding the tomb (28:4) parallel those soldiers who kept watch over Jesus at the cross (27:54). Both witness an earthquake, and both are seized by fear. The guards at the tomb, however, do not confess; and, unbelieving, they become as dead men. The angel disregards them and speaks only to the women who have come "to see the tomb" (28:1). It becomes clear that the stone has been rolled back only to enable them to peer inside to see that Jesus is not there (28:6). No canonical Evangelist dares to describe the actual resurrection of Jesus; they only report its aftermath (contrast the details offered by the *Gospel of Peter* 9:35-10:42). The reason for this reticence is that the resurrection is not something open to human experience. That is why it is necessary for an angel to make the announcement of the resurrection, the divine explanation for the empty tomb. "An angel brings the decisive word, thus protecting God from the prying gaze of human beings yet conveying to chosen witnesses an understanding of meanings hidden behind the events" (P. S. Minear, "Matthew 28:1-10," *Int* 38 [1984]: 60).

Just as a woman was the first to recognize that Jesus must die and needed to be anointed for his burial (26:6-13), so the women who loyally witnessed his crucifixion (27:55-56) and burial (27:61) are the first to get the news of the resurrection. They are told to report the news to the disciples and to jog their memories that Jesus promised to go before them to Galilee where they will be reunited (26:32). Going back to the Galilee of the gentiles (4:15) where Jesus began his ministry is a move away from the corrupt power structures of Jerusalem and the first step in going to all the world. The women depart from the tomb with the same great joy as that of the magi when they saw the star that led them to the newborn king (2:10). Jesus then appears to them himself to reassure them that what they have been told by the angel is not a fantasy. The appearance confirms that the risen Jesus is the same as the earthly Jesus they knew. Jesus' command to go tell "my brothers" (28:10, not "the disciples" as in 28:7) serves notice that all is forgiven and emphasizes the importance of their reunion.

The empty tomb is assumed by Matthew to be an incontestable fact. If it were not empty, the leaders could easily refute any preaching about the resurrection by displaying the corpse. Their dilemma, as Matthew presents it in 28:11–15, is therefore to come up with some plausible explanation as to why the tomb was empty to counter what the disciples might say. Ironically, they sought to prevent the disciples of Jesus from deluding others (27:64) but foist on the people an even worse fraud of their own. They are clearly the deceivers, not Jesus (27:63) or his disciples.

"Silver" turns up once more as the leaders try to cover up the resurrection with lies and bribes. The high priests first gave silver to Judas to betray his master (26:15; 27:3). Now they give it to the guards (28:12, 14), and they ultimately betray the people who are led to believe that the body of Jesus was stolen. These false leaders operate on the assumption that everyone has his price, even the governor, whom they promise to satisfy if he gets wind of the conspiracy.

In the context of Matthew's story, the guilt of this action is monstrous. The scribes and Pharisees had asked Jesus for some corroborative sign that God was working in Jesus and were told that the only one they would get is the sign of Jonah, which, in Matthew, is connected to the resurrection (12:38–40; and also 16:1–4). The Jewish leaders therefore conspire to undercut the only sign that this generation will receive and that they themselves had demanded. The guards did as they were *taught,* and the narrator is aggrieved that the teaching is spread "among Jews" to this day (see Justin, *Dialogue* 108, who accuses the Jews of continuing to spread lies regarding the filching of the body by the disciples). Matthew's account shows the rumor to be a lie based on the laughable testimony of witnesses who admit to sleeping through the whole event. "God's authentication of Jesus, says Matthew in effect, has been made so abundantly plain, by portents and angelic deeds at tombs, that no one who is not corrupted (by self-interest like the chief priests or bribes like the soldiers, 28:11–15) should resist the claims of Christian faith: belief is no option, it is, morally and by its evidences, obligatory" (Houlden, *Backward into Light: The Passion and Resurrection of Jesus according to Matthew and Mark* (London: SCM, 1987], 35–36). The Jewish leaders have palmed off a trumped-up story for the truth and in the process bar themselves and their followers from the kingdom.

The last paragraph of the Gospel (28:16–20) is tied together by the word "all:" *all* authority, *all* the nations, *all* things, *all* the days. The mountain, the place of divine revelation (5:1; 8:1; 17:1, 9; 24:3) and succor (15:29) in the Gospel, again figures in the story as the place where the risen Lord reveals himself to his disciples. Several themes in the Gospel reach their climax in this grand finale: (a) Jesus' authority (7:28; 11:27; 21:23–27); (b) the need for stout faith (8:10, 13; 9:2, 22, 28, 29; 15:28; 17:20; 21:21, 22; 6:30; 8:26; 14:31; 16:8); (c) the identity of Jesus as God with us (1:23; 18:20; 26:29); (d) Jesus as the teacher (4:23, 5:2, 19, 21–48; 7:29; 9:35; 11:29; 17:5; 23:8, 10; 24:35); (e) the universal offer of salvation (2:1–12, 4:14–16; 5:13–14; 8:11–12; 10:18, 22; 12:17–21; 13:31–32, 38, 47; 15:21–28; 22:9; 24:14, 31; 25:31–32; 26:13; 27:54); (f) the transformation of the hope of Israel (8:11–12; 21:43); and (g) the mission of the disciples that now will include making other disciples (4:19; 5:13–16; 9:35–10:42; 24:14; 26:13) and the creation of the church through baptism and instruction (16:18).

(a) Jesus' authority is underscored by the disciples' reaction to him and his announcement to them. Both the women and the disciples respond to the risen Jesus by worshiping him and prostrating themselves before him (28:9, 17). To prostrate oneself before another is not a normal form of greeting but a token of absolute submission that is offered only to gods or kings (see 18:26; Suetonius, *Vitellius* 2.5). Unlike Satan, Jesus has never insisted that he be worshiped. When Satan tried to entice him to pay homage to him, Jesus responded from Scripture that one may worship and serve only God (4:9–10). When the disciples bow down before the resurrected Jesus, they acknowledge that he is due the same honor and service as God. Their worship means that the story has come full circle. The magi came to worship him as the king of the Jews at the beginning (2:2, 11). At the conclusion, however, Jesus declares to his disciples that he is the supreme sovereign of the cosmos and owed unconditional obedience. Satan had only pledged to give Jesus "all the kingdoms of the world," but Jesus grasped after nothing and has received much more through his faithful submission to the will of his heavenly Father – all authority in heaven and earth (see Ps 2:7–8). The promise in 26:64, alluding to Daniel 7:13, is therefore considered by Matthew to be fulfilled in this announcement in 28:18, which alludes to Daniel 7:14.

(b) The second theme has to do with the disciples' need for faith. When they first encounter the resurrected Jesus, they are torn between adoration and doubt (28:17). The resurrection exceeded all of their expectations in spite of Jesus' predictions, but their doubt need not imply a skeptical attitude devoid of faith nor a state of bafflement. The verb translated "doubt" (*distazein*) denotes that "the person is divided in his conviction. The facts are present but the action on them is lacking" (I. P. Ellis, "But Some Doubted," *NTS* 14 [1968]: 576). The disciples' doubt is therefore not unbelief but another case of little faith, as in 14:31 when Peter stumbled out of the boat that was being rocked by the seas (see 6:30; 8:26; 16:8; 17:20). The disciples are initially hesitant, but they have been like that throughout the narrative. Matthew understands that the fluctuation between worship and indecision is every disciple's struggle. What is needed is confidence that Jesus is Lord of all and present with them at all times.

(c) A comparison of the differences between the resurrection appearances recorded in Luke-Acts and John and Matthew's account highlights another Matthean theme: the assurance of Jesus' abiding presence as God with us (1:23; 18:20; 26:29). In Matthew, Jesus has not warned the disciples in advance that he will depart from them as he does in John (13:33; 16:5–7, 10, 17; 20:17). Nor does he ascend from the midst of his followers into heaven as he does in Luke-Acts (24:51; Acts 1:9). The role of the Spirit and its coming is ignored in Matthew's conclusion to the story. Instead, Jesus promises his constant presence with them until the end of the age; and Matthew mentions nothing of his final departure from them.

The resurrection invests Jesus with the same latitudes as God in his relations with his people and insures his lasting presence with them (1:23). When the Lord commissioned Moses to take the Israelites into the promised land, the Lord tells him to be strong and of good courage, "I myself will be with you" (Deut 31:23). In Isaiah 41:10, God reassures the people, "Fear not, for I am with you" (see also Isa 43:5; Gen 26:24; 46:4; Exod 8:12; Deut 31:6). Because disciples waver, it is necessary for Jesus to go with them every step of the way to strengthen their weak faith (Ellis, "But Some Doubted," 580) and to continue to instruct them (18:20).

(d) A fourth theme has to do with the presentation of Jesus as the authoritative teacher and the need for all to be obedient to his words (7:24-27). Again, a comparison with Luke and John helps its features to stand out more clearly. In both Luke and John, Jesus assuages the misgivings of his followers about his resurrection by performing some action: displaying the marks on his body (Luke 24:39; John 20:20, 27) and eating with them (Luke 24:30, 35, 41-43; John 21:12-13; Acts 1:4; 10:41). In Matthew, Jesus' visual appearance is passed over in silence, and he does not dispel their doubt by sight or touch. Only his words are important. He has not appeared to them to satisfy their questions about the reality of the resurrection but to speak to them with a command and a promise (28:18-20; Barth, "Matthew's Understanding of the Law," 132).

The disciples encounter the risen Jesus when they are obedient to his words. In 28:8-10, Jesus appears to the women as they were obediently carrying out the command of the angel. In 28:16-17, he appears to the disciples, whose numbers are now down to eleven, after they obediently followed his command to rendezvous with him in Galilee. Now, Jesus commissions them to make disciples of the nations by teaching them to obey what he has taught. With this charge, he makes it clear that his commands are invested with the same authority as the commands of God (see Exod 7:2; 29:25; Deut 4:2; 7:11; 12:14; Josh 1:7; 1 Chron 22:13; 2 Chron 33:8; Jer 1:7). Jesus saves his people through his death and resurrection, but they can find life (7:14), security (7:24-27), and rest (11:29) only when they submit to his yoke.

(e) The allusion to Daniel 7:14 in 28:18 clarifies another theme in the Gospel, the universal offer of salvation. In Daniel 7:14, dominion, glory, and kingdom are given to the son of man "that all people, nations, and languages should serve him." The scope of Jesus' authority now extends beyond Israel (10:5-6), and he breaks down the geographical and racial barriers to command a universal mission to the nations centered on baptism in his name and the teaching of his commandments.

(f) The death and resurrection is, for Matthew, the pivotal moment in salvation history; and it results in a transformation of Israel's hope. Isaiah prophesied:

> [2]In the days to come the mountain of the Lord's house shall be established as the highest of the mountains, and shall be raised above the hills; all the nations shall stream to it. [3] Many peoples

shall come and say: "Come, let us go up to the mountain of the Lord, to the house of the God of Jacob; that he may teach us his ways and that we may walk in his paths." For out of Zion shall go forth the law, and the word of the Lord from Jerusalem. (Isa 2:2–3)

Matthew's conclusion to his Gospel revolutionizes this expression of Israel's traditional hope in four ways. First, it is Jesus, not Jerusalem, who is exalted (28:18). Second, the nations are not to come to the temple where God is presumed to dwell because it will soon be destroyed (23:38; 24:2). Instead, Jesus' disciples are to go out to the nations; and Jesus, as "God with us" (1:23) and as "something greater than the temple" (12:6), goes with them (28:20). Those in Israel who have not responded to the mission of the disciples lose their special status as the people of God (21:43) and simply become one of the many nations that must be evangelized. Third, "the word of the Lord" has now become the teaching of Jesus, and salvation comes from walking in his paths (28:20; see 17:5). Finally, the word of the Lord does not go forth from Jerusalem but from the despised outpost of Galilee (28:16).

(g) A final theme in this concluding passage has to do with the mission of the disciples. They are to make other disciples. The earthly life of Jesus comes to a close, but he continues to confront the world as a living presence in the community of his disciples who must faithfully continue the mission (25:31–46). They are not to obey Jesus' commands just among themselves in an insular society but are for the first time in the Gospel given authority to teach others to observe his commandments as well. All are to come under Jesus' authority as they are incorporated into his church through baptism and instruction. It is assumed that the task of making disciples of the nations will not end until the end of the age.

The glorious setting of the commission may be misleading, however, since the process of making disciples of the nations will often be inglorious. All authority in heaven and on earth has not been given to the disciples as they go to the nations who will "all hate them" (24:9). The disciples are to follow in the steps of their Lord who has been crucified. They are supported by his presence and assured of their own vindication, but they are not preserved from the threat of suffering the same earthly fate as their Lord. Some disciples of little faith may hesitate; but, according to Matthew, the mission to the world is their very reason for existing (5:13–16).

The life and death of a church depends on how much its members are willing to proclaim the gospel to the world. If its ministers are satisfied merely with performing their functions and counseling religious people, if its members confess their faith as far as it is socially acceptable, the church will grow more and more into a sterile institution that is far from the living church of the New Testament. (E. Schweizer, "The Church as the Missionary Body of Christ," *NTS* 8 [1961]: 1)